1457–2012

555 Years
of the Moravian Church

1457–2012

by Evald Rucký

COPYRIGHT INFORMATION

555 Years of the Moravian Church
All Rights Reserved.
Copyright © 2023 Mgr. Evald Rucký Th.D. Ep. Fr.
First English Edition

Original title: 555 let Jednoty bratrské v datech
Translated from the Czech by Anna Černá, Lenka Pohunková, Tereza Černá, Jan Procházka
The Czech edition was published in 2015 by Jednota bratrská

The opinions expressed in this manuscript are solely the opinions of the author and do not represent the opinions or thoughts of the publisher. The author has represented and warranted full ownership and/or legal right to publish all the materials in this book.

This book may not be reproduced, transmitted, or stored in whole or in part by any means, including graphic, electronic, or mechanical without the express written consent of the publisher except in the case of brief quotations embodied in critical articles and reviews.

Outskirts Press, Inc.
http://www.outskirtspress.com

ISBN: 978-1-9772-6058-1

Cover Design by Ester Rut Vognerová (FS Interactive, s.r.o.) © 2023 Evald Rucký.
All rights reserved - used with permission.

Outskirts Press and the "OP" logo are trademarks belonging to Outskirts Press, Inc.

PRINTED IN THE UNITED STATES OF AMERICA

ACKNOWLEDGMENTS

Special thanks go to Professor PhDr. Jan Kumpera, CSc. (Czech historian) whose texts inspired me to write the first chapter of this book. I also want to thank a number of collaborators to whom I owe the final form of data: Bishops Petr Krásný and Samuel Gray, documentarist Jan Horálek, archivist Lydie Halamová, proofreader Noemi Rucká, and graphic designer Ester Rut Vognerová.

Many thanks to Kay Windsor for reviewing the book and Rev. William Andrews and Lorraine Parsons for helpful advice and insight.

TABLE OF CONTENTS

Acknowledgments	5
Table of Contents	6
Preface	10
Foreword	12

PART I
From the origins until the death of Bishop Comenius

Predecessors of the reformers	16
The first generation, the founders of the work	17
Appointment of priests	19
The conflict between the majority party and the minority party	23
The second generation lays a foundation of Brethren theology	24
The third generation closer to the German reformation	29
The fourth generation takes care of exulant brothers in Poland and Prussia	33
The fifth generation creates spiritual and literary values	39
The sixth generation aims for politics	46
The seventh generation is leaving into exile	50
The Polish branch of the Unity of Brethren	56
Conclusion	57

PART II
Since the renewal in Herrnhut to this day – 280 years of Brethren's mission

The beginning of a new generation of Unity's fathers	60
Rebirth of the Moravian Church and the beginnings of the Moravian mission	64

West Indies
- Danish colony (since 1732) – St. Thomas Island, St. Croix Island, St. John — 66
- British colony (since 1753) – Jamaica, Antigua, Barbados, St. Christopher Island, Tobago, Trinidad — 69

Greenland (1733–1900) — 75

North America (since 1735) — 78
- Among the North American Natives — 80
- Among the Delaware Indians (1765–1903) — 82

- In the Far West	86
- Among the Cherokees (1801–1896)	87

South America – Suriname — 88
- Among the Arawaks (1738–1808) — 88
- Among the Bushmen (from 1765) — 89
- Among the black peoples in the colonies (from 1754) — 90

South Africa — 93
- Among the Khoi people (from 1736) — 93

Labrador Peninsula (from 1752) — 96

Other mission efforts — 99
- Among the Saami and Samoyedic people (1734–1737) — 99
- Among the Jews in Amsterdam (1738–1743) — 100
- Guinea Coast (formerly Gold Coast, modern-day Ghana) (1736–1769) — 100
- Algiers (1740) — 101

Mission efforts in the Orient — 102
- Constantinople (1740) — 102
- Romanian Wallachia (1740) — 102
- Among Kalmyks (1742–1822) — 103
- In the Caucasus among the Tartars — 105
- Persia – today's Iran (1746–1750) — 105
- Egypt and Ethiopia (1752–1782) — 106

Mission efforts in East India — 107
- Ceylon – modern Sri Lanka (1740) — 107
- Bay of Bengal and Nicobar Islands (1758–1787) — 108
- Bengal – modern-day India (1776–1792) — 110

The Unity of Brethren in Europe — 112
- Moravian congregations in Silesia — 114
- Further development of ministry — 117
- Diaspora in Livonia (1743–1914) — 121

Nineteenth century missions — 126

South Africa — 126
- Among the Xhosa people (from 1818) — 126

TABLE OF CONTENTS

South America – British Guiana (from 1835)	128
Central America – Nicaragua (from 1849)	130
Mission efforts in Australia	133
- Victoria Colony (1850–1907)	133
- Queensland (1891–1919)	135
Ladakh and South Asia (from 1856)	136
- Kyelang	136
- Pooh	137
- Ladakh – Leh	138
- Raipur in India	139
Alaska (from 1885)	140
East Africa – later Tanzania (from 1891)	142
- Nyasa – Southern Tanganyika Mountains	142
- Unyamwezi – West Tanganyika	144
Europe – crisis and recovery	145
Extension of work in the twentieth century	147
Central America – Honduras (from 1930)	147
Central America – Costa Rica (from 1968)	148

PART III
From awakening in Herrnhut and subsequent missionary movement to a church

The life and development of the Unitas Fratrum in the world	152
- Jesus Christ, the Chief Elder of the Moravian Church	153
- Constitutional Synods (1764–1775)	154
- Following General Synods (1782–1857)	156
- Back to the land of forefathers (1862–1957)	160
- Unity Synods (1967–2012)	163
List of provinces in 1967	165
List of provinces in 1995	167
List of provinces in 2009	169

PART IV
Back in the Land of Fathers – from the promulgation of the Patent of Toleration to the Velvet Revolution

Introduction	172
The pioneer from Nowa Sól	173
First Moravian Church congregations	176
Registration	177
Brethrens' orphanages	178
Diaspora in Volhynia	180
Ústí nad Orlicí – the renewal of the congregation	181
Progress of other work	183
Uneasiness between two World Wars	185
- The Czech district	190
- The German district	191
Moravian Church congregations in 1937	192
German occupation and the war years	192
Post-war period	195
Arrival of totalitarian regime	197
Independence of the Czechoslovak Province	198
Spiritual and social crossroad	200
List of congregations in 1961	200
List of congregations in 1989	205

PART V
Current mission of the Moravian Church in its homeland

Events of the past years in the Moravian Church	208

APPENDIX

List of Unitas Fratrum Bishops until 2014	218
Bibliography	228
Bibliography reference list	232
List of images	234

PREFACE

In 2007 the spiritual descendants of Jan Hus celebrated the 550th anniversary of the founding of the Moravian Church (Unitas Fratrum). Professor Jan Kumpera, PhD, prepared an interesting booklet titled: *Jednota bratrská – zbožnost, mravnost, tolerance* (The Unitas Fratrum – piety, morality, tolerance) which gave readers a simple and readable recounting of the first 160 years of the history of this church.
As I read the booklet I was inspired to build upon Dr. Kumpera's work by writing an ordered and readable account of the history of this church from 1457 to date. In Czechia some older people may remember a little bit about Jan Blahoslav, Czech grammarian and musicologist, or John Amos Comenius, the last bishop of the early Moravian Church from school. However, few people know that the Moravian Church did not end with Comenius but became a unique spiritual gift and jewel to many nations thanks to its selfless mission.
I am not a historian, and I certainly make no pretentions that this is a scholarly or comprehensive history. That is why I have chosen to present our story as a series of important events, people and dates. I am grateful for the help I received as I researched many sources in the library of the Moravian Church Archive in the Czech Republic, the Unity Archives in Herrnhut, Germany, and in addition from Poland and the USA.
This book is arranged chronologically. The first chapter deals with the Ancient Unity and covers the first 160 years of the Moravian Church. The second chapter focuses on the renewal of the church in Herrnhut in the early 1700s, and the remarkable mission that took place over the course of three centuries. The third chapter describes the gradual formation of the church structure into its current state. The fourth chapter outlines the much longed for return to their homeland in Bohemia after almost one hundred years in exile. The fifth and final chapter outlines the most important events from the modern period. As it is not yet concluded I leave its evaluation for future generations to consider.
A work of this size and scope cannot detail all the dates or events of the period it covers and deals only marginally with some topics. For example, I regret that the second chapter gives only a glimpse into the significant story of Moravian missions.

The history of Czech bishops of the Unitas Fratrum is also one of the important themes of the book. Bishops in the Ancient Unity were spiritual leaders with executive power. This decision-making role was assumed by the Provincial Elders' Conference in the renewed Unity and bishops be-

PREFACE

came spiritual pillars and shepherds. Today, Moravian bishops serve not only in their Province but also in the whole Unity. Their principal responsibility is helping the church to remain faithful to Christ and the gospel in doctrine and practice. Bishops represent the church during the rite of ordination and are called to serve in a pastoral role to ordained ministers. Not many current members of the Moravian Church in the Czech Republic grew up in a church. They have come to faith from a secular and atheistic environment and are unfamiliar with the history of the church. We are a church open for all generations. My deep desire is to introduce the history of the church not only to its members, but also to teachers, civil servants, fellow citizens and friends in towns where the Moravian Church is serving today. As they learn about the church's origin, roots and spiritual legacy they can understand and appreciate the significant influence the Moravians have had on the history Czechia and of many nations.

The Unitas Fratrum has endured for more than five and a half centuries. This book gives an overview of the faith of at least twenty generations that, through their obedience and trust in God, became a valuable gift spreading far beyond the borders of their country.

Mgr. Evald Rucký, Th.D. Ep. Fr.

The author became a follower of Jesus on his 18th birthday. In 1997, he was ordained as a deacon and pastor in the Moravian Church. He has served on the Provincial Board since 1998, as its chairman since 2008. In 2011, he was consecrated as the 345th bishop of the Unitas Fratrum. Evald is married and together with his wife Rut, they have three adult daughters.

One of his favorite quotations is Hebrews 10:5.7: *"...Sacrifice and offering you did not desire, but a body you prepared for me;... 'Here I am – I have come to do your will, my God.'"*

FOREWORD

Sometimes we think that "history" is a thing of the past. We forget that every day we are living history! The things that God is doing all around us today will be looked back on many years from now as part of the history of the church of Jesus.

It is refreshing, intriguing, and yes, sometimes challenging, to read about more recent events in the history of the Unitas Fratrum and to see how they are connected to the events of the more distant past. In this well-researched and well-presented chronology, the development of the Unitas Fratrum, its extension into "all the world," and the obstacles and challenges that it faced in various times and places, can be seen in a clear and concise way. Besides being a rich resource for those who live in the "land of the fathers," the book provides a helpful summary (especially in Parts II and III) of the mission efforts (whether ultimately successful or not) that have been carried out throughout the world. The chronological bullet-points format makes it easy for anyone to pay a visit to a particular point in the overall story and then see how that portion of the story fits into the overall story – the story of God's mission in and through the Unitas Fratrum.

The photographs, lists and other graphics help the story come alive and remind us that our history has taken place, and continues to take place, in the "real world" (sometimes places that we recognize in the photographs!) and with real people (even some whom we have met!). All of this serves to invite us into the story and helps us realize that we, too, have a part in what God is doing.

Thank-you, brother Evald, for your work. May it blossom and bear fruit in the fatherland and beyond.

Bishop Sam Gray
Pastor
New Philadelphia Moravian Church

FOREWORD

PART I

PART I

From the Origins until
the death of Bishop Comenius

PREDECESSORS OF THE REFORMERS

1325 (?) Jan Milíč of Kroměříž, a reformer, was born. He worked in the royal office; he would accompany Emperor Charles IV to Germany. Later, he said of the Catholic church of the time: *"Behold, a war is coming, but not a war against a sect and tyranny, but as many fights as there are attacks against the Gospel truth… Behold, first! Your princes are friends of thieves, everyone longs for bribes, everyone follows rewards, they do not give the orphan the justice and the case of the widow does not reach them… Behold, your field is filled with weeds, behold, a garden full of nettle. Root out the evil and plant the good, so that no one shall tell of you and your field: I passed by the field of a lazy man and behold, it was all filled with nettles… Behold; on all sides of the world be war or plague or hunger, and the wrath of God rages against all peoples. Take the censer of the heart and fill it with the fire of the warmest love, sacrifice yourself, standing between God and the people, so that the plague would cease."*[1]

1350 (?) Matěj (Matthew) of Janov, a reformer, priest and preacher was born. He was a student of Milíč of Kroměříž. Matthew received a word from the Lord: *" 'Son of man, break the wall!' And so, I obeyed the voice of my God and I broke it thrice: by preaching to the people daily, by hearing confessions always and by writing these treatises conscientiously by day and by night."* Matthew thus prophesied the rise of the Moravian Church* almost a century before its founding: *"Now the anger of the enemies of the truth has prevailed over us, but it shall not be this way forever. For a small people without a sword and without power will rise, and it shall not be overcome. How to bring about the remedy? A return to Christ, to the law of God, a turn away from the Antichrist, a return to the apostolic calling, so that the first church would be renewed. All the works of man, ceremony and tradition shall be rooted out. And only the Lord our God shall be praised, and His word will remain forever. I believe for this age that there will rise a new people, created from the new man, which is according to God. From it, new clerics and priests will arise, hating both greed and the glory of this world, rushing to the heavenly fellowship. That shall all be done by the Spirit of Christ, the Holy Spirit, who only can revive humankind… Thus…a People of God without a sword will arise, and it shall prevail."*[2]

| *Theological disputation*

---

* In this chapter, the Moravian Church is referred to as the Unity of Brethren or simply the Unity in keeping with the original Czech appellation Jednota bratrská (Unitas Fratrum).

1371 Jan Hus, later a magister and a rector of
(?) Charles University, was born in Husinec. A significant Czech preacher who manifestly criticized some of the practices of the Catholic Church.

1374 **29 June** Priest Milíč of Kroměříž died in Avignon, France.

THE FIRST GENERATION, THE FOUNDERS OF THE WORK

1390 Petr of Chelčice was born. F. M. Bartoš, a
(?) Czech historian, identifies him as a yeoman from Záhorčí near Chelčice. He was a Czech spiritual thinker and the spiritual father of the Moravian Church (Unity of Brethren). Prophetically, he saw in brother Řehoř Krajčí a captain of God's people about whom Matthew of Janov prophesied that *"without a sword will once arise, and shall prevail."* [2]

1393 **30 November** Matthew of Janov, a priest and a reformer, died.

1414 Jan Hus was called to Constance by the Pope.

1415 **6 July** Hus was condemned as a heretic and burned at the stake. The ash of his body was poured into the Rhine. His death started a revolution in Bohemia, which changed into the Hussite wars. Radical outbreaks of Hussitism ended with the Battle of Lipany in 1434.

1419 –1436 The Hussite wars broke out with all their consequences lasting until the year 1479.

| *Monastery Na Slovanech where Gregory the Patriarch lived*

1420 Gregory the Patriarch, the future founder
(?) of the Unity, was born.

1430 Tůma of Přelouč was born.
(?)

1436 Compacts of Basel were agreed on as a result of discussions between the Council of Basel and the representatives of the Hussite Bohemia. Their cardinal point was granting communion under both kinds for the members of the Bohemian Hussite movement.

1442 Matěj (Matthew) of Kunvald was born.
(?) Both brothers later belonged among the three priests of the church chosen by lot (1467) and were first among equals.

1446 Gregory the Patriarch renounced all property and entered the Hussite monastery Na Slovanech in Prague.

PART I

1448 Jan Rokycana, archbishop-elect of Prague, who was never acknowledged as such by the Pope, received the presbytery in the church of Týn in Prague. That was the beginning of his work in the church of Týn. The generations of the first Brethren, Gregory the Patriarch and his company among them, would come there to hear his preaching.

1453 – 1454 Petr of Chelčice criticized in his writings both the papal Catholicism and the official Hussite (Utraquist)* church. He also denounced the feudal teaching on separation of the people into *three peoples*** and demanded adherence to Christian morality. All the while, he refused violence in solving religious and political conflict. He expressed the desire for the renewal of the church on an apostolic and prophetical ground.

| *Jan Rokycana with Masters and Petr of Chelčice*

1455 (?) Laurentius of Krasonice, a close associate to Luke of Prague, was born.

1456 (?) Jan Černý (the older brother of Luke of Prague) was born, a doctor and a significant personality of the Moravian Church. He treated some of the Brethren; among them lord Vilém von Pernstein.

1457 or 1458 The Unity of Brethren was formed. Its supporters, gathered around Gregory the Patriarch, were granted refuge in the dominion of Litice, belonging to George of Poděbrady, in the village of Kunvald near the town of Žamberk.

1459 or 1460 A gathering took place in Kunvald. The teaching of the Taborites and the Picards*** on the sacrament of the altar was abolished. The community named itself *Brothers of Christ's law*.

1460 (?) The spiritual father of the Unity, Petr of Chelčice, died. The same year, first persecution against the Unity took place. Services were banned in Kunvald. The Brethren found a new refuge in Rychnov nad Kněžnou, in the domain of Jan of Rychnov. Michal, the Hussite priest from Žamberk, came to the fore (tradition has it that he was the very first bishop of the Unity).

- Luke of Prague was born in Prague, later to be known as the second significant member of the Unity.

1461 In March, George of Poděbrady restored the validity of mandates of Emperor Charles IV against heretics, initi-

---

* Utraquism denoting the manner of receiving the Holy Communion, sub utraque specie, meaning both the bread-body and the wine-blood. / ** i.e. those who pray, those who work and those who fight / ***The Taborites were a Hussite movement settled in the town of Tábor and the Picards were a more extreme movement within them. The term Picard was later used as a general pejorative term for a heretic.

ating a wave of persecution against the Unity. It was not very thorough. Despite that, Gregory the Patriarch and other Brethren were imprisoned by the magistrate of Prague's New Town.

- Until 1467, the Unity was going through an internal struggle over the issue of whether to separate from the Utraquists.

1464 *Agreement on the Mountains of Rychnov* – this is de facto the first ever covenant to be concluded in the Unity between the members of the church and God. It stated the first rules of brotherly life: *"the rights and duties to reprove the brothers."* The first punishment was also defined: exclusion from the sacraments. *"And then those who will live in delusions and mortal sin will be excluded from the Unity of Brethren."*³ New members were accepted conditionally with a probationary period of up to two years.

APPOINTMENT OF PRIESTS

1467 The Brethren first met to agree upon a way to appoint the priests. They submitted fully to God's leadership and decided to select them by lot. All other brothers were ordered to pray and fast to plead for God's guidance. They met again some time later and prayed that God would reveal whether he wanted the appointment to take place. And they recognized he did. They waited once more and then gathered in Lhotka near Rychnov on the estate of Duchek. There were about sixty of them. At first, they appointed twenty judges and then proceeded to elect the

| *House in Kunvald – the place of the first Brethren gatherings*

priests. They approached it very responsibly and it was very probable that nobody would be elected. Nine Brethren were chosen as candidates. Nine of the slips of paper were blank; three said *it is he*. A child then distributed the papers to candidates. Three brothers drew the marked papers. Everyone saw this as a sign of God's assent and so the three brothers were elected: Matthew of Kunvald, Tůma of Přelouč and Eliáš of Chřenovice. Following this significant event, modeled after the appointment of the first apostles, Matthew of Kunvald became the first senior (bishop). He then ordained more priests and gave blessings.

The Unity of Brethren thus became a presbyterian-type church voluntarily separating from Catholic ordination. By this act, the Brethren detached themselves from both the Roman and Hussite church making the Unity one of the first reformed churches in the world.

Though the Brethren saw in this appointment a sign confirming the priesthood and concluded that they need no further ordination, they would still undertake another step and called out to Stephen, the bishop of the Waldenses. They did this *"for the certainty of brothers weaker in their faith."*[4] This step brought an encouraging change. More and more communities from both Bohemia and Moravia were joining the nascent Unity, as were some of the Waldenses coming to the Czech lands from Austria. The Waldenses' Bishop Stephen was therefore asked to grant the ordination of Bishop to Michal of Žamberk. However, Bishop Stephen fell into the hands of the inquisition in Vienna and was burned at the stake. The request of the Brethren was most likely granted

Jan Rokycana

by the eldest of the Waldenses' priests of Bohemia, probably by the name of Martin. Michal of Žamberk was sent to meet him to be entrusted with the 'confirmation of the authority of bishop.' Brother Michal then transferred this by ordination to the three appointed priests and they would then ordain him, as he renounced the Catholic ordination. By this, the Unity established its own independent priesthood. However, by their separatism, the Brethren overstepped the law as the so-called compacts (law of the land from 1436) did not allow life in other churches than the Roman or the Hussite. Furthermore, George of Poděbrady swore in his coronation ceremony that he would lead

Bohemia out of all sectarianism and heresy and would bring the Bohemian nation to a unity of faith. Therefore, he ordered that the established Unity be harshly persecuted. Nevertheless, the Brethren overcame the first persecution and joyfully worked to turn their ideals into reality even though many had to flee into exile.

1468 Even Jan Rokycana publicly renounced the Brethren and wrote a sharp letter against them. The Waldenses were persecuted at the same time. A second, and a much more thorough, wave of persecutions took place.

1471 22 March The king George of Poděbrady died. He was succeeded by Wladyslaw II Jagiello, king of Bohemia and Hungary. The persecutions were temporarily halted.

1473 The Land Assembly of nobles held a meeting in Benešov. The issue of picards* was put on the table. King George's widow, lady Johana, pushed through a resolution that Brethren be arrested and imprisoned. The following persecution was not that serious as the Unity of Brethren had already had some powerful protectors.

- The Brethren were granted a public hearing with the masters of theology in Prague. However, it turned out fruitless.

1474 12 August Gregory the Patriarch, the founder of the Unity, died in Brandýs nad Orlicí. Before his death, he had urged Bishop Matthew that he *"bears in memory those learned."*[5] The Unity grows in size and some nobles, townsmen and educated people join it.

| Brandýs nad Orlicí – place of work of the Brethren from the very beginnings of the Unity

*i.e. sectarians or heretics

1478 Another public hearing – a colloquium – took place at Prague University, in Charles College, presided over by Václav Koranda. The debated issue was the ordination of the Brethren and the Eucharist (Brethren also defended themselves from false accusations of someone called Jan Ležka). At that time, a baptism outside of the Unity was considered null by the Brethren.

1480 The Unity was strengthened by the arrival of more Waldenses from the land of Brandenburg. They came to two German-speaking parts of Bohemia – the region of Lanškroun (Landskron) in east Bohemia and the region of Fulnek in north Moravia.

- A controversy over human salvation took place among the Brethren (whether salvation depends on acts or on faith). So far, Gregory's maxim had always applied that faith without good deeds is dead. Prokop the Bachelor attempted to strike a compromise.
- The church in Mladá Boleslav (Jungbunzlau) was established most likely this year. Later, several bishops of the Brethren served there, e.g. Luke of Prague or Jan Augusta.
- A school of the Brethren was established near the church followed by a printing workshop in 1518.

1485 A Land Assembly of nobles was in session in Kutná Hora. The Utraquists made a truce with the Catholics but this agreement did not apply to the Unity of Brethren. Along with the Unity's numbers, enmity also grew towards it.

| *Mladá Boleslav – the venue of important synods and assemblies even in times of persecution*

THE CONFLICT BETWEEN THE MAJORITY PARTY AND THE MINORITY PARTY

1490 An assembly of Brethren took place in Brandýs nad Orlicí – the Inner Council* was authorized to decide on contentious issues: brothers could accept public offices (if necessary but they should not seek it). This decision opened a new path for the Unity. Brothers Prokop the Bachelor, Jan Klenovský, as well as brothers Michael and Matthew of Kunvald were advocates of this direction. The decision was soon opposed by a group of Brethren from the region of Prácheň. This group was later called the "minority party". Two of its members – Jakub, a miller from Štěkeň, and Amos, a wax maker, sent a letter to Rychnov to Brother Matthew. The ensuing conflict in the Inner Council ended in resignation of Prokop the Bachelor and Jan Klenovský (1491). (The minority party parted ways with the Unity in 1496 and ceased to exist in 1546.)
- This year, Jan Roh of Domažlice was (most likely) born, later to become a bishop of the third generation of Unity.

1491 Brothers attempted to find a church corresponding to the model of the New Testament. Four Brethren – Luke of Prague, Kašpar the Walden, Mareš Kokovec and Martin Kabátník set out on a journey to the Holy Land and to the Near East; it was funded by Bohuš Kostka of Postupice. Martin Kabátník started his journey on 1 March 1491. After his return in 1492, a book entitled *The Journey from Bohemia to Jerusalem and Cairo in 1491–1492* was created based on his memories (published in press for the first time in 1518).

Jan Roh of Domažlice

1494 **5 May** An assembly of Brethren took place in Rychnov. There was a complete turn in the direction of the Unity. The former ascetic rigorousness was defeated, replaced by a renewed "statement" of Brandýs. Jan Klenovský and Prokop the Bachelor again became members of the Inner Council, joined by Vavřinec of Krasonice and Luke of Prague. Matthew of Kunvald remained a bishop but retained only his power to ordain. The direction of Unity was taken up by Prokop the Bachelor as the judge. Amos, the wax maker, refused to obey until the Unity returns to the teachings of Brother Gregory.

The formerly dominant position of a bishop was taken by a judge (the chairman of the Inner Council) – the *primus inter pares* in the Inner Council with fourteen members. His authority was limited though as the Inner Council was

---
*An executive body of the Unity. Its role was clarified at the Assembly session of 1499 (cf. Decrees of Unity).

granted, after Christ, the original authority in the church. The assembly also put together rules for trade and craft.

1495 The Inner Council (with eighteen members by this point) reached a crucial decision during its session in Rychnov: *"unconditional respect belongs only to the Lord, not the writings that have come from the Unity so far."* Thus the binding power of teachings of Gregory and Petr of Chelčice is taken away with Gregory's teaching even called *"immoderate and intemperate."*[6]

- **29 April** Jan Vilímek of Tábor, a member of the Inner Council, died in Litomyšl.

THE SECOND GENERATION LAYS A FOUNDATION OF BRETHREN THEOLOGY

1497 and 1498 saw more Brethren's assemblies taking place.

1498 Luke traveled to Italy. This journey led him to a conclusion that there is no church for the Brethren to join in. Since then, he emphasized an independent direction for the Unity.
- **9 November** Jan Klenovský, a writer and a leading representative of the Unity, died.

1499 Assembly of Brethren in Prostějov led to a definitive prevalence of the majority party seeking to understand the society of the time and dealing with the relation to the nobility: *"We give place to the temporal powers among us… Joining the army is possible as a duty, but not voluntarily for pay."*[7] This assembly also clarified the position of deacons, members of the Inner Council, bishops, the judge and the Inner Council as an executive body. Consecration of Tůma of Přelouč and Elijah of Chřenovice took place.

Parents and children attend catechism together

1500

23 January Possibly this year, Matthew of Kunvald died at age 58 in Lipník. He was the first and thus far the only bishop
- of the three priests chosen by lot in 1467. A resolution was passed on how to act
- concerning craft.

19 April An assembly of Brethren in Rychnov nad Kněžnou elected and consecrated two bishops (Luke of Prague and Ambrosius of Skuteč) with a resolution that *"the highest position in the entire Unity will not belong to any of them or to all of them collectively but to the whole council."*[8] Tůma of Přelouč became the judge after Matthew of Kunvald. Both Tůma of Přelouč and Elijah of Chřenovice affirmed the offices of brothers Luke of Prague and

Ambrosius by blessing and laying on of hands. Furthermore, the election of bishops was officially put in the hands of the Inner Council though in practice it was done by Brethren's assembly.
- Jan Augusta was born in Prague; he would later become a bishop of the third generation of Unity.

1501 It was resolved that the eldest of the bishops would also be the judge presiding over sessions of the Inner Council. The bishops were now also called *senior**, i.e. elders. Each bishop was entrusted with administration of one region leaving the leadership of the Unity in the hands of relevant bishops. The most influential bishop was Luke of Prague (seated in Mladá Boleslav); other bishops were brother Ambrosius, seated in Štěkeň, who presided over the Prácheň region (in South Bohemia) and brothers Tůma and Elijah divided Moravian region between them (seated in Přerov and Prostějov, respectively). Tůma became a judge.
- An agenda of priests was passed. Priests and deacons were only to be appointed by the Inner Council. (Petr of Chelčice once required that they be elected by their communities). It was also resolved that priests, especially younger ones, should live by the work of their hands. Until then, priests had been celibate; from that point on, they could marry (this had been, in practice, pursued since late fifteenth century). However, they could not leave their designated congregation without assent. Priests served the Holy Communion and heard either private or public confessions and they were also charged with administration of the resident folk in matters of morality. They were assisted by deacons

Tůma of Přelouč – his manuscript "About the origin of Unitas Fratrum"

and boards of elders which administered the property and resolved disputes among Brethren. Churches were not only places of service, but also homes of the priests and deacons, acolytes** and sometimes even elders – and they were called Brethren houses or congregations (*sbor* in Czech). The Brethren's houses were also to be a refuge for old priests and traveling brothers and they served as a centre of all life in the community.
- **12 April** A priest Michal of Žamberk died. He was the one who had blessed Matthew of Kunvald, the first bishop of the Unity in 1467.
- During these years, the influence of Luke of Prague was predominant as he was in a certain sense the second founder of the Unity. Brother Luke laid foundations persisting in the church to this day. According

---

*The name was used during the sixteenth and early seventeenth century. In this book, however, we use the current title „bishop".
** Acolyte – lay helper

to him, church matters were divided into three categories: things essential, ministerial and incidental. *The Essentials* are important for the salvation of man, i.e. the relationship with the Triune God as expressed by faith, hope and love. *The Ministerials* are these serving the essentials but independent of them they are of no value. *The Incidentals*, i.e. manners in which all of these things are practiced: the Scripture, sacraments, the church, preaching – all of this serving the only thing substantial, i.e. the relationship with Triune God. This is a special approach to the theology of the Brethren. Brother Luke kept as a part of Sunday services regular reading of the Gospels and the Epistles as well as observing fasts and holy days. He also wanted to be forthcoming to human imagination and to enrich the services – he reinstated the use of candles, ritual vessels, tablecloths and singing. By this he also gained supporters among the nobility. Opponents of the Unity started considering him a dangerous "pope of the Brethren" for his authority. In these times, also thanks to a generational change, the Unity became an open and communicative church.

Luke's treatise *O požívání krve a těla Páně*
- (On Consuming the Blood and Flesh of the Lord) was written – it was the first formulation of this teaching by the Brethren (converging to the opinions of the Taborites and of John Wycliffe).*

1502 Brother Luke wrote a catechism of the Unity entitled *Otázky dětinské* (Children's Questions). It was somewhat returning to Hussite and Taborite teachings.

Since the early sixteenth century, first schools had been founded by the congregations. Over time, they raised several generations of clerics, teachers, musicians, craftsmen etc. Later on, those schools would give rise to leading personalities such as Jan Amos Komenský (John Amos Comenius) or Jan Blahoslav. Several towns would also have hospitals of the Brethren (Litomyšl, Prostějov, Ivančice).

1503 **2 February** Matěj (Matthew) Kabátník died – he was one of the travelers sent by Brethren and traveled as far as Egypt.
- A session of the Land Assembly regarding the suppression of the Unity took place. Luke of Prague reacted by a written apologia or confession sent to king Wladyslaw II meaning to prove that the Brethren were not heretics.
- **5 September** Elijah of Chřenovice, one of the first three bishops, died in Prostějov.
- **2 November** Six Brethren were burned at the stake due to persecution in Bor near Domažlice

1505 Jiří Izrael, who later became a bishop, was born.

1506 It was resolved on how to act regarding suitable and inappropriate, proud and lustful clothing.

1507 Luke wrote a treatise *Dosti činící z víry* (Apology of Faith) putting a greater emphasis on faith than before.
- **13 September** Prokop the Bachelor from Jindřichův Hradec died – he was a judge of the Unity and a significant personality of the church.

1508 King Wladyslaw issued a St. Jacob's Mandate (decree) – a resolution of the chamber of all three Estates of the realm

---
* *John Wycliffe (1320–1384) – English theologian and an advocate of reform in the Roman Catholic Church*

intending to suppress the Unity entirely. The resolution became law of the realm by entering into the Land Tables* which could then be used against the Unity at any later time. The Brethren could not assemble, their treatises were to be burned and their priests were to be arrested and forced to adhere to utraquism or the Catholic Church. After the death of king Wladyslaw II (1516) the mandate ceased to be valid but it was later repeatedly renewed and became a permanent threat for the Unity for the following hundred years.

1509 Jan Černý (Nigranus), later a bishop and
(?) a judge of the Unity, was born.

King Wladyslaw II of the House of Jagiello

1510 Luke wrote his treatise *On the Righteousness*.

1512 An Inner Council meeting taking place in Brandýs nad Orlicí resolved that: *"Collected resolutions or decrees of the Unity of Brethren, the old and the new, be read to priests and through them delivered to the people…"*[9]

1514 A wave of persecution ended (taking place since 1508) most likely thanks to the intervention of Albrecht Rendl (a burgrave of Prague and a secret member of the Unity) and of prince Bartholomew of Münsterberg.

1517 **15 August** Martin Škoda was consecrated as Unity bishop.
■ **31 October** Martin Luther's famous appearance took place in Wittenberg. Lutheran reformation commenced in Germany.

1518 **23 October** Tůma of Přelouč, a bishop and a judge, died in Přerov and soon after him, Ambrosius of Skuteč died as well (1520) leaving the only remaining bishop of the Unity – Luke of Prague. With consent of the Inner Council, he asked Martin Škoda to assist him. Jan Roh of Domažlice was ordained as a priest. Luke of Prague became the judge of Unity.

1521 **21 February** Matěj Červenka, who he later became a bishop, was born in Čelákovice.

1522 Contacts between the Unity and Martin Luther were established. A message to Luther was delivered by brothers Jan Roh and Michal Weiss. Luke of Prague,

Old Czech source of law

unlike J. Roh and M. Weiss, kept his distance from Lutheranism. He also starkly approached the Swiss reformer U. Zwingli whose teachings were spread in the Unity by a man called Čížek, a former monk from Wroclaw.

1523 Luther wrote a treatise *On the Unity of Brethren* (it was a critical writing because of Luther's doubts about Brethren teaching on the Holy Communion).
- Luke of Prague reacted to Luther's treatise.
- **20 February** Jan Blahoslav was born. He was to become a bishop of the fourth generation of fathers of the Unity.

1526 Ferdinand I was elected the Czech throne and marked the entrance of the House of Habsburgs to the region. Their long-term goal was to dispose of Czech Protestantism. First of all they wished to get rid of the Unity of Brethren.
- A group of people established a new religious movement: Unity of Brothers from Habrovany. Their teaching was a mix of various protestant theses. They only recognized two sacraments: baptism and the Holy Communion, both only as symbols. This group was also opposed by the Unity leadership led by Luke of Prague just as the minority party was a few years before.

1528 11 December Luke of Prague, the second founder of the Unity, died in Mladá Boleslav. In Brethren accounts it is said: *"Brother Luke was a good and erudite man who found everything in the Unity of Brethren and gained from it as well while acquiring for the Unity the favors of the world and the blessings of God."*[10]

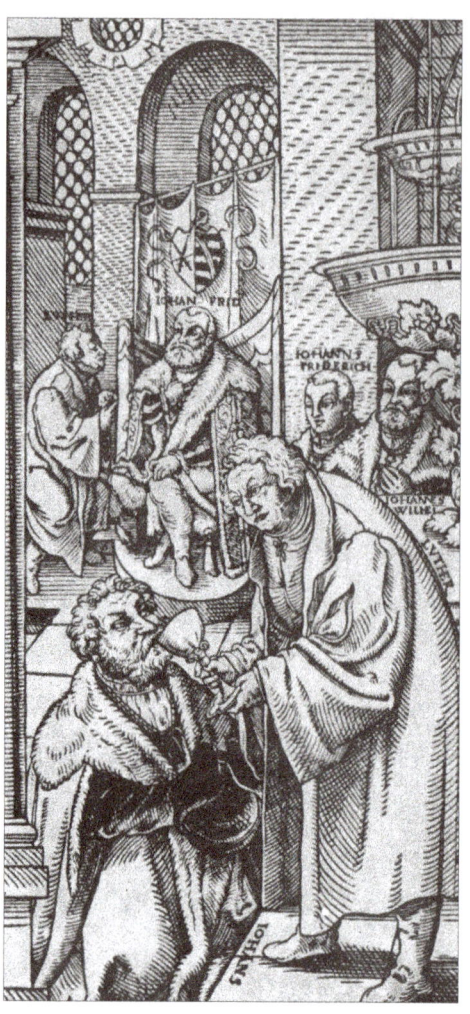

| *Luther serves the Holy Communion to the prince-electors of Germany*

- About this year, Ondřej Štefan was born in Prostějov and later became a Unity bishop.

1529 21 September A Synod of the Unity took place in Brandýs nad Orlicí.* Martin Škoda became the successor of Luke of

---

* Over the course of the 16th century, Assemblies of the brethren were renamed Brethren Synods.

Prague in the office of the eldest bishop and judge. Three more bishops were elected: Jan Roh of Domažlice, Václav Bílý and Ondřej of Ciklov.

- **28 October** Bishop Ondřej of Ciklov died. In the same year, Václav Bílý was removed from his office of bishop due to a moral transgression (as the only one in a long line of bishops in the Unity).

1530 At an assembly in Mladá Boleslav, several noblemen publicly and ceremoniously joined the: Konrád Krajíř of Krajek, Friedrich of Donín, Jan Křinecký of Ronov, Burian Špetle of Janovice and Arnošt of Jilemnice. Up to this time, the noble supporters of the Unity often did not publicly proclaim their confession. Konrád Krajíř gave the brothers in Brandýs nad Labem an Utraquist church building. Later, the Brethren built their own church house there.

1531 Jan Augusta was ordained as a Brethren priest. His first place of service was Benátky nad Jizerou where he was in service of lord of Donín.
- Mach Sionský was also ordained as a priest of the Brethren serving in Brandýs nad Orlicí.

1532 25 January Vavřinec of Krasonice, a historian of the Unity, died in Litomyšl. Martin Škoda died as well.
- **14 April** Three new bishops were elected (besides the pro-lutheran Jan Roh): Beneš of Bavoryň, natural brother of Martin Škoda, Vít Michalec and Jan Augusta. The Unity now had four bishops again. With this new generation, the Unity of Brethren became closer with Lutheranism. Mach Sionský was elected as a member of the Inner Council.

Brethren church in Brandýs nad Labem

THE THIRD GENERATION CLOSER TO THE GERMAN REFORMATION

After 1532, Jan Augusta, in particular, was promoting rapprochement with the Lutheran centre in Wittenberg and he was adapting Brethren teaching to the Augsburg confession (celibacy became voluntary, he put emphasis on justification by faith, adapted the sacraments and the Lord's Supper). In the end, Martin Luther could approve of the Brethren teaching by saying, *"After many conversations, I have found that the brothers profess our faith in somewhat different words."*[11]

1533 At the request of the Brethren, Martin Luther wrote a laudatory preface to their apologia *Rechenschaft des Glaubens* (Ac-

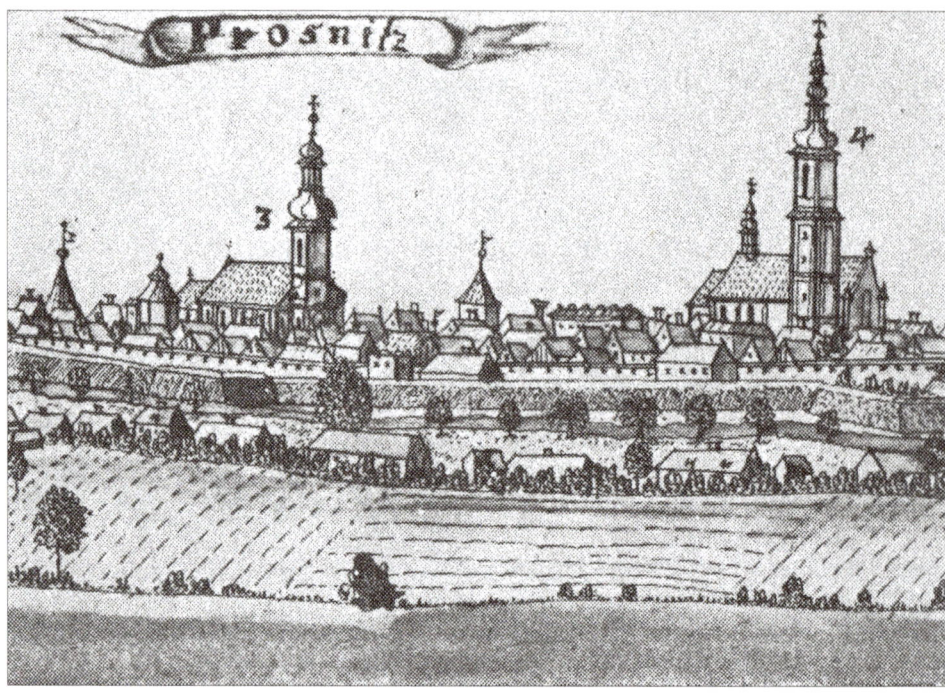

| *Prostějov – the seat of a higher Brethren school and the place of work of Jan Černý*

count of Faith) which he published that year in Wittenberg.
- Bishop Jan Roh moved to Mladá Boleslav.

1535 A synod took place in Prostějov. There, preachers were warned that they had been placing too much emphasis on foreign theological writings.
- A new Brethren's confession (with pro-Lutheran orientation) was written and was presented by Konrád Krajíř from Krajek, Jan Křinecký and Mr. Domanský in Vienna to Ferdinand I. The king verbally allowed them to believe in what they wanted but warned them against attempts to overthrow religious conditions in the Czech Kingdom. His promise, however, was not sincere.
- A persecution of brothers began in southwestern Bohemia; they were expelled from the royal towns of Vodňany, Klatovy and Domažlice. The local protectors of the Unity of Brethren, Oldřich and Smil from Janovice, were taken to the chamber court for protecting Brother Jan Zborník and then imprisoned in the Black Tower of the Prague Castle.
- **25 August** Bishop Beneš of Bavoryň died.

1536 3 March Bishop Vít Michalec died. In his and Beneš' place two brothers were called to become bishops in 1537: Martin Michalec and Mach Sionský.
- Jiří Strejc (Vetter) was born. He came from Zábřeh in Moravia. He grew up in

a Brethren family and studied in Mladá Boleslav and at universities abroad. He later became a well-known translator of the Psalms.

1537 No other bishop election took place yet but bishops Jan Augusta and Mach Sionský *"were little at peace together."*
- Jan Černý (Nigranus) was ordained a priest at the Prostějov Synod.
- The king Ferdinand I sought to separate the Unity of Brethren from the Utraquists (in an effort to unite the Utraquists with Catholics). This increased tensions between the Unity and the Utraquists. Under the influence of the German Reformation, the Utraquists were divided into two groups: conservative traditional Utraquists and Lutheran-oriented neo-Utraquists. The latter were much closer to the Unity. Jan Augusta exacerbated the controversy with two writings against the Utraquist priests.

1538 After three years, Jan Zborník, a protégé of families of Janovický and Krajíř, was released from prison.

1540 The first public and ceremonial ordination of Brethren priests and deacons took place in Mladá Boleslav. One of the brothers was, for example, Jiří (George) Israel.
- It was probably this year that Jan Augusta established contacts with the Swiss Reformation (M. Bucer, J. Calvin, W. Capiton) through Matěj Červenka. At the same time, opposition to Jan Augusta was growing in the Unity of Brethren. Opposing brothers blamed Augusta for *"leading the brothers away from the*

Jan Augusta

teachings of Brother Luke by associating with Luther."[12] Many of them, such as the governor of Moravia Václav of Ludanice, expressed their protest by leaving the Unity of Brethren.

1541 The Utraquist administrator Mystopol demanded a mandate against the Unity from the king under the pretext of Augusta's anti-Utraquist tracts. Jan Augusta was saved from prison only thanks to his trip to Wittenberg.

1542 During Augusta's last visit to Wittenberg, Martin Luther declared: *"Be apostles of the Czechs, I and my brothers will be apostles of the Germans."*[13]

1543 A new wave of persecution began.

1544 **15 September** Šimon Teofil Turnovský, later a bishop of the fifth generation of the Unity of Brethren, was born in Turnov.
- Augusta's sharp anti-Utraquist tracts irritated the whole party under both kinds. Jiří Sládkovský (an official of Jan of Pernštejn) demanded and obtained an arrest warrant for Jan Augusta from the king.

1545 New mandates against the Unity of Brethren were issued. Yet another persecution of brothers in south-western Bohemia was under way (in Klatovy, Domažlice and on the Hluboká estate, namely in Račice).
- The Land Assembly held a meeting on the restoration of the Land Tables destroyed by the fire of the Prague Castle in 1541. The Assembly rejected the request of Unity nobles that the St. Jacobs's Mandate against the Picards (from 1508) be deleted from the new records.
- Another wave of persecution against the Unity of Brethren was rising.

1546 A synod was held in Mladá Boleslav. The synod diverted from Lutheranism when Jan Roh himself (known for his previous contacts with Luther) publicly admitted that he did not find anywhere, not in the German Reformation, nor with any men of the Reformation, *"as complete and thorough teaching as in the Unity of Brethren because, illusively, I did not acknowledge merits of my church glorifying a foreign church…"*[14] It was really moving when the crying old bishop confessed to those present that he had strayed: *"I did not understand and could not know and did not know how great and pure things Unity of Brethren has."* Jan Roh repented and returned to Brother Luke's legacy in tears, especially to the *Priest Messages*. The brothers present at the synod read the whole book and found in it *"the wholeness of faith and the meaning of it"*[15] and decided to be satisfied with that and not seek anything else.
- During the fire in Litomyšl*, all documents brothers had stored there burned down. The new archive of the Unity of Brethren was then founded by Jan Černý. Matěj Červenka, the scribe of the Unity of Brethren, was entrusted managing and supplementing it with historical records and his work was continued by Jan Blahoslav who was originally Černý and Červenka's assistant.

1546–1547 The Unity of Brethren supported the neo-Utraquist opposition. The Moravian printing office printed their writings, leaflets and pamphlets against the Pope, Emperor Charles V and King Ferdinand I.

1547 **25 January (?)** Bishop Martin Michalec died in Prostějov at the age of 63.
- **11 February** Jan Roh, bishop and judge of the Unity of Brethren, died in Mladá Boleslav. Therefore, Jan Augusta once again leaned towards Luke of Prague's emphases and defended priestly celibacy.

THE FOURTH GENERATION TAKES CARE OF EXULANT BROTHERS IN POLAND AND PRUSSIA

1547 **25 April** Imperial-Catholic forces won the battle of Mühlberg (ending the Schmalkaldic War). That marked the beginning of a catastrophe for the Czech

---
* One of the key centers of the Ancient Unity.

estate opposition, especially for the Brethren nobility. Its main leader Vilém Křinecký from Ronov escaped from certain death only by fleeing. Families of Kostka and Kramář were punished by extensive confiscations of their estates where the Brethren still lived under their protection. Unlike royal cities, however, that were to be cleansed of the Unity, the Brethren nobility could retain its affiliation with the Unity.

- **5 October** King Ferdinand I renewed the St. Jacob's Mandate first issued by Wladyslaw II Jagiello in 1508.

1547 – 1549 He Unity of Brethren in Bohemia again faced severe persecution performed mainly by Utraquist priests led by the administrator Mystopol. Persecutors compiled lists of suspects and encouraged denouncing, arrests and imprisonment.

1548 20 January The king issued a new anti-Brethren order in Augsburg. This order commanded strict implementation of the previous mandate. Brethren meetings were to be banned, priests imprisoned, and congregations handed over to Catholic or Utraquist preachers. Brothers were forced to renounce their faith the easy way or the hard way.

- **25 April** Šejnoch, the new governor of Litomyšl, cunningly lured Jan Augusta and his assistant, Jakub Bílek, to a meeting and captured them. Jan Augusta was imprisoned for sixteen years altogether; first at Prague Castle and then at Křivoklát Castle.
- **5 May** King Ferdinand I issued a new royal mandate valid in all his lands. All Brethren living in royal cities and on royal estates (many of those acquired by previous confiscation) were to be expelled within six weeks.
- **Mid-June** Brothers left royal domains in Bohemia in great numbers, mainly the Rychnov, Litomyšl, Býnov, Brandýs

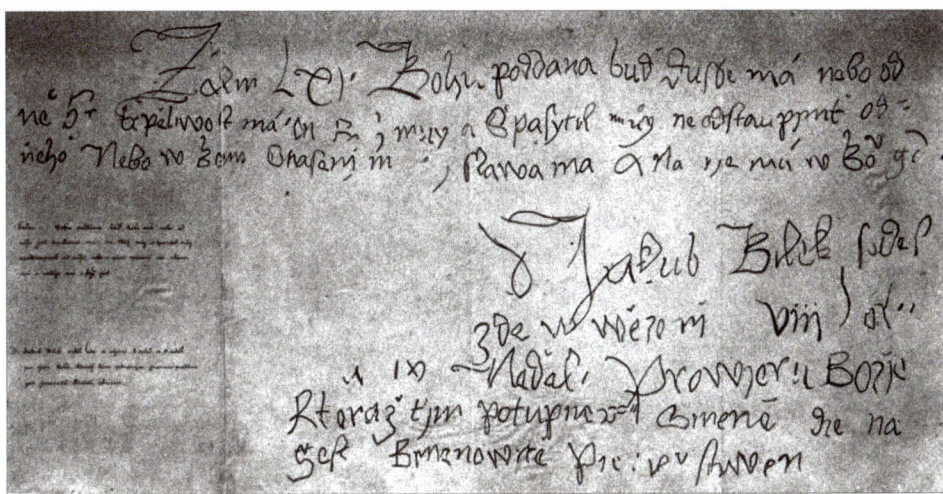

| Facsimile of the inscription of Jakub Bílek in the prison at Křivoklát Castle

estates and Solnice. About six hundred people with sixty carriages then traveled towards Wrocław and further to Poznań in Wielkopolska (Greater Poland). A second group from Brandýs and Turnov followed them about a week later. The emigrants were led by Matěj Orel, Urban Hermon, Jan Korytanský and Matěj Tatíček.

- **25 June** The first brothers arrived in Poznań where its Protestant mayor, Lord Ondřej of Górka, took care of them against the will of Bishop Izbiński.
- **4 August** Bishop Izbiński of Poznań demanded an anti-Unity mandate from King Sigismund II Augustus of Poland. Brothers thus were to be expelled from Poznań and Poland.
- **At the end of the summer**, the brothers left Greater Poland for Prussia (at the invitation of Albert, Duke of Prussia). Jiří Izrael and Mach Sionský, the only

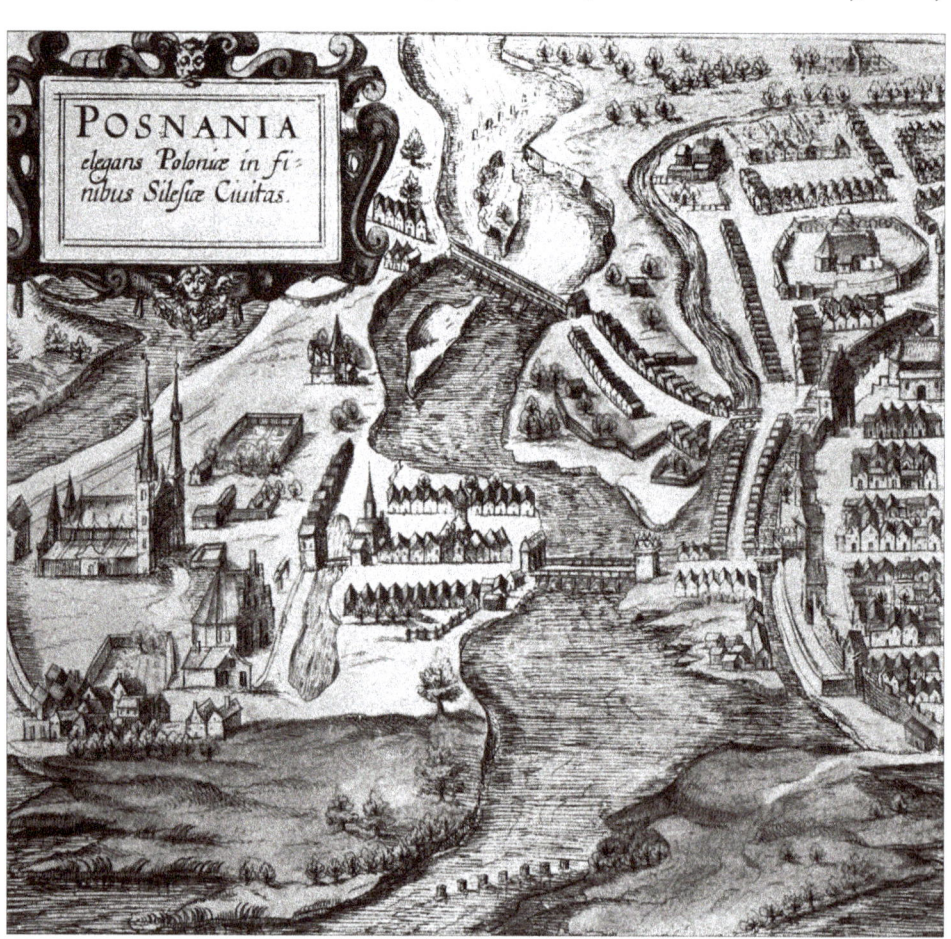

Poznań – one of the most important centers of the brothers in Poland along with Leszno

bishop at liberty after Augusta's arrest, also found refuge in Prussia. The Brethren remained there until 1574 but they had to adapt to the Prussian Lutheran Church.

1549 Bishop Mach Sionský returned to Poznań for some time. The centre of the Unity of Brethren was secretly established in the house of Lord Ondřej Lipčinský. Matěj Orel, Matěj Červenka and Jiří Izrael also worked there as well.

- **13 December** Matěj Červenka was ordained a Unity priest.

1550 **1 January** Matěj Červenka was elected to the Inner Council.

- At a Moravian Diet in Brno, King Ferdinand I unsuccessfully tried to suppress the so-called sectarianism in Czech lands. The Moravian* governor, Václav of Ludanice (formerly a follower of the Unity), and with him the whole Moravian nobility, stood up for resistance. Moravia therefore became the main centre of the Unity of Brethren.
- Pavel Jesenský (Jessenius) was born in Uherský Brod. He later became a Unity bishop and a translator of the Kralice Bible.

1551 **16 April** Bishop Mach Sionský died in Doubravna, Prussia. At that time, the Unity of Brethren had only one Bishop – Jan Augusta. However, he was in prison and exercised his office through written communication with Jan Černý. At that time, there was no one who could ordain new priests.

1552 Jan Černý (Nigranus) established the main seat of the Unity in Bohemia at his residence in Mladá Boleslav under the protection of Arnošt Krajíř of Krajek.

- Jan Němčanský who later became a bishop and arranged publishing the six-volume Kralice Bible, was born in Uherský Brod.

1553 Despite the original resistance, brothers began to assert themselves in Greater Poland with the support of powerful Polish evangelical families. Jiří Izrael became an administrator of a Brethren community in Poznań and the influence of the Unity of Brethren was spreading to other cities in Greater Poland, such as Leszno.

- **8 June** A synod took place in Prostějov. After breaking contact with imprisoned Jan Augusta, brothers elected new bishops – Jan Černý and Matěj Červenka. They received consecration from the oldest members of the Inner Council, Matouš Strejc and Pavel Paulin, with others joining them in laying on of hands on behalf of the whole Unity.
- **13 June** Bishop Matěj Červenka was appointed a scribe of the Unity of Brethren.
- Jan Blahoslav was ordained a priest. Jan Černý (living in Mladá Boleslav since 1552) who had already had an influential position during the life of Bishop Mach Sionský, became the real head of the Unity of Brethren.
- Jan Kálef was ordained a priest.

1554 **9 March** King Ferdinand I issued a new mandate against the brothers ordering the closure of their churches.

- **23 March** The Brethren church in Mladá Boleslav was ceremonially consecrated.

Moravia – eastern part of Czech lands.

1555 The Unity of Brethren in Greater Poland together with Protestants from Lesser Poland held a synod where they discussed possible fusion of both directions.
- Jan Blahoslav met with Pfauser in Vienna. He was the court Lutheran preacher of Archduke Maximilian II.
- Jan Blahoslav went again to Vienna to see Pfauser who promised to help the Unity of Brethren.
- Jan Augusta's conditions in prison were eased and he could reconnect with his brothers in the Unity.
- **18 March** Arnošt Krajíř of Krajek died. He was the owner of the Mladá Boleslav estate and the leading protector of the Unity of Brethren in Bohemia.

1554 – 1555 Jiří Izrael helped to organize about twenty congregations and preaching stations of the Unity in Poland; the most important of which also had their spiritual administrators. Vojtěch Serpentin took care of the church in Kožmínek followed by Jan Rokyta; Jiří Fillipenský was appointed to the congregation in Lobženice; the priest Jan Rybinski served in Barcin; Petr Skalník was appointed to Marszewa etc. These congregations together with older ones established in 1548 (most important of which were on the estates of Ondřej Górka in Szamotuły, Leszno and Kurnik) totaled to forty.

1556 Bishop Jan Černý (Nigranus) became the judge of the Unity of Brethren.

1557 Efforts to release Jan Augusta were renewed with the intervention of Christoph – Duke of Württemberg, former

Jan Kálef

papal legate Pavel Verger, and Polish Protestant lords. However, all efforts turned out to be fruitless.
- Another synod took place in Žeravice and the opposition against Jan Augusta won. It was unanimously decided: *"that no one alone, as one head, is to be favored or treated the way the Pope is in the Church of Rome with everything relying on him."*[16]
- Flacius II, a Lutheran fundamentalist, attacked the Unity of Brethren saying it is as a heretical sect directly following the Waldensian movement.
- **24 August** The Unity of Brethren celebrated its centenary with a synod which took place in Ślęzany. Brothers from Bohemia, Moravia and Poland were joined by their Polish protectors Jan Krotoský, Jakub of Ostrorog, Rafael Leszczynský

and others. The Brethren confession was declared a norm in matters of faith (against the will of Polish lords who preferred the Lutheran confession of Augsburg). A senior was appointed for the regions of Poland and Prussia.

Jan Blahoslav and Jiří Izrael were elected bishops meaning the Unity of Brethren had four bishops again. Jiří Izrael was called to administer Polish and Prussian congregations. The synod introduced means for greater decentralization of the church with the power of the elected council increasing at the expense of the bishops: *"the council elected by the synod represents the assembly of the faithful and becomes not only the supreme authority but also the executive power and the centre of life and work."*[17] The Synod also strengthened the position of laity and the growing Calvinist influence.

- Ondřej Štefan was ordained a priest and became an assistant to Matěj Červenka in Přerov.
- After 1557, Polish Protestant theologians Laski and Lismanin spoke out against the Unity and criticized the Brethren confession, especially the teaching of the Lord's Supper. Based on these intrigues and disinformation, Swiss reformers (J. Calvin, T. Beza, W. Muskulus) wrote an unfavorable report on the Brethren confession and sent it to Poland.

1560 The Unity sent Brother Rokyta and Petr Herbert to Switzerland. Negotiations with the reformers were successful and rectified all misunderstanding. Petr Herber returned home with friendly letters from Swiss theologians.

Title page of the Szamotuły hymn book

1561 Jan Blahoslav was the key person behind publishing the Szamotuły hymn book called Songs of Divine Worship.

1562 Ferdinand I (the Holy Roman Emperor at that time) handed over the imprisoned Jan Augusta to the Catholic clergy. Augusta refused to accept Catholicism in order to be set free. However, he took sides with Utraquists (or rather Lutheran neo-Utraquists). The Inner Council condemned this and deprived Augusta of his episcopate and membership in the Unity.

1564 The Emperor and King Ferdinand I died and a new King Maximilian II raised hopes for better times in the Unity of Brethren.

- Jan Blahoslav published his translation of the New Testament.
- **26 March** By the king's intercession, Jan Augusta was released from prison and forbidden to preach in public.
- **April** Jan Augusta met with the Inner Council, explained all misunderstandings they were reconciled. Augusta was allowed to return to his office resulting in the Unity having two judges.
- Brothers published a hymn book of Ivančice – the pride of Czech typographic and woodcarving art.

1565 **5 February** Jan Černý (Nigranus), a bishop and a judge of the Unity of Brethren, died in Mladá Boleslav.
- Jan Augusta tried to unite the Unity of Brethren with the Lutherans (neo-Utraquists) and to gain the leadership of all Czech and Moravian non-Catholics.

1566 Brothers presented their confession and hymn book to King Maximilian II but they received only a verbal promise that they would continue to be tolerated.
- **27 December** Ján Jesenský, also known as Jan Jessenius, was born in Wrocław. He later became a renowned doctor, politician and philosopher of the Unity of Brethren. As a doctor, he performed the first public autopsy in Reček's college in Prague from June 8 to June 12, 1600.
- Matěj Cyrus, later a bishop of the Unity, was born in Třebenice. He became an important personality in the sixth generation of the Unity of Brethren before the Battle of White Mountain.

1567 Another synod took place in Přerov and brothers refused Augusta's efforts to unite with the Lutherans. However, Augusta carried on with his efforts personally. Jiří Strejc (Vetter) was ordained as a priest and also called as an administrator in Hranice.

1568 Blahoslav's translation of the New Testament revised by Jan Němčanský was published again. The translation became the basis for the last sixth volume of the Bible of Kralice.

1569 **12 December** Matěj Červenka, bishop and administrator of the Přerov region, historian and composer of many songs, died in Přerov at the age of 48.
- Matouš Konečný, later an administrator in Mladá Boleslav and a bishop, was born in Strážnice.

Maximilian II, Holy Roman Emperor

1570 The Unity of Brethren held negotiations with Lutherans and Calvinists in Sandomierz, Poland. All three Protestant schools in Poland reached an agreement to recognize each other's creeds (so-called Sandomierz Agreement). The Unity of Brethren still maintained its independence.

- **March** Jan Cyrill (Cyrillus) Třebíčský, the last preacher of the Bethlehem Chapel, was born.

THE FIFTH GENERATION CREATES SPIRITUAL AND LITERARY VALUES

1571 Blahoslav's books, *Gramatika česká* (Czech Grammar), which he had begun writing in 1551, and *Vady kazatelův* (The Failings of Preachers), were completed and published.

- **11 October** Jan Kálef, Jan Lorenc and Ondřej Štefan were consecrated as bishops in Ivančice.
- **24 November** Bishop Jan Blahoslav, one of the greatest personalities of the Unity of Brethren, died in Moravský Krumlov at the age of 49. Brethren memoirs say: *"Jan Blahoslav died in Krumlov. He was one of the four leaders and a scribe, a father and a charioteer of the Lord's people of the Unity, a man so great and excellent, devout and diligent and very amiable to everyone from a young age. His reputation was known among other nations. A great and precious jewel of the Unity, whom the Lord has taken, in our judgment, too soon."*[18] Ondřej Štefan then became a scribe of the Unity of Brethren.

Augusta's further work in Unity was marked by new conflicts that arose from a series of misunderstandings with the new generation of bishops. Historical evidence suggests that Augusta showed little willingness to submit to the collective decisions of the Inner Council and he acted independently. The tension escalated into an open conflict in which Augusta was again removed from his Episcopal office and thus of all influence in the Unity.

Jan Blahoslav

1572 **13 January** Jan Augusta died in Mladá Boleslav. With Augusta's death, the pro-Lutheran direction in the Unity was significantly weakened.

1573 **28 February** Šimon Teofil Turnovský was ordained a priest and called to be a church administrator in Lutomierzice.

Former town hall in Prague – the place where the Bohemian Confession was written

1575 Non-Catholic estates wrote a draft of the Bohemian Confession. The Confession was submitted for approval to the Land Assembly. At first, King Maximilian II verbally gave his permission providing that Protestant nobility agreed to the election of his son Rudolf II as a Czech king. Ultimately, however, he banned printing the Bohemian Confession altogether and issued a manifesto which instructed the regional governors to strictly abide by anti-Brethren decrees (by Wladyslaw II and Ferdinand I).

- The Unity of Brethren began to participate in the Bohemian Confession. Specifically, Ondřej Štefan (who became a scribe of the Unity after Blahoslav) and Jan Kálef (the oldest bishop after Blahoslav's death). George Israel resided in Poland with Bishop Jan Lorenc and they did not interfere in Bohemian and Moravian affairs. In addition to the two former brothers, Jakub Veliký, Jan Javornický, Izajáš Cibulka and Jiří Strejc also took part in negotiations.
- After accepting the conditions (partly thanks to Pavel Pressius, a professor at the University of Prague, and Kryšpín, the scribe of the Old Town of Prague), the Czech Confession was a mixture of Brethren and Lutheran teachings.

The teaching about the Lord's Supper is inspired by Melanchthon's formulation but in an effort to conform to Calvin. *"According to Lutheranism, faith is salvific and also only those good deeds that come from faith. But he who neglects deeds will drive away faith and turn away the Holy Spirit."*[19]

The Bohemian Confession included a second part – a proposal to change the ecclesiastical establishment of church in Bohemia. The Confession was a big compromise and the Unity remained reserved. But they needed to be by the side of other Protestants.

1576 Brother began translating the Old Testament from Hebrew into Czech. Bishop
–
1577 Ondřej Štefan invited brilliant experts in Hebrew – Master Albrecht of Kamének and Lukáš Helič of Poznań who came from a Jewish family.

1577 21 June Bishop Ondřej Štefan died in Prostějov.

- **30 August** A synod took place in Holešov. The Synod decided that the oldest bishop George Israel and Bishop Lorenc (residing in Poland) would head the Unity of Brethren as judges. Brothers Zachariáš Litomyšlský (from Mladá Boleslav) and Jan Eneáš Boleslavský were chosen to be new bishops alongside Bishop Jan Kálef. Izaiáš Cibulka, who was also on the Provincial Board, was called to continue with the translation of the Old Testament under the supervision of Bishop Jan Eneáš Boleslavský.
- Brothers were invited by Count Palatine John Casimir to attend the Calvinist Synod in Frankfurt am Main. However, the Unity of Brethren was in contact with the Lutherans at the time so the delegates only expressed their sympathies at the Calvinist Synod because for tactical reasons they had to adhere to those who belonged to the Augsburg confession.
- After 1577, the Unity of Brethren sent its students to Calvinist schools, especially to Heidelberg, as an expression of further convergence with the Reformed. The administration of the Unity of Brethren was more in the hands of the laity at that time. Educated clergy did not lose its influence, but unlike Lutheran priests (servants of the superior nobility), they rather became friends, guides and confidants of their nobles. The Brethren's

Title page of the six-volume Kralice Bible

priests were increasingly giving up their voluntary celibacy and they did no longer live off the work of their hands as often as before.

1578 The printing office was transported from Ivančice to Kralice nad Oslavou together with the extensive library of the Unity of Brethren.

1579 The six-volume Kralice Bible was printed
– in Kralice under the protection and with
1594 the financial contribution of Jan Starší of Zierotin. People who were involved in the translation and publishing of the Bible, apart from Bishops O. Štefan, J. Eneáš

and Hebrew linguists, were: Jiří Strejc, Jan Capito, Pavel Essen and Jan Efraim. Even though the Unity of Brethren was getting closer to the world, it was still filled with the spirit of its founders. While in Bohemia, Moravia, and Poland, where the Unity was active, there was church decline and moral depravity, the Unity of Brethren *"was a remarkable school of perfection and purity, and, in a generation soaked in selfishness, it represented the cultivation of ideals, dedication and devotion."*[20]

1580 The Emperor and King Rudolf II issued an order about printing offices and prints mainly to prevent Brethren from further publication of the bible.

1581 Brothers published another edition of the hymn book (Ivančice hymnal). It was first published in 1564 and 1576 in Ivančice. After the printing office moved, it was printed in Kralice. The third version was published in 1583 and 1598.

- **27 November** Jakub Bílek, a fellow prisoner of Jan Augusta and a Brethren author, died.

1582 A Jesuit Václav Šturm published a treatise against the Brethren *Srovnání víry a učení bratří starších* (Comparison of the Faith and Teaching of the Brethren). The author tried to prove the variability of opinion and ambiguity of Brethren's dogmas.

- On the order of the highest Czech chancellor Vratislav of Pernštejn, Brethren's congregations in Litomyšl, Lanškroun, Potštejn and Kostelec were closed.
- **25 August** Isaiah Cibulka, one of the translators of the Bible of Kralice, died.

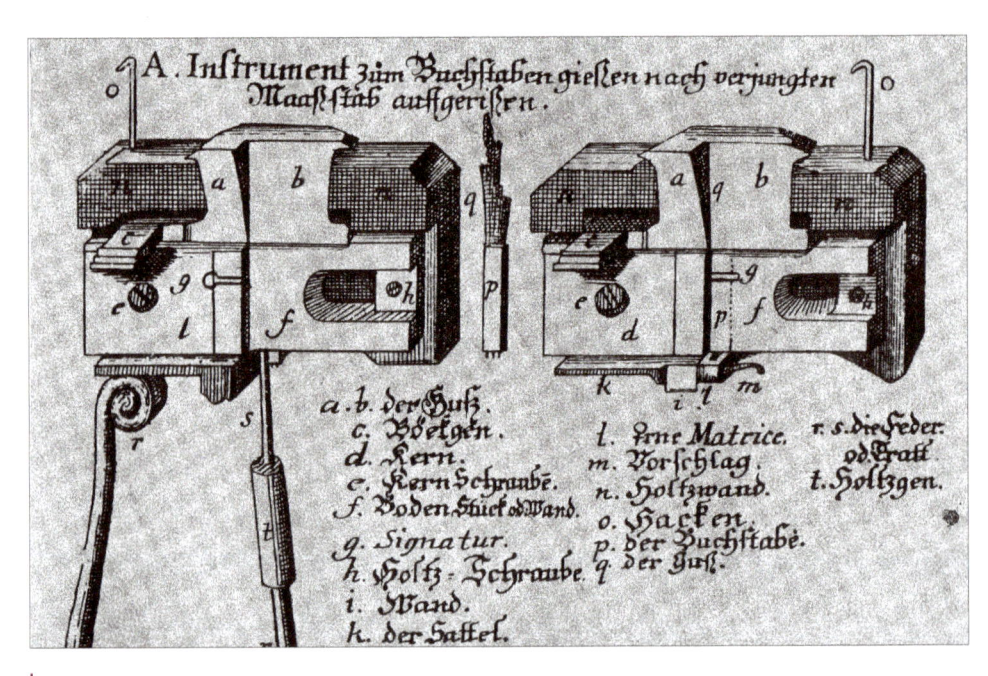

| *Old tools for casting block letters*

He had prepared the first three parts for printing.

1583 The persecution of the Unity of Brethren reappeared; this time on the estate of Václav Berka of Dubá in Rychmburk.

1584 **7 January** The king Rudolf II issued a mandate against the brothers.
- Jan Capito, a Brethren author, was called to service in the Inner Council. He also participated in the translation of the Kralice Bible.

1585 Jiří Strejc (Vetter) was elected to the Inner Council.

1586 *Postilla*, a book written by Jan Capito, was published for the needs of Brethren's churches.

1587 **9 July** Bishop Jan Lorenc died in Ostrorog, Poland. Bishop Zacharias fell ill. Therefore, Bishops Jan Abdiáš and Šimon Teofil Turnovský, who became the leading Bishop of the entire Polish branch of the Unity of Brethren, were to help him. This decision was made at the synod in Lipník in Moravia.
- Jiří Strejc (Vetter) published a work called *The Psalms – Songs of St. David* in Kralice.

1588 With the death of Adam Krajíř of Krajek, the Krajíř family, powerful supporters of the Unity, died out. The position of the congregation in Mladá Boleslav was thus seriously endangered.
- **15 June** The Unity Bishop of the Polish branch, Jiří Izrael, died at an age of more than 80. Bishop Šimon Teofil Turnovský took over the administration of Polish congregations.

Rudolf II, Holy Roman Emperor

- **24 June Bishop** Jan Abdiáš died in Přerov.
- **12 December** Bishop Jan Kálef died in Brandýs nad Orlicí leaving behind three bishops: Zachary Litomyšlský who was old and ill, then Jan Eneáš Boleslavský and Šimon Teofil Turnovský.
- The fifth volume of the Kralice Bible finishing the translation of the Old Testament was published. Blahoslav's idea finally became a reality.

1589 **5 June** Two new bishops were elected to serve alongside Bishop Zachariáš of Litomyšl: Jan Efraim and Pavel Jesenský who served in Lipník for a total of six-

teen years. Jan Němčanský was called to the Inner Council.
- **31 December** Jan Capito died in Třebíč.

1590 **4 April (?)** Bishop Zachary Litomyšlský died in Sležany at the age of 68.
- Pavel Fabricius, later a Unity bishop, was born in Strážnice.

1592 **28 March** John Amos Comenius, an important personality in the seventh generation of the fathers of the Unity, was born (either in Uherský Brod or in Nivnice).
- Zachary Ariston, later a bishop, was called to the Inner Council.
- In fall, Daniel Strejc, called Vetter, was born in Hranice in Moravia. He was the first Czech to visit Iceland with his companion Jan Salmon in 1613.

1594 **5 February** Jan Eneáš Boleslavský, bishop and leader of the staff of translators of the Kralice Bible, died in Ivančice. He was one of the most important shepherds of the Unity of Brethren. He was attacked by soldiers, beaten and tortured during his pastoral service in Kounice near Ivančice. *"Brethren's memoirs call him a special jewel of the Unity, a pious and exemplary man, a vigilant guardian of God's servants."*[21]
- Blahoslav's translation of the New Testament was published again, this time as the sixth volume of the Bible of Kralice and revised by a group of translators.*
- **24 May** Bishop Pavel Jesenský died in Bezuchov and was buried in Dřevohostice. Brethren's records describe him very realistically. They speak of him as a bright and erudite man, but

Bishop John Amos Comenius

also a proud man. He left behind debts, because among other things, he had an extraordinary house built in Lipník.
- The Sandomierz Agreement of 1570 was re-adopted and approved at the General Synod of the Polish Protestant Churches in Toruń.
- **14 July** Brothers met at Synod in Přerov. Bishops Jakub Narcissus and Jan Němčanský, who was a scribe of the Unity, were consecrated there. Šimon Turnovský became a representative of the Unity of Brethren in Poland where he served.

1596 **8 March** Zachariáš Solín, the printer of the Bible of Kralice, died.

---
* Some sources say it was in 1593.

1598 The Synod met in Mladá Boleslav. Bishop Šimon Turnovský pushed a compromise doctrine between Lutheranism and Calvinism and rejected purely Calvinist orientation (e.g. the doctrine of the Lord's Supper).

- **16 September (?)** Bishop Jan Němčanský died in Drahotuše near Hranice.

1599 Bishop Š. Turnovský unsuccessfully negotiated on the initiative of Prince Kryštof Radzwil and Konstantin of Ostrorog on unification with the Greek Church. It was a reaction to the Union of Brest from 1596 when the Orthodox Church in the Polish-Lithuanian Commonwealth united with the Roman Catholic Church.

- **23 January** Jiří Strejc (Vetter), a translator of the Psalms, died in Židlochovice.
- **6 July** Samuel Sušický and Zachariáš Ariston were called as collaborators and bishops alongside Bishop Š. Turnovský. However, on August 6 of the same year,

Uherský Brod – an important centre of the Ancient Unity

Samuel Sušický died. He belonged to the younger generation of translators of the Scripture. Zachariáš Ariston was commissioned to review the text of the New Testament and to expand the expository notes. Unity of Brethren had four bishops at that time.

1600 **22 October** Bishop Jan Efraim, a collaborator in the translation of the Kralice Bible, died in Prague. He was buried in Mladá Boleslav in the grave of Jan Augusta. The obituary highlighted his piety, erudition and philanthropy. *"But he was too anxious not to punish or offend anyone. Yet, deep inside, he was worried and cried when alone."*[22]

Jan Efraim

THE SIXTH GENERATION AIMS FOR POLITICS

1601 **11 May (?)** Bartoloměj Němčanský and Jan Lanecius were appointed as bishops by the Synod in Mladá Boleslav.

1602 St. Jacob's Mandate from 1508 was renewed on the initiative of the highest hofmeister* Kryštof Popel of Lobkowicz.
- The church in Mladá Boleslav was closed and two imperial commissioners also took over a Brethren's house and a school.

1603 Protestant estates confronted Emperor Rudolf II at the Land Assembly. Wenceslas Budovec, on behalf of a knighthood, demanded religious freedom for fellow believers who adhered to the Bohemian Confession from 1575.

1604 The Synod in Žeravice rejected Turnovský's pro-Lutheran position on the Lord's Supper and accepted Calvinist teaching which states that in the Eucharist, there is only a symbolic presence of the body and blood of the Lord.

1606 The Czech Protestant nobility made use of the following three years of a dynastic and political crisis of Habsburg states and tried to strengthen their positions.
- **8 February** Bishop Zachariáš Ariston died in Ivančice. Brethren's memoirs write of him that during the Bocskai uprising in Moravia (in 1605) he suffered great sorrow. Bocskai's regiments set fire to a number of Brethren's church houses, raped women, murdered brothers, and dragged

---
* Second highest administrative position in the kingdom.

women and girls into captivity. On top of that, a wave of plague struck the region of Moravia. Zachariáš Ariston died of tuberculosis in the end.

1608 22 March Bishop Šimon Turnovský died at the age of 64 in Ostrorog, Poland. He was buried in a Brethren's church between the altar and the northern column and his obituary says: *"In him left a man so zealous and exemplary in his teaching and spiritual calling; tireless bishop, honorable in every respect."*[23]

- **30 August** Matěj Rybinski and Martin Gratianus were elected bishops in Lipník.

1609 29 April (?) Jan Cruciger was elected by lot and called in place of Bishop Ariston. The Unity of Brethren, therefore, had five bishops again.

- Matouš Konečný was called to Mladá Boleslav with Jan Brož as his assistant.
- **9 July** Rudolf II issued the Letter of Majesty which guaranteed in writing a free and undisturbed practice of the Protestant religion. The emperor wanted to secure the support of Czech Protestant estates in the dispute with his brother Matthias and to keep at least the Czech crown* for himself. The basis of the Letter laid in the Bohemian Confession from 1575. No side, Catholic nor Protestant, may insult or persecute each other for religion. The nobility and cities were free to build churches and schools on their land. No lord may force his subjects to adopt his faith. Estates were to decide on the members of a

| *Church in Mladá Boleslav – built by Matteo Borgorelli in 1544–1554.*

---

* Rudolf II was King of Bohemia but also Holy Roman Emperor and until 1608 King of Hungary and Croatia.

consistory which would watch over ordinations of Protestant clergy, discipline and faith. The university also passed into the hands of estates. The estates form a standing committee to defend their rights – *the defensors* – whom the emperor then confirmed in office. Protestants were still to be called by their common name: Utraquists. The Letter of Majesty became a fundamental article of the code of law. It was accompanied by a settlement written by both Catholics and Utraquists. This was to prevent new disputes between them. Brothers immediately began with creating a joint Bohemian Lutheran-Brethren church. The Protestants established a new consistory with twelve members: six Lutheran priests, three brothers from the Unity of Brethren (Matěj Cyrus, Jan Cyrill Třebíčský and Jan Korvín) and three members of the university. Lutheran Eliáš Šúd from Semanín became the administrator of the consistory. University professors were usually laymen. Ordinations of priests were performed by an administrator and a senior.* Otherwise, each party retained its own teachings, customs and orders, as well as full freedom in the education of priests. It was, however, a process of convergence and many compromises (especially by the Unity of Brethren).

■ **16 November** Bishop Bartoloměj Němčanský, Jan Němčanský's brother, died. Matouš Konečný, who had been consecrated as bishop in October, was called in his place.

| Bethlehem Chapel in Prague – Matěj Cyrus's place of work

* Representative of the Unity of Brethren – bishop.

- **4 December** The Bethlehem Chapel was placed under the administration of the Unity of Brethren and Matěj Cyrus became a preacher there.

1611 **27 March (?)** Bishop Jakub Narcissus died.
- Matěj Cyrus, an administrator in the Bethlehem Chapel, was consecrated as bishop. He had been a member of the Prague Consistory since 1609.

1612 **22 May (?)** Bishop Matěj Rybinski died in Ostrorog, Poland. Bishop Jan Turnovský, nephew of Teofil Turnovský, was consecrated and called in his place.
- **22 October** Bishop Jan Cruciger died in Ivančice and in his place, Jiří Erastus was consecrated as bishop. There were thus six bishops in the Unity of Brethren (J. Lanecius, M. Gratianus, M. Konečný, M. Cyrus, J. Turnovský and J. Erastus).

1613 After the previous revision, the one-volume Kralice Bible without expository notes was published again. The press was launched due to great interest in the previous edition, but also due to the need to have the Bible in a larger and more readable format than before. This edition is referred to as the last edition of Kralice owing to the fact that a few years later (after the Battle of White Mountain in 1620) the Unity of Brethren had to end its activities.

1616 A synod was called to Žeravice. The *Ratio disciplinae ordinisque ecclesiastici in Unitate fratrum Bohemorum* (About discipline and ecclesiastical order in the Unity of Czech Brethren) was accepted as the norm for the future. The treatise expressed will and desire to maintain Unity's originality, discipline and church organization even after full unification with other Protestants (this order was re-approved at the Synod in Leszno in 1532 and then published in the press). At the Synod on April 26, John Amos Comenius was ordained a priest of the Unity of Brethren.

1618 **16 March** Bishop Matěj Cyrus, the administrator of the Bethlehem Chapel, died in Prague where he was also buried.

Remains of a Brethren's church in Ivančice

- **11 May** Despite the opposition of the Prague Old Town Mayor F. Osterstock, Jan Cyrill Třebíčský became the new administrator of the Bethlehem Chapel.
- **15 May** J. C. Třebíčský was consecrated as bishop.

1619 26 August Bishop Jan Cyrill Třebíčský (member of the consistory under both kinds) and administrator Jiří Dikast crowned Frederick V of the Palatinate as Czech King.

THE SEVENTH GENERATION IS LEAVING INTO EXILE

1620 8 November The Imperial and Bavarian army defeated the Bohemian Estates' army in the infamous Battle of White Mountain. The defeat of the Estates' Uprising paved the way for implementing Habsburg absolutism and Catholic Counter-Reformation.

1621 13 March A mandate was issued to expel Protestant preachers from their homeland.
- **21 June** Twenty-seven Czech noblemen were executed on the Old Town Square in Prague. Among them were also some personalities of the Unity of Brethren, such as Wenceslas Budovec of Budov, Jindřich Otta of Los or Jan Jessenius.
- **2 August** Emperor Ferdinand II annulled Rudolf's Letter of Majesty.
- **In December**, Prince Karl I of Liechtenstein issued an order to expel members of consistory, bishop Jan Cyrill Třebíčský and administrator Jiří Dikast, from the country. The consistory of the Protestant party under both kinds is thus effectively dissolved.

Execution on the Old Town Square

1622 8 February Bishop Matouš Konečný died in Brandýs nad Orlicí. Before that, in December 1620, he had hidden rare writings and documents of the Unity of Brethren under the threshold in a house in Mladá Boleslav.*
- **21 July** All non-Catholic priests were expelled from Moravia.

1623 24 July Ferdinand II issued a new mandate ordering a banishment of all non-Catholic clergy from Bohemia.

1624 Catholic Reformation was introduced in towns and villages.

---

* These documents in two boxes were discovered during house remodel in June 2006.

1626 17 November Bishop Jan Lanecius died in Kralice leaving the Unity with only four bishops.

1627 In May A renewed code of law was issued ordering even higher estates to convert to Catholicism within six months. Otherwise, they were to sell their land and move out of the country.
- In Greater Poland, the Polish branch of the Unity of Brethren was completely merged with the Calvinists. Therefore, after arriving in Poland, Brethren exiles did not unite with the Polish branch of the Unity of Brethren, but continued to live as a separate church with its own hierarchy. Both of these branches of Unity lived side by side. Their common seat was Leszno. The Polish Bishop of the Unity of Brethren, Martin Gratianus, and Bishops of the Bohemian Unity of Brethren, Jan Cyrill Třebíčský aand Jiří Erastus, also resided there.

1628 8 February A wave of exiles led by John Amos Comenius arrived in Leszno, Poland.
- **21 April** Another mass escape of non-Catholics from Bohemia took place.

1629 6 March (?) Bishop Martin Gratianus died in Leszno, Poland.
- **8 April** Another bishop, Jan Turnovský, died. Only two bishops, Jan Erastus and Jan Cyrill Třebíčský, remained.
- **6 July** Pavel Paliurus and probably Daniel Mikolajewski were elected bishops of the Polish branch, in Leszno.

Wenceslas Budovec of Budov – representative of Brethren nobility

1632 30 May Bishop Jan Cyrill Třebíčský (the last preacher in the Bethlehem Chapel) died right during his sermon.
- **1–7 October** A Synod was held in Leszno. Brothers elected new bishops: Vavřinec Justýn, Matěj Prokop, Pavel Fabricius and John Amos Comenius who also became the scribe of the Unity of Brethren. The consecration was performed by Jiří Erastus. (Pavel Fabricius was consecrated later due to his absence.) The Unity had then seven bishops. The Synod also confirmed an ecclesiastical order and a system of organization of the Unity which were both published in print.

1633 **11 April (?)** Bishop Daniel Mikolajewski died in Debnice.
- **17 April** Bishop Martin Orminus was appointed head of the Polish branch of the Unity of Brethren and Bishop Jan Rybinski was appointed his deputy. At that time, the Unity of Brethren had the following bishops: J. Erastus, V. Justýn, M. Prokop, P. Fabricius, John Amos Comenius, M. Orminus, J. Rybinski.

1636 In Ostrorog, a church house was taken away from the Unity of Brethren. Leszno thus remained the only Brethren's village in Greater Poland and Unity's last refuge until 1656.
- **16 February** Bishop Matěj Prokop died in Leszno.

1638 **13 September** Bishop Jan Rybinski died.

1643 **8 May** Bishop Jiří Erastus died in Leszno. Bishop Vavřinec Justýn became the judge.

1644 **1 January (?)** Bishop Martin Orminus died. Only three bishops, V. Justýn, P. Fabricius and John Amos Comenius, remained. Bishop Martin Gertich was elected to join them. He was called to be the judge of the Polish branch of the Unity after Orminus. Jan Bythner was elected as another bishop (on April 15). Eventually, the Unity of Brethren had five bishops.

1648 **18 April (?)** Bishop Vavřinec Justýn died in Leszno and Bishop Comenius became the judge of the Bohemian-Moravian branch of the Unity of Brethren in Poland.

Leszno in Greater Poland (Wielkopolska)

- The Peace of Westphalia was ratified. It buried all hopes for return of the Unity to its homeland and Bishop Comenius wrote *The Bequest of a Dying Mother, the Unity of Brethren*. Only three churches: Roman Catholic, Lutheran and Reformed (Calvinist) were recognized in Europe by the Peace of Westphalia.

1649 3 January Pavel Fabricius, bishop of the Bohemian-Moravian branch of the Unity, died in Leszno. The Polish branch still had two bishops; the Bohemian-Moravian branch had only one.

1650 Bishop Comenius visited Czech exiles in Slovakia (then part of Hungary). He also accepted the invitation of Prince Sigismund Rákóczi of Transylvania to realize his ideal of an "omniscient school" on Prince's estate in Šaryšský Potok (Sárospatak). To put his ideas into practice, Bishop Comenius wrote eight school plays *Schola ludus* and prepared the first picture textbook *Orbis Pictus* (The World in Pictures). After Rákóczi's death, he could not finish his work there anymore.

1654 Bishop Comenius returned to Leszno.

1655 The Polish-Swedish war broke out and became a disaster for Czech emigration. The Polish branch of the Unity of Brethren practically disappeared. It was scattered to England, Germany, the Netherlands, the Swedish Baltics and Hungary.

1656 29 April Leszno was burned down by Polish Catholic troops. Bishop Comenius lost all his property and alongside all Czech exiles left the city.

1660 20 November Daniel Ernest Jablonský (later chief court preacher of the Reformed Church and bishop of the Polish branch of the Unity of Brethren), grandson of Bishop John Amos Comenius, was born in Nassenhuben (modern-day Mokry Dwór near Gdańsk).

- Bishop John Amos Comenius wrote *The Sorrowful Voice of the Pastor Banished by the Wrath of God*. Like in his *Bequest of a Dying Mother*, he also bade farewell to his sons and at the same time, he prophetically saw the renewed future of the Unity of Brethren. It was a prophetic prayer where he proclaimed that "…*kingdoms of the earth, and among others our country, fall into ruin, and churches of the nations, and our Unity among them, are collapsing; but let us not be dismayed for He who has power, and who is wise, knows what He does. For we know that no wise homesteader would tear his house down, but he would build himself a new one. He would not tear anything down, except when he wanted everything new from the ground. Let us hope, then, that the one who said: 'I do everything new' knows why he does not want to countenance the old… So whatever happens, hope that the Lord does not do those things for nothing, but something great lies beneath it…*"

"*Dear sons, return your hearts to your fathers first, and since you have the Order of Unity, you will find there (if the Lord takes us old ones and keeps you) how to build a temple on old grounds and honor God in it and how to serve God's people... And therefore I do not grieve too much that dying myself, I see you, my dear mother, the Unity, dying. I, like Abraham, command myself and you to God who raises the dead. Although I, the last gatekeeper of yours for this time, shut*

J.A. Comenii
DIDACTICA OPERA
OMNIA.
Ab Anno 1627 ad 1657.
continuata.

the door behind me, you shall not be shut not to be able to come out of your grave. But the glory of the power of God will be revealed in you all the more when even if you fall, you will arise and when you die, you will become alive."[24]

1661 Bishop Comenius published a German hymnal and catechism for his German-speaking friends and brothers practicing their faith in secret in Fulneck, Moravia: *"…that you may remember these things even after my departure … that we have led you only to a solid prophetic and apostolic teaching. You do well to take care of it like a candle shining in a dark place until dawn."*[25]

1662 Bishop Comenius published *Brethren's Confession* from 1535.
- **5 November** The Synod in Milenczyn decided that each branch of the Unity of Brethren – Polish and Bohemian-Moravian – would have more bishops. Mikuláš Gertich was chosen to become a bishop alongside Bishop Jan Bythner and Petr Figulus alongside Bishop Comenius.

1663 Bishop Comenius published *History of Severe Adversities of the Bohemian Church* and *History of the Passion and Death, the Funeral and Resurrection of Our Lord Jesus Christ* and reissued *The Labyrinth of the World and Paradise of the Heart* and *Centrum Securitatis* (The Centre of Safety).

1668 Bishop Comenius published a writing *Unum Necessarium* (The One Thing Necessary).

These books then served those who were scattered with reinforcement and encouragement.

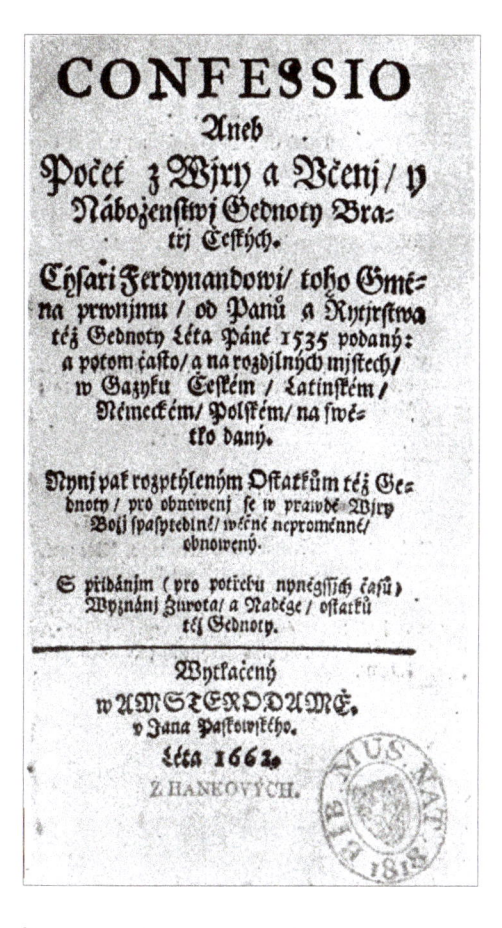

| Title page of the Brethren's Confession published in Amsterdam

1670 **12 January** Bishop Petr Figulus died in Klaipėda, Lithuania. Bishop Comenius thus remained the last bishop of the first part of the Unity's history.
- **15 November** Bishop Comenius' death in Amsterdam symbolically ended the first period of the Unity of Brethren.
- **20 November** Bishop John Amos Comenius was buried in Naarden, the Netherlands.

55

THE POLISH BRANCH OF THE UNITY OF BRETHREN

Other bishops of the Polish branch of the Unity of Brethren were:

Bishop	Date of Consecration	Date of Death
Jan Bythner	1644	2. 2. 1675
Mikuláš Gertich	1662	24. 5. 1671
Adam Samuel Hartman	28. 10. 1673	29. 5. 1691
Jan Zugehör	13. 8. 1676	29. 11. 1698
Joachim Gulich	26. 6. 1692	14. 11. 1703
Daniel Ernst Jablonski	10. 3. 1699	25. 5. 1741

Brethren's consecration was then transferred to Herrnhut thanks to Daniel Ernst Jablonski.

Bishop	Date of Consecration	Date of Death
Jan Jakobides	10. 3. 1699	1709
Salomon Opitz	11. 7. 1712	1716
David Cassius	4. 11. 1712	1716
Pavel Cassius	26. 2.1725	?
Kristian Sitkovius*	1735	1762

Other bishops continued the work of the Polish branch of the Unity. However, this line is no longer connected with the genealogy of Moravian Church bishops.

Bishop	Date of Consecration	Date of Death
Samuel Vilém Kasur	1719	1732
Albert Jounga	1742	1746
Bedřich Vilém Jablonský	1742	1760
Jan Alexandr Cassius	1746	1788
Jan Teofil Elsner	1761	1782
Pavel Ludvík Cassius	1770	1775
Bedřich Klofe	1776	1794
Kristian Teofil Cassius	1790	1813
Jiří Vilém Behr	1798	1808
Jan Benjamin Bornemann	1810	1828
Samuel David Hanke	1817	1841

*62nd bishop after Matthew of Kunvald

Polish congregations of the Unity were then reorganized and Brethren's consecration was transferred to Poland.

Bishop	Date of Consecration	Date of Death
Rudolf Siedler	1844	?
Karel Gobel	1858	?
Eugen Borgius	1883	?

Before World War I, only five congregations remained in Poland: Poznań, Waszków, Łasocose, Orzeszowo and Leszno.

In Leszno, a few Polish families remained served by preacher Bickerich. He learned Czech so that he could read from old Brethren books and cultivate Brethren tradition and piety. After World War I, the congregations found themselves in the Republic of Poland but the number of members dropped to only 1,400. Many German members moved to neighboring Germany.

With Bickerich's death, Polish services ceased in 1934. Several small churches remained from the former Polish branch of the Unity of Brethren. They kept the name "Unitätsgemeinden" and the title of senior for their spiritual leader, although this designation was rather an honorary title. By confession, these brothers were already completely Reformed as part of the united church of Lutherans and Reformed in Poland. World War II definitely ended this era. After the liberation of the occupied territory, all German members were expelled and thus the last remnants of the Unity of Brethren in Poland completely disappeared.

CONCLUSION

According to historian Ferdinand Hrejsa, the Unity of Brethren had about 40,000 members before the Battle of White Mountain in 1620. Brothers served in 245 congregations and places in Moravia and 187 congregations and places in Bohemia.

Between 1457 and 1620, 160 writers were born from this church and 500 literary works that we know of were written in addition to those lost in the White Mountain disasters. Compared to one Catholic printer and two Hussite printers, the Unity had three printers in Bohemia and Moravia. At the same time, they printed their books not only at home but also abroad. The Unity of Brethren had its own excellent school system and also thanks to that Czech schools were ranked among the best in Europe. The Unity's writers paid special attention to history, Czech language and were excellent composers.

The author is sorry that not all personalities of the Unity of Brethren could be recorded here. There are many other witnesses of faith about whom we have not received enough information. But they are written in the Book of the Faithful and their memory is not forgotten in God's eyes.

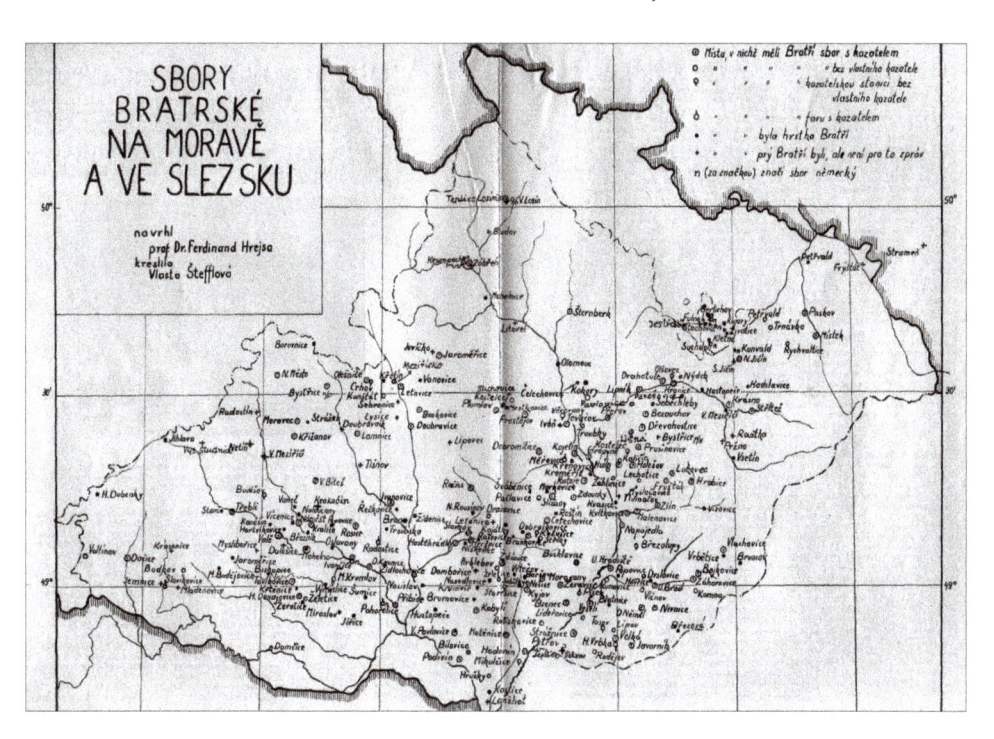

Brethren's congregations in Moravia and Silesia until 1620

PART II

PART II

Since the renewal in Herrnhut
to this day – 280 years of Brethren's mission

THE BEGINNING OF A NEW GENERATION OF UNITY'S FATHERS

1685 13 June Polycarp Müller, a descendant of Czech exiles, later a missionary and a bishop of the renewed Unity of Brethren, was born in Stolberg in Saxony (then Prussia). Under his leadership, groups of exiles were accepted in Prussia and later Czech colonies of the Brethren were established.

1688 Johann Andreas Rothe was born in Upper Lusatia. He became a Lutheran preacher in Berthelsdorf and served there when the Unity was renewed (he never joined the Unity of Brethren himself).

1692 17 February Carpenter Christian David, cofounder of Herrnhut, was born in Ženklava.

1693 12 or **13 August** David Schneider, grandson of M. Schneider, was born. His grandfather was a member of the Unity in the 'pre-White Mountain' period.* This family connects the history of the Moravian Church from the beginning of the seventeenth century to the present day.** David Schneider made history thanks to his ability to display the original Unity of Brethren. He encouraged the exiles to Moravian traditions and thus he was helping the renewed Unity to have true historical continuity. He died on July 14, 1755 in Eberndorf.

1695 18 December David Nitschmann, later the first bishop of the renewed Moravian Church was born in Suchdol nad Odrou.

Daniel Ernst Jablonski

- Ernest Julius Seidlitz, well-known benefactor of the exiles and founder of Brethren's colonies in Silesia, was born.

1698 David Sigmund Kriegelstein, later a missionary in Livonia, was born in Bautzen. He worked for a long time in Herrnhut as a doctor and he laid the foundations of Herrnhut pharmacy.

1699 On the synod of the Polish branch of the Unity in Greater Poland (which was already united with the Reformed at that time), Daniel Ernst Jablonski, a Reformed court preacher, was elected and consecrated a bishop.

1700 7 February Friedrich von Watteville, later a close associate of Count N. L. Zinzendorf and a bishop of the renewed Unity of Brethren, was born in Bern.

*Before the Battle of White Mountain in 1620. ** Eugen Edmond Schmidt married into this family – see Part IV, year 1872 and onwards.

- **26 May** Count N. L. Zinzendorf, the second bishop of the renewed Unity of Brethren, was born.

1701 Melchior Zeisberger, later missionary working in the north of Europe was born in Suchdol nad Odrou.

1702 14 March Jan Raschke, the co-founder of village Nízký (Niesky) in Upper Lusatia, was born.

1703 20 September David Nitschmann the Syndic was born. Later he was elected as bishop of the renewed Unitas Fratrum.

1704 15 July August Gottlieb Spangenberg, a bishop of the renewed Unity, was born. He studied in Jena where he met count Zinzendorf in 1728. Then he worked in America for many years.
- Andreas Grassmann, later a missionary and a bishop of the renewed Unity, was born in Ženklava. He was active mainly in the north of Livonia, Sweden, Finland, Lapland, Moscow, and also in Archangelsk.

1706 In June, Johann Beck, a missionary in Greenland, was born in Kreuzendorf.
- Leonhard Dober was born. He later became one of the first Moravian missionaries and bishops of the renewed Moravian Church. He belongs to the pioneers of the Moravian mission together with David Nitschmann with whom he sailed to the island of St. Thomas in 1732.

1709 3 April Jan Jílek, a Moravian exile, was born.

Young count N. L. Zinzendorf

- Evangelical Lutheran Church was established in Cieszyn. Many non-Catholics even from great distances were secretly attending the services.
- **30 September** Georg Schmidt, the first missionary among the Khoikhoi people, was born.

1711 Johann Nitschmann, Jr., a missionary and a bishop of the renewed Unity of Brethren, was born in Kunín. Since 1766 he worked among Kalmyks in the Russian colony in Sarepta where he remained until his death in 1783.
- **11 February** Matouš Stach, a Moravian missionary, was born in Mankovice, Moravia. For many years, he was working in Greenland where several congregations of the renewed Moravian Church were built (see Greenland

Missions, p. 75). He died on December 21, 1787.

1716 Friedrich Wenzel Neisser was born in Žilina. When he was 5 years old, he arrived in Herrnhut. He later became a Moravian missionary. In 1741, he became a member of the General Conference.*

1717 Christian David came in contact with non-Catholics. He was influenced by pietism and became one of the traveling preachers.
- **4 March** Jan Theofil Elsner, a teacher at Leszno Gymnasium, was born in Węgrów, Poland. Since 1747 he was a preacher of Czechs in Berlin whom he had served for thirty five years. Later, he became a preacher of the Polish branch of the Unity of Brethren. He was publishing old Brethren's writings and also works of Bishop John Amos Comenius.

1721 **2 March** David Zeisberger was born to become the Apostle of the Indians.
- Saxon Count Nicholas Ludwig Zinzendorf, a follower of Protestant Pietism, met with Christian David. They discussed the establishment of a new home for secret Protestants from the German-speaking area around Kravaře, North Moravia, where the Brethren's tradition has still survived.

1722 **12 June** The first Moravian immigrants came to Berthelsdorf: two families of Neisser and Christian David's family.
- **17 June** Christian David struck his axe into the first tree for the construction of a new exile's settlement called Herrnhut.

Christian David

1723 Christian David's interpretations of the Eight Beatitudes aroused a spiritual awakening in Suchdol area in Moravia. The persecution intensified immediately and made brothers to flee to Herrnhut. In the course of several years, about 550 people from Suchdol and another 100 from Nízký Jeseník arrived to Herrnhut.

1727 Zinzendorf presented so-called *General rules* for this new settlement and village. These rules, together with *Manorial Injunctions and Prohibitions*, were read for the first time on May 12 and later revised.

* The managing body of the Moravian Church

- **4 July** The statutes of the Christian community were drawn up and they were called *Brotherly Agreement*. The statutes were written by Count Zinzendorf but it was preceded by interviews with Moravians. Christian David urged the Count to read a book by Bishop Comenius about orders of the Unity of Brethren. So during his stay in Silesia, Count Zinzendorf translated part of the book into German.
- **4 August** The Count presented some selected parts of the book to the Moravians, especially those passages that were in accordance with his statutes. *Manorial Injunctions and Prohibitions* and *Brotherly Agreement* along with the spiritual renewal happening throughout August changed life in this Brethren's settlement. Moravians saw God's action in it and the Count's authority rose among them. The Brethren actually made an agreement together similar to the one 263 years ago in the *Agreement of the Mountains of Rychnov* in 1464.

The spiritual fruit of this agreement of the newly resurrected Unity of Brethren appeared five years later. The renewed Unity kept the form and ecclesiastical independence of the Ancient Unity but filled it with new mission goals.

Herrnhut, Brethren's house of prayer

REBIRTH OF THE MORAVIAN CHURCH AND THE BEGINNINGS OF THE MORAVIAN MISSION

1727 **13 August** Brethren held a memorable Lord's Supper in Berthelsdorf. They accomplished the reconciliation and unification process of the initially diverse streams of the Renewed Unity. This event is still commemorated in the Moravian Church as a Day of Renewal.

- **26 August** The first prayer group was established in Herrnhut. During May, June and July, settlers were already experiencing a special wave of God's power which led them to more and more intense prayers. Prayer meetings were getting longer and a lot of participants wished to stay in prayer even all night long. At that time, several brothers decided to go regularly to the nearby Hutberg hill at night to pour out their hearts in front of God in prayers and songs.
- **In August**, Count, along with fourteen brothers, was praying on Hutberg all night long. During the following days, prayers continued and people were not able to go home. Therefore, the Brethren decided to set certain hours and to establish a prayer watch meaning they would come in groups at a certain time to pray and experience fellowship with the Lord. They used Lev. 6:12–13 as a motivating text. At first there were, in total, twenty four brothers who started the so-called *prayer watch*. They were inspired by the words of the Scripture from Isaiah 62:6: "I have set watchmen upon thy walls, O Jerusalem, which shall never hold their peace day nor night…" Brothers were convinced that it was necessary to designate people who would

Brethren's cemetery and the hill Hutberg

continually pray for the church, brothers and sisters at home and on the road, and for God's kingdom in the world. The prayer watch lasted for a hundred years.

1728 **3 May** For the first time, Count Nicholas Ludwig Zinzendorf began to use Daily Watchwords of the Unity of Brethren.

1731 **1 January** Daily Watchwords were published in print for the first time.
- In Copenhagen, the coronation of the Danish King Christian VI took place and attending Count Zinzendorf was intrigued by a black servant named Anton. He had told the Count about the misery of slaves working on plantations in Dan-

ish colonies. Back in Herrnhut, Zinzendorf was movingly telling what he had heard from Anton. Immediately, two brothers, Tobias Leupold and Leonhard Dober, decided to go to these slaves and tell them about the cross of Jesus. At the invitation of Zinzendorf, Anton came to Herrnhut to recount his testimony of the misery of his siblings to everyone. This encouraged another wave of volunteers who were ready to go to these slaves. Like Zinzendorf, Matthew Stach cared for Greenland as well. But the island of St. Thomas was more important. A lot decided it would be carpenter David Nitschmann and potter Leonhard Dober who would set out on a journey.

1732 21 August This day is considered the beginning of the Moravian mission. About two hundred settlers left Herrnhut and became missionaries on four continents in the early years. Many of them had lived through imprisonment and suffering for faith while still in Moravia. Instead of taking advantage of their new refuge in Herrnhut, they did not hesitate to go further into the unknown. They were leaving without resources, experiences and knowledge for strangers who were not even considered humans at that time; to slaves and to those who lived in wilderness and did not have the opportunity to hear the gospel. Even Count Zinzendorf participated in many journeys in Europe and America. He had been thinking about mission since childhood and later, especially under the influence of pietism in Halle and the study of Comenius' writing *De regula fidei judicium duplex* (Double Investigation on the Rule of Faith), he revived and consolidated this idea.

| *Commemorative stamps issued for 200 years of the Moravian Mission (1932)*

WEST INDIES
Danish colony (since 1732)

Saint Thomas Island

1732 **21 August** Leonhard Dober and David Nitschmann embarked on their first mission. They walked through Wernigerode to Copenhagen where they were searching for a ship to transport them to Saint Thomas in the West Indies. In Copenhagen, many people tried to talk them out of the journey and warned them of difficulties.

- **8 October** Brothers Dober and Nitschmann set sail and on a ship, they learned bloodletting from Dr. Grothausen and received some valuable tools from him.
- **13 December** Brothers arrived to Saint Thomas. Local authorities did not allow them their original intention to become slaves. So they started to work for white owners of plantations and searched for a way to establish contact with slaves. It was not easy. Plantations' owners were French but the main language spoken on the island was Dutch. David Nitschmann went back to Herrnhut after less than six months. His job was just to explore the place and to report on it.
- Dober remained alone on the island. He tried to get as close as possible to slaves living in subhuman conditions but he was not always successful. The area was also affected by hurricanes.

1733 The Danish West India Company bought the island of Saint Croix from France. The company's president Pless requested twelve Brethren from Herrnhut as guards for his plantations.

Leonhard Dober

- **18 August** Brothers from Herrnhut set out on their journey to establish a Brethren's colony on St. Croix. The oldest of them were D. Nitschmann – father (57) and D. Weber (55). The head of the expedition was Tobias Leupold who was the first to enroll for mission together with Dober. The journey across the sea was very difficult; they had to stay in Norway over the winter.

1734 **11 June** At first, they landed on St. Thomas and met with Dober who learned of his election as a senior elder and immediately returned to Herrnhut (see p. 152). Brothers tried to establish a settlement **New Herrnhut**. During this time, two men and one woman fell ill and died.

Saint Croix Island

1734 **1 September** Brethren continued to St. Croix. One of the children died during the short cruise so the first service in their new home was a funeral. Drinking water was rare. The water which missionaries found was mostly polluted and at that time, people did not know how dangerous it can be. One by one they fell ill and died. After three months, only nine survived out of the original eighteen people.

1735 Tobias Leupold died on the island in January.
- **25 February** Eleven men and women set out on their journey from Herrnhut (they had not received any information about the situation on both islands yet).
- **28 May** The group arrived to St. Thomas and then continued to St. Croix. At both places, they found the remaining members of the first group bedridden. Within six weeks, four of the newcomers died. By then, the news of what had happened arrived in Herrnhut. Some brothers doubted whether it was right to send people to death. Brethren sent a message to the island to tell everyone to return home by the first ship. Andreas Hickel was sent for them. Only eight out of the original twenty nine missionaries who left Herrnhut survived the journey home. This tragic event was dubbed 'The Great Dying'.

1736 **23 May** Another three men landed on St. Thomas – Frederic Martin, Johan Bonicke and doctor Theodor Grothaus who

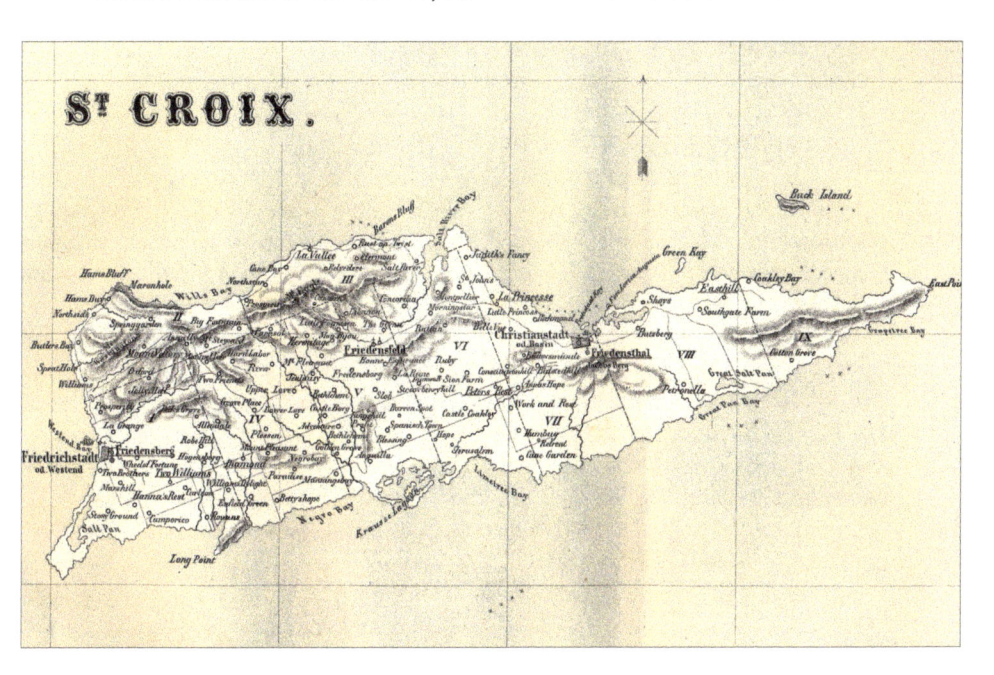

Mission map of St. Croix

died shortly after his arrival. Frederic Martin had been imprisoned for his faith at home, in Moravia. One night he had managed to outwit the guards and he had arrived to Herrnhut ten days later. Faith, he suffered for, was very precious to him. He could not refuse the calling to spread the gospel even if it meant to die for it.

- **30 September** The first three new believers were baptized. A. Spangenberg was visiting St. Croix at the time so he baptized them.

Frederic Martin used five important principles in his work:
- *self-sufficiency* – therefore he acquired a plantation for the Unity which provided Brethren with a livelihood.
- *systematic discipline* – he taught new believers to help each other. He made sure they were diligent, honest and obedient.
- *education* – he set up a school where he taught black people to read and write although initially, this was forbidden.
- *personal conversation* – he wanted to get to know each black man or woman personally and to gain their trust this way.
- *management* – after his ordination, he appointed helpers and other authorities creating thus the core of an independent church.

Brother Martin soon found himself in a conflict with authorities and a local Reformed priest because he wedded black slaves. In those days, slaves were not allowed to get married properly but Martin did not respect this ban. He was arrested and imprisoned and only the unexpected arrival and intervention of Zinzendorf helped him to regain his freedom.

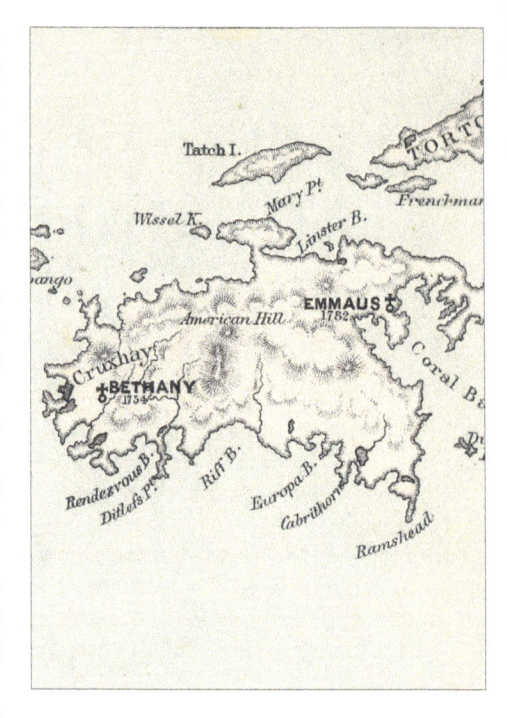

Island of Saint John

Saint John

1740 Brethren started work on the island of Saint John and Frederic Martin became an important personality even there. Two more men were sent to help him: learned theologian Albin Feder and tailor Gotlieb Israel. However, their ship wrecked in the Caribbean Sea and Albin Feder drowned. Gotlieb Israel arrived to New Herrnhut few weeks later. Jens Rasmus had been the only preacher on St. John for several months.

Brother Martin later bought a plantation on the island for his own money and the first station **Bethany** was built there in 1754.

1750   Frederic Martin passed away. Zinzendorf called him a faithful witness and apostle of black people. His grave on the Brethren's plantation has been preserved to this day.

1754   The three islands were transferred under the direct administration of the Danish government.

1755   The first mission station **Friedenstahl** was founded in St. Croix. Thus, at the cost of many lives, mission in Danish West Indies had started. In St. Thomas only, 160 missionaries died during the first fifty years. Brother Martin's death marked the end of the pioneering era. After that, the mission continued to develop for another thirty years. Since 1762, Martin Mack took over the mission work. Also, the education of slaves' children was finally allowed.

1774   The Danish king issued an edict in favor of the mission and both governors and plantation owners were quite friendly to Brethren. Missionaries could therefore establish more stations. They founded **Niesky** in St. Thomas, **Friedensberg** (1771) and **Friedenfeld** (1805) in St. Croix, and **Emmaus** (1782) in St. John.

1808–1815   The islands came under the rule of Britain. From that time, English was the main spoken language and Creole, the language of the blacks, started disappearing rapidly. In the late nineteenth century, a biblical seminar was opened for a short time in St. Thomas.
The work of the Unity of Brethren in these islands has continued to this day.

Frederik Martin

WEST INDIES
British colony (since 1753)

Jamaica

1754   Jamaican owners of plantations asked elders of the Unity of Brethren in Britain to provide spiritual administrators for their slaves. That year the first missionaries – George Caries, Thomas Shalleross and Gottlieb Haberech – landed in Jamaica. Heinrich Rauch, who was originally sent by Zinzendorf as an inspector, was a successful missionary among the Indians. In Jamaica, however, his strictness almost destroyed the mission. He introduced strict rules and refused to baptize new Christians until they reached a high lev-

PART II

el of Christian knowledge. Another reason for initial lack of success was health problems and high mortality.

1764 – Friedrich Schlegel worked in Jamaica during these years and at that time, the
1770 mission came back to life.
Then the work was often moved from one place to another and plantation owners became hostile to the missionaries.

1780 5 October Part of the island was hit by a violent hurricane and not a single house remained standing.

1815 – The work renewed and more stations were established: **Irwinhill**, **Neu-Eden**
1823 and **Fairfield**. These soon became the centre of the mission in Jamaica.

1831 Slaves organized a great uprising but black Brethren did not participate. Uprising was violently suppressed. Some preachers had to run away and even Moravian missionary H. G. Pfeifer was unjustly arrested and brought before a court. Luckily, he and other brothers were released again.
Brothers disagreed with the slave system and wanted to find a solution for blacks. They also knew that it was necessary to prepare black people for their future freedom. That is why they founded schools for them and educated them.

1838 Slavery was finally abolished in Jamaica. From that time, mission work was growing rapidly. New stations, **Beaufort**, **Bethany**, **New Nazareth**, **New Hope**, **Litiz** and **Bethabara**, were founded. Schools became full of children.

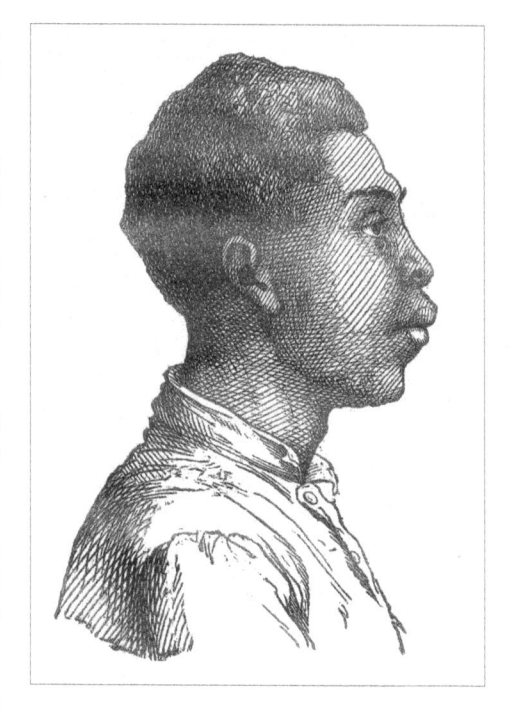

Peter Blair, local teacher in Jamaica

1842 Brethren founded a school for teachers in Fairfield and soon afterwards, they established another station **Springfield**.

1861 A school for female teachers was opened.

1876 Theological seminary for indigenous workers was opened.

1906 Twenty missionaries and seventeen indigenous collaborators served in eighteen places to 15,197 baptized people.

1979 Jamaica became independent province of the Moravian Church and was separated from other mission locations of the Caribbean.

Antigua

1756 During the first fourteen years, it seemed that mission on this island was hopeless. Samuel Isles, the first missionary, founded only one mission station named **Saint John** and baptized the first fourteen new believers. According to his letters, the cause was not in wrong methods, but in an exceptional depravity of local slaves. Day after day, they got drunk, someone was stabbed or poisoned. Plantation owners had to execute culprits every week. Then it all changed.

1769 Peter Braun led the mission in Antigua
– and during that time, two more grow-
1791 ing stations, **Bayleyhill** and **Gracehill**, were established and the total number of new believers increased to more than 7,000. His success had two reasons. The first one was financial: Braun and his colleagues still had to earn a living but, on the other hand, they received some plots from brothers from North America. So, unlike Jamaican missionaries, they had more time for spiritual work. Another reason was Braun's character. According to B. Harvey, one of his successors, Braun did not acquire black people only by eloquent preaching, but also by amazing tact and good character. He visited them in their huts, he talked to them on the fields, ate with them. In the evening after the hard work, the blacks walked sometimes even several kilometers to listen to God's Word. Braun became a recognized authority.

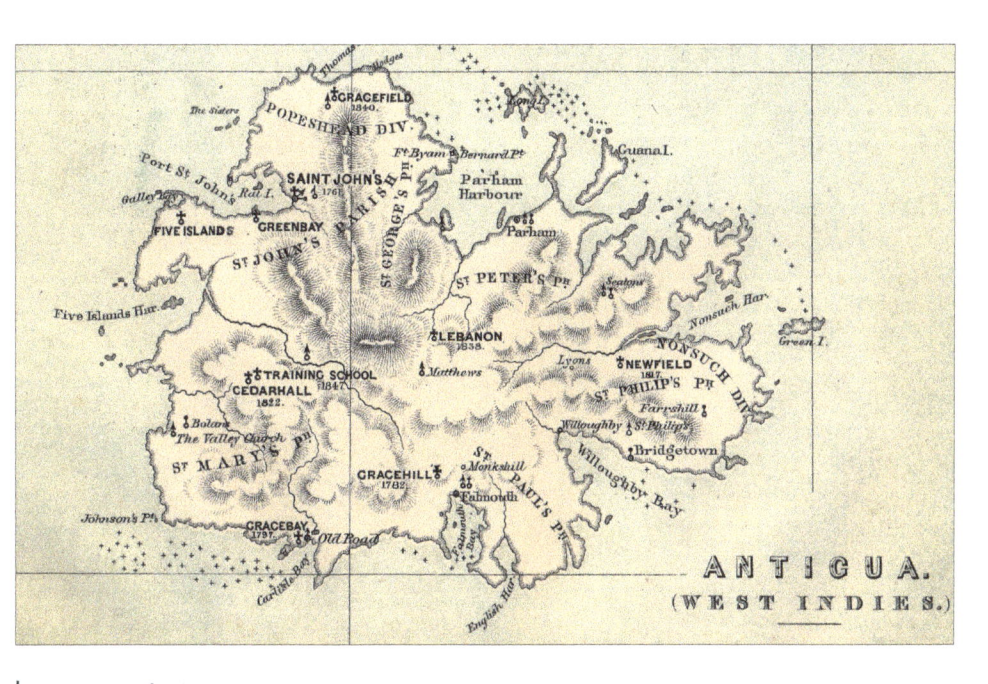

Mission map of Antigua

1797 A third station was established on the south coast – **Gracebay**.

1816 Local plantation owners saw black people changing under the influence of the Moravian mission so they supported establishment of other stations – **Newfield** (1817) and **Cedarhall** (1822).

1832 The great uprising of black people on other islands did not affect Antigua very much. On the contrary, biblical and missionary fellowship arose even more among local blacks.

1834 The 'emancipation' of black people was declared – that is the abolition of slavery. Brethren had been preparing slaves for a long time. Therefore it could take effect without a trial period which was common on other islands. This was another success for the mission.

1855 An educational institution for indigenous female teachers was established.

1900 A theological seminary for education of indigenous clergy was established.

1906 Eight missionaries and six indigenous collaborators served in eight places in Antigua. In total, they were taking care of 7,272 people. Compared to Jamaica, there was a decline in membership, because other missionary companies began to operate there and the black people always sought out the nearest one.

Barbados

1765 Andreas Rittmansberger and Brother Wood started the work in Barbados. It

Station Gracebay in Antigua

was very difficult. Missionaries were dying really fast – A. Rittmansberger (1765), Johann Fozzard (1766), Benjamin Brookshaw (1772), Johann Bennet (1772), Herr (1773) and Angerman (1775). The main cause was a fever caused by the climate and poor water. And although the local clergy were friendly and one pious plantation owner allowed them to preach on his land, no real development was possible.

1780 10–11 October A powerful hurricane caused extensive damage and Brethren lost their housing. Plantation owners and slaves lost faith in God's goodness.

1794 A mission station **Sharon** was founded and five years later, brothers also built a church there.

1816 Local black believers did not participate in uprisings either. This also helped the Moravian mission gain recognition and missionaries were invited to preach on plantations not only on Sundays, but also during the week.

1826 Brethren founded another station **Mount Tabor**.

1831 Another devastating hurricane hit the island killing 4,000 people and destroying both stations.

1832 The work in both places was renewed and had a total of 1,100 members.

1836 Brethren built a church in **Bridgetownu** and also another station **Cliftonhill** (1841).

1854 The island saw a cholera outbreak which killed 20,000 people. Brothers, together with their wives, faithfully cared spiritually and practically for the sick and dying.

1906 Four missionaries and three indigenous collaborators worked at four stations and looked after 3,517 baptized.

Saint Christopher Island (Saint Kitts)

1777 Missionaries were sent to the island at a special request of a pious owner of a Gardinera plantation who personally came to London to meet with representatives of the English Unity of Brethren.
- **14 June** Jan Daniel Gottalt and James Birkby set out for a journey. Gardiner gave them a house in **Basseterre**.

Station Mount Tabor in Barbados

1779 Brethren performed the first baptism and the desire for the gospel arose among the black people.

1785 In Basseterre, Brethren built the first church; it was soon too small. Missionaries worked intensively, especially Gottalt's successor Schneller. By 1800, the number of members had risen to 2,500.

1819 Brethren started working in the Cayon area, known today as **Bethesda**, and continued to **Bethel** (1832) and **Estridge** (1845). At the new emerging mission places around 700 slaves were taught to read and write.

1906 Four stations were active in St. Kitts. Three missionaries and four native helpers looked after 3,775 members.

1914 The local Unity of Brethren handed over its schools to the state because it could no longer keep those financially.

Tobago

1790 This mission was founded thanks to one of the local plantation owners, John Hamilton. The first missionary was John Montgomery. The island was under French rule and at that time, French Revolution was underway. The island was also affected by a hurricane. Montgomery's wife died and he himself was sick and left the island.

1799 Brethren made another attempt at mission. Brothers Schirmer and Church arrived and worked among the blacks. But after four years, the mission ended again.

1827 Brethren made a third missionary attempt with Ricksecker and his wife and the work grew rapidly.

1828 A **Montgomery** station (named after the first missionary) was founded. Missionaries soon built a church but it shortly did not suffice.

1848 A second station – **Moriah** was founded.

A hurricane hit the island again but the work did not stop. The black population was receiving the gospel and becoming faithful Christians. Other mission companies started to work in this area as well.

1906 Five Moravian missionaries and one local helper worked there and they looked after 4,262 people.

John Montgomery's maid

Trinidad

1890 The work in Trinidad started and a mission station was founded in the capital **Port of Spain**.

1906 At that time, there were three missionaries who took care of 700 people.

Conclusion

Islands Antigua, Barbados, St. John, St. Croix, St. Kitts, St. Thomas, Tobago, and Trinidad are nowadays part of the Moravian Church as its province Eastern West Indies (today's Eastern Caribbean).

GREENLAND (1733–1900)

1733 **19 January** The first free Herrnhut missionaries went to Greenland.
- **20 May** Christian David and Matthäus Stach with his nephew Christian arrived in Godhaab. They called their new home **New Herrnhut**. But Inuit (formerly Eskimos) refused to talk to them; some even told them the sooner they leave the better. Like many others, they thought they were the best nation in the world. They called other people *kablunat* – barbarians and themselves *inuit* – people. But their self-satisfaction was not entirely unfounded. They seldom argued, never cursed, murders were hardly ever committed among them. They did not know how to brew beer so they were rarely drunk. Disputes were settled not by fists, but verbally. Most men were faithful to their wives. And old people who could no longer take care of themselves were cared for by their children.

1734 After a year, Christian David and Christian Stach returned home and they were replaced by Friedrich Böhnisch and Johann Beck.

For five years, missionaries preached with no results. However, during these years they had several experiences. One of them was smallpox epidemic. Within nine months, the epidemic spread rapidly throughout the west coast of Greenland. Estimated number of deaths was 2,000. Missionaries turned their homes into a hospital, visited hundreds of sick people, buried the dead and they were telling the sick and the dying of the risen Christ. When the epidemic ceased, the Inuit listened with pleasure if there was talk about seals. When it came to faith,

New Herrnhut on Greenland coast

they either responded with apathy, or they ran away.

Another fact that greatly influenced missionaries was the conversion of young Inuit Kajarnak. Johann Beck was working on the translation of the Gospels and by simply reading a passage from Matthew's Gospel, this young Inuit was touched. Beck later told him the whole Passion narratives. Then also other Inuit asked missionaries to teach them how to pray. The dogmatic theology which had been preached until that time never touched the Inuit, but the stories of the Gospels were captivating and began transforming the natives.

1739 29 March Kajarnak was publicly baptized as the first one of the Moravian Greenland mission.

Then Andreas Grassmann arrived in Greenland as an inspector. He was exhilarated by the teaching that Zinzendorf began to preach, the so-called theology of blood and wounds of the Lamb. Brethren then changed the way they preached; not only because of Kajarnak, but because they were convinced by this teaching themselves. Thus began a new era of Greenlandic mission. Before that, Brethren had preached an abstract theological doctrine, but then they adopted a living form of narration. The Inuit themselves soon noticed the difference. Beck wrote to Zinzendorf that from that time, they would preach nothing but love of the slain lamb. As the Inuit began to repent, Grassmann noticed that it was time to establish the Unity as a church in Greenland. Mat-

| Baptism of people in Greenland

thew Stach was ordained in Marienborn to continue serving as a proper clergyman in Greenland.

1741 12 December Missionaries of the Unity of Brethren were authorized by the King of Denmark to baptize, marry, and to serve the Lord's Supper. When Matthew Stach returned to Greenland, brothers arranged New Herrnhut as a settlement of the Unity of Brethren. They wanted to allow believers to live together in one village so they could look after their spiritual life better. The Inuit gladly agreed and New Herrnhut became a thriving settlement. At the request of the new inhabitants, a church was built, followed by houses for single men and women. The gatherings were held several times a day. The most significant assistant to Matthew Stach was Johann Sörensen. Brethren became known for their service of justice and faith. New Herrnhut was soon over populated with 512 members.

Two other villages were founded further in the south – **Lichtenfels** (1758) with 374 members and **Lichtenau** (1774) with 336 members. These three settlements became the basis of the mission in Greenland. Johann Beck worked there for forty-three years, he died in 1777. His son followed in his father's footsteps and served in Greenland for fifty-two years.

The Inuit were literally decimated by other epidemics and the settlements often ended up in ruins.

Natives on a hunt

1823 The first comprehensive Greenlandic translation of the New Testament was published.

1824 Station **Friedrichsthal** was established.

1864 Station **Ogdlorpalit** was built.

1861 **Umának** station was built in the northernmost point of Greenland.

1900 The Unity of Brethren handed over this mission to the Danish State Church.

NORTH AMERICA (since 1735)

The beginning of the mission was also closely connected with the beginning of the work of the Unity of Brethren in America. More and more exiles from Silesia gathered at the estate of Count Zinzendorf. Therefore, in 1733 a decree was issued for immigrants to leave the area.

1734 August Gottlieb Spangenberg started negotiations with the British Government about the possibility to resettle thirty families in Georgia. They were promised 500 acres of land in Savannah, given permission to preach the gospel to the natives, and the government also promised them exemption from military service. Zinzendorf was satisfied with the conditions and he sent the first Moravian colonists to America. August G. Spangenberg was the head of the expedition.
- **20 November** They set out on a journey from Herrnhut on foot.

The natives in Lichtenau say goodbye to missionaries

1735 **7 April** Missionaries landed in Georgia.

1736 Another group arrived in Savannah. One of them, Anton Seifert, went to the Indians to learn the language.

1738 Fifteen-year-old David Zeisberger came to Georgia with another group.
- The colony, built with great effort, was abandoned after five years because a war broke out between England and Spain. Brethren refused to fight on either side and therefore were asked to leave Georgia.

1739 They set out on a long journey to the north, to Pennsylvania. There, under the leadership of Spangenberg, began to build **Bethlehem** on the Leigh River.

1741 **28 June** Brethren laid the foundations of Bethlehem, later an important center of Unity of the Brethren, and built **Nazareth**.
- The beginnings were modest. Everyone capable worked and earned money to support others. They then sent help not only to all missionaries in North America, but also in West Indies.
- Spangenberg founded a missionary school that he called "the Savior's Armory". He was more than just an excellent organizer and a man of great vision. No one had as much enthusiasm and determination as he did. His goal was to convert all native tribes in North America. David Zeisberger also studied at this school.

1742 Fifteen traveling preachers who worked mainly among German settlers set out. By 1748, thirty one places were established in Pennsylvania, Maryland, New Jersey, New York; Rhode Island and Maine.

1744 **25 July** Spangenberg was consecrated a bishop in Marienborn, Germany. At the end of October, he took over the leadership of Moravian work in America. He oversaw traveling preachers, led missionary work among the natives, directed economic matters and planning new settlement construction projects, and he was partly responsible

Bethlehem

for the missionary work in West Indies and Suriname.
- The work continued to develop; more brothers were involved in the service of Bethlehem and Nazareth. They developed trades and founded farms. All of this brought resources for work and mission support not only in America. In 1748, there was already a lively trade with Europe. And the mission ship Irene was in constant operation between New York and the European continent.

Among the North American Natives

1740 **16 August** Christian H. Rauch arrived in New York. He was called as the first missionary among the natives. He worked in the Mohican village of **Shekomeko**. People there either fought or in peace, they indulged in alcohol. They first looked at Rauch as a fool, later they threatened him with death. But the way he spoke about God and Jesus Christ soon touched the Chief Tschoop. He was a renowned drinker but in a few weeks he converted and soon after that, a greater awakening began.

1741 Zinzendorf arrived in America. During his stay, he visited the natives three times.

1743 He visited work in Shekomeko and also attended meetings with representatives of six tribes of Iroquois nations. During these meetings, the Brethren requested to live among the natives and to learn their language.

1742 **7 September** The first native congregation was founded in Shekomeko.

Brethren's settlement Bethabara (Winston-Salem, NC)

The fiercest natives became exemplary Christians; the largest drinkers became sworn abstainers. Shekomeko became a model village.
- Two new missions were established. Native Brethren quit their nomadic life, started to work the land, followed Brethren's orders, and sent children to school. Drunkenness and theft were eliminated and care for the sick and wounded improved instead. The gospel changed the inner man and the change manifested itself in everything.

But this work soon found its opponents among colonists and local merchants. As a result, Brethren were forced to leave this territory. Rauch was later called to West Indies and David Zeisberger took over the mission among the natives. He had an aptitude for languages and soon learned Indian languages. However, on his way to the Mohawks, he was accused of spying for the French and was arrested for some time.

1746 **In June**, some natives set out on a journey with their brothers to Pennsylvania. They stayed temporarily near Bethlehem in the village of Nazareth.
- During the summer, they went across the Blue Mountains and, on a Brethren's land, founded an Indian settlement called **Gnadenhütten**. Other Indians arrived as well and the settlement grew very soon. In 1748 there were about 500 baptized Indians.

1747 Brothers founded more settlements, all built and administered by the model of Herrnhut and followed order. The natives learned to cultivate land and to provide for their livelihood which was new to them. They also built a water wheel, mill and sawmill and became economically independent.
1748

1752 The mission continued to develop successfully. At that time, Zeisberger stayed in Onondag in the centre of the Iroquois and he worked among the natives whose biggest enemy was alcohol. There he also wrote the Iroquois dictionary.
1754

1755 The Seven Years' War broke out between France and Britain – it was also called the French and Indian War. Some native tribes were more or less drawn into the war. Brethren tried not to be aligned but that caused suspicion on the side of France and Britain as well.
- **24 November** Gnadenhütten was attacked by pro-French natives at night. Eleven people – missionaries with their families – were killed or burned and part of the settlement burned down. Some managed to escape. Zeisberger then brought about 600 Moravian natives to Bethlehem and Nazareth to protect them, not only from other natives, but also from the white settlers during the war.

Zinzendorf meets the Iroquois

1757 Brethren built together settlements **Naim** and **Wechquetang**. Thus they survived until the end of the war in 1763.
1760

1763 – 1765 The war was hardly over and the so-called Pontiak's uprising began. The natives fought for independence; this time against the white settlers. The natives from Moravian settlements had to flee and they spent two years living in Philadelphia where they were under government protection by the governor's intercession. But they were dying of fever and smallpox there.

Among the Delaware Indians (1765–1903)
Pilgrimage of the natives in western Pennsylvania and Ohio

Once the truce was declared, it opened the way to the Delawares (Lenni Lenape). Brothers did not want just to preach to individuals, they were out to convert the whole nation. Zeisberger proved that he was not only an excellent preacher, but also a builder and an organizer. At that time, his ministry was at its peak. However, the situation was complicated by the fact that Zeisberger with the natives' church had to travel from place to place because they always came across adversity and persecution, both by the other natives or by the white colonists.

1765 They relocated to a deserted native village northwest of Bethlehem and built a settlement of **Friedenshütten**. The new settlement soon gained an excellent reputation. The natives no longer engaged just in fishing and hunting, but also in agriculture. They learned to farm and trade and built a school for children. They were very affected by Zeisberger's sermon. The settlement was a center of awakening for two years.

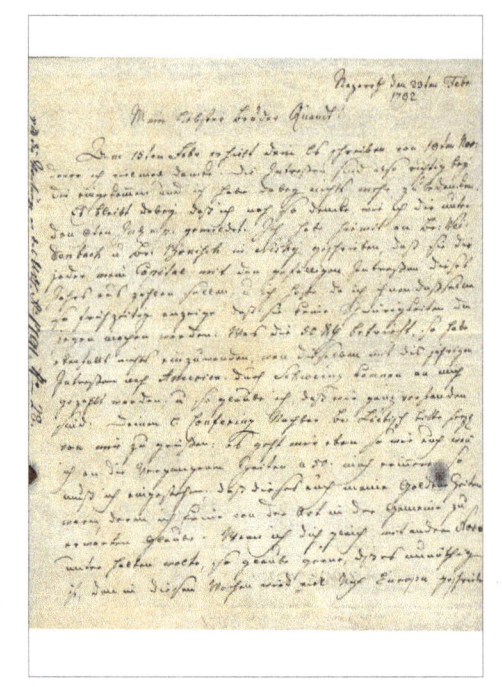

David Zeisberger's letter from the mission

1768 At a special invitation of the Delawares, Zeisberger with another brother went to the Delaware village of Goshgoshunk in northwest Pennsylvania where they were warmly received. Zeisberger preached there, built a missionary house and, with the approval of the Council, he could also ban the sale of alcohol in the village. However, pagan magicians soon began to spread rumors and defame missionaries and Brethren were repeatedly threatened. Zeisberger knew that it was not possible to maintain permanent work there. Yet six families converted and Brethren left with them.

1769 Because of the persecution, the natives and the brothers left Friedenshütten and moved to **Lavunnakhanek** where the first baptism took place. D. Zeisberger and others joined them there as well. But they were once again expelled.

1770 Together they sailed down the river on sixteen ships to the Ohio borders where they founded **Friedensstadt** settlement and many natives were baptized and joined the congregation.

1772 Brethren were expelled from Friedensstadt as well. Natives had to leave the land of their fathers and go from Pennsylvania to Ohio. In Ohio, they had lived for ten quiet years and the mission grew joyfully.

1772 –1780 D. Zeisberger established friendly relations with the Delawares. He was also accepted by Chief Netawatwees himself from whom he received allocated land for the construction of new settlements. Zeisberger preached among the Delawares and his sermon was the first Protestant sermon in Ohio.

- Brethren established settlements **Schönbrunn**, **Gnadenhütten**, **Lichtenau** and later **Salem**. Schönbrunn grew into a beautiful city led by a council of missionaries and local Delaware helpers.
- Public prosecutor for natives' issues Colonel Morgan even said that the natives in Zeisberger's villages were not only fully civilized, but even an example for the whites.

Zeisberger emphasized the gospel. But he still had one more desire in his heart: to establish a Christian state of Native Americans in Ohio. This idea was

David Zeisberger preaches to the natives

supported by the Delaware Chief Netawatwees. This plan could not be realized without the permission of the British government. However, during the preparatory negotiations, another war broke out – the American War of Independence (1775–1783).

As the war approached Ohio, Zeisberger and the others decided to maintain total neutrality. He asked the Bethlehem Council to appeal to Congress to issue a law that would prohibit American officers from calling Christian natives into military service. But the more they tried to maintain neutrality, the more they were exposed to unjust suspicion.

1781 They were attacked by a group of Indians in the English service and they were all dragged north to **Sandusky**. D. Zeisberger, along with other missionaries, was dragged to Detroit for questioning. However, after a proper trial, they were declared innocent and were given permission to establish a new settlement in Sandusky.

1782 Sandusky was threatened by hunger so a group of people, including women and children, secretly went back to Gnadenhütten to harvest the crops in the fields.
- **8 March** That group was attacked by American soldiers who massively slaughtered and scalped ninety-six people including children. (Their remains were later buried properly and a memorial stone was erected on the site.)

1783 The remaining natives moved north to Canada where they were allowed to build the village of **Neu Gnadenhütten** on the British territory.

David Zeisberger

1786 After the war, the settlement of 117 people moved south and founded **Neu Salem**. However, they had to escape again in 1791 from the forthcoming war.

1787 The Society for Propagating the Gospel among the Heathen was established in Bethlehem and it began to support the missionaries significantly.

1792 The settlement of **Fairfield** was established and two years after that, Brethren opened a chapel there. They lived in peace for the following twenty years and did the mission work.

TRAVELS OF THE NATIVE BRETHREN

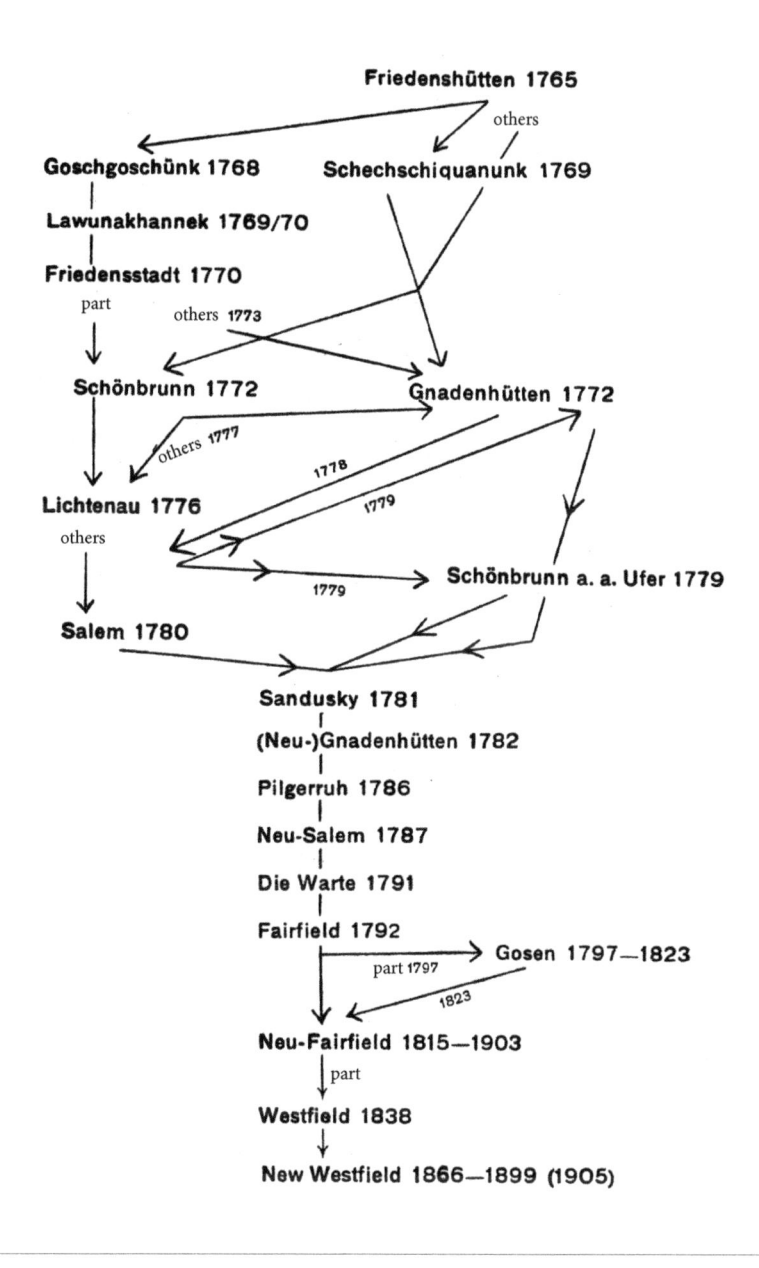

Friedenshütten 1765

others

Goschgoschünk 1768　　Schechschiquanunk 1769

Lawunakhannek 1769/70

Friedensstadt 1770

part　　others 1773

Schönbrunn 1772　　Gnadenhütten 1772

others 1777　　1778

　　　　　　1779

Lichtenau 1776

others　　　　　　Schönbrunn a. a. Ufer 1779

　　　1779

Salem 1780

Sandusky 1781

(Neu-)Gnadenhütten 1782

Pilgerruh 1786

Neu-Salem 1787

Die Warte 1791

Fairfield 1792　　→　Gosen 1797—1823

part 1797

1823

Neu-Fairfield 1815—1903

part

Westfield 1838

New Westfield 1866—1899 (1905)

1797 – 1798 Brethren received more land from American government. Some of the natives and Zeisberger moved there and Zeisberger founded the thirteenth (and his last) settlement **Goshen**. Brothers then continued to other areas to preach to the natives (e.g. the Chipewyan) but that was not always successful.

1808 17 November David Zeisberger died in Goshen at the age of 87. He was an Apostle of the Indians and a veteran missionary serving for sixty-three years. In addition to his hard work, he also wrote textbooks, dictionaries, readers, songbooks in various Native American languages and also translated parts of the Bible and some other writings.
He lived among his Red Brothers and he also laid down on the deathbed among them. He was buried in Goshen.

1813 Fairfield was demolished in another war.

1815 After a visit from Bethlehem, **New Fairfield** settlement was built on a Canadian territory near the former Fairfield. The congregation settled for many decades and the work could grow joyfully.

1842 17 September Brethren celebrated the 50th anniversary of the church on Canadian territory. That day, 101 adults and 432 children were baptized.

1848 13 August Brethren inaugurated a new church.

1903 The natives were increasingly influenced by the English language and the English way of life.

David Zeisberger's grave in Goshen

■ **1 June** This ministry was handed over to the Methodists who worked in the area among the rest of the Delawares as the English state church.

In the Far West

1837 Some natives along with missionaries Vogler and Mikš left New Fairfield for the west to find a new home. They founded **Westfield** in the Native American's region of Kansas. The church consisted mainly of the Delaware peoples.

1853 The congregation had to leave again.

1860 Brethren founded **New Westfield**. However, it was impossible to maintain a Christian village with ethnically mixed inhabitants as a mission station in the long term. The era and conditions were not favorable. The place was handed over to the American Moravian Church for its purposes in 1900. Nowadays the Moravian Church is no longer active there.

Among the Cherokees (1801–1896)

1801 After Brethren from Salem made several missionary expeditions among the Cherokees to the northern Georgia, Brothers Abraham Steiner and Byhan founded **Springplace** settlement there and continued the mission.

1807 Brethren also tried missionary work among
– the Muscogee Creek on the Flint River in
1813 Georgia but the effort was unsuccessful.

1817 Brother Charles R. Hicks, half Native American, was elected a second Chief of the Cherokee tribe.

1821 Thanks to Hicks' influence and awakening, another mission station **Oochelogy** was established.

1838 The desire of white men for the land caused all natives to be forcibly expelled from Georgia. The missionaries went to Arkansas with them.

1840 Missionaries were gathering scat-
– tered natives again and again. They
1843 established small Cherokee churches **Kannan** and **New Springplace** and a branch of Mount Zion (1849).

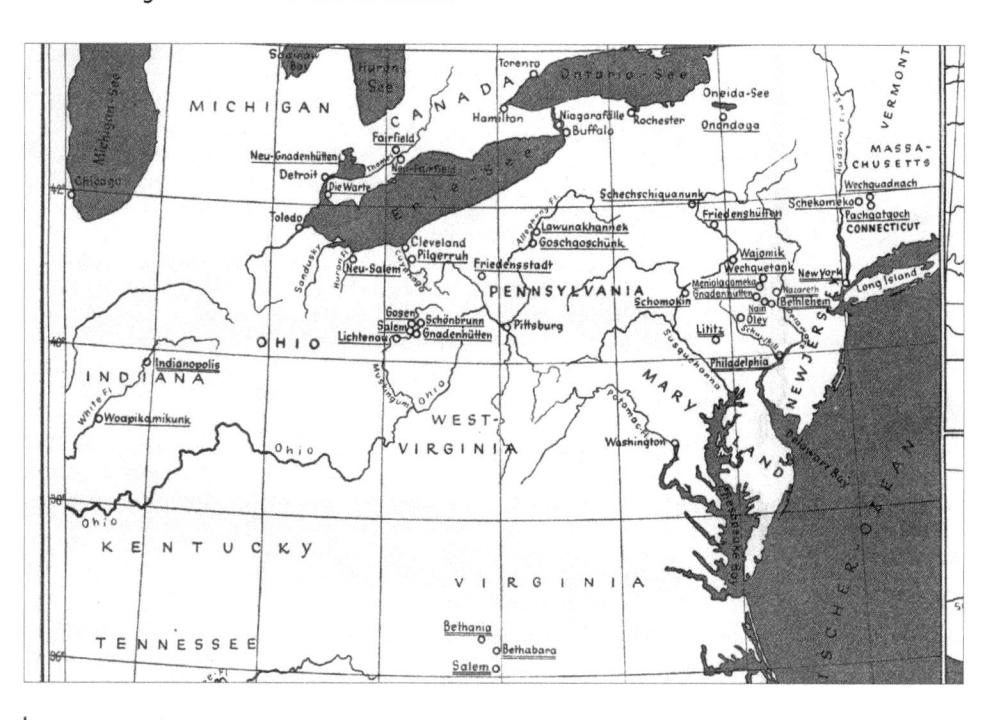

Mission map of North America with Brethren's settlements

1861 Both places were demolished during the American Civil War.

Nevertheless, they built **Woodmound** and **Talequah** but, for similar reasons as in Westfield, the work among the natives was discontinued in 1896 and stations were handed over to the American Unity of Brethren.

1899 The General Synod in Herrnhut decided that the work of the Moravian Church in North America would be divided into two provinces: northern and southern.

SOUTH AMERICA – SURINAME

1734 Since the Suriname colony belonged to the Dutch government, Spangenberg went to Amsterdam to negotiate the conditions under which the Brethren could settle in Suriname.

1735 **7 March** The first colonists set out on their journey. They bought a small plantation and cultivated it. Due to the influx of other people, riots began to arise and brothers soon left the site while the mission was successful in other places. The mission was among indigenous peoples, Bushmen and enslaved black people.

Among the Arawaks (1738–1808)

1738 A ministry was established in the area around the Demerara River, home to the native tribe of Arawaks. At first, it was a Dutch colony, later British Guiana (see also p. 128).

Missionary Schumann with an Arawak man

1740 Arawak station **Pilgerhut** was founded on the river Wironje. The first missionaries were Johannes Güttner and Ludwig Ch. Dähne.

1748 Preaching the gospel among the natives began to bear fruit. The work was started by the theologian Solomon Schumann who was not only erudite, but also very capable. He soon learned the language of the natives and also cut down trees, cultivated his own garden, and taught the natives to value work. He soon took care of 260 natives of which 180 were baptized. He translated the Gospel of John, the Epistles and the story of Passion of Jesus. He also wrote an Arawak dictionary and grammar.

1757 Brethren founded **Sharon** station on the Saramaka River, and in **1759** they established **the Ephrem station** which had to be transferred upstream due to frequent floods and was named **Hoop**. However, the area was plagued by epidemics and famine.

1760 **6 October** Solomon Schumann passed away at just 41 years old.

1763 An uprising broke out among the blacks and confusion and violence spread rapidly. Pilgerhut was burned and the brothers had to flee.

1779 The work in Sharon was also cancelled. The natives, threatened by frequent attacks by Bushmen and troubled by food worries, were increasingly abandoning the area. Brethren therefore focused on working at Hoop station.

1789 This year, the work started once again thanks to missionary J. Fischer. He thought that the mission would benefit if the natives were tied to one place. Soon, the first natives were baptized. But work was generally declining because many native had become addicted to alcohol.

1806 The station was mostly burned down and in **1808** the mission definitely ended.

Among the Bushmen (from 1765)

The Bushmen were escaped black slaves who had been hiding for decades and lived in forests. They were divided into four large tribes: the Auka, the Saramaka, the Matuari, and the Koffimaka.

Surinamese natives

1765 The black uprising ended, slavery was abolished, and the Bushmen gained complete freedom. In order to maintain political stability in the country, the governor asked the Moravian Church to launch a mission there. As the Aukan people refused to accept missionaries among themselves, brothers started to work among the **Saramaka** people on the Suriname River.

It was a challenge for the first missionaries Rudolf Stoll and Thomas Jones. The way to the Bushmen led only down the river with large waterfalls and the great heat together with the haze of the humid forest was life-threatening to Europeans. Jones soon died and other brothers, who arrived later, were dying as well.

Brethren gained the favor of Chief Abini who heartily supported the mission. He even became famous as a preacher and two of his sermons have been preserved to this day. With his help, Stoll translated all our Gospels into 'Black English'.

1771   Abini's son Arabi was the first one to be baptized.

1773   **Bambey** station was founded and a group of Bushmen moved here. Brethren then moved with them.

1777   Rudolf Stoll, the first Apostle of the Bushmen, died.

1784   **New Bambey** was established and brothers had to move there. About twenty Bushmen came to listen to the gospel at that time.

1790 – 1791   The Bushmen's desire for education was growing. Brothers visited them from time to time but many illnesses and deaths prevented missionaries from developing this service.

1813   The ministry in New Bambey was interrupted due to the lack of interest of younger people, in particular, and the lack of missionaries. Only some faithful maintained contact with missionaries in town and served as indigenous collaborators.

1830 – 1840   Bushmen were once again expressing a desire for education. They followed brothers to town until work in New Bambey was re-established.

1840 – 1859   New servants and teachers were coming to this place, but no one was there for a long time because of the unhealthy climate. The missionaries either fell ill and left or, in the worst case, died. This resulted in the Bushmen leaving the area completely and living scattered in the bush.

Bushmen

Among the black peoples in the colonies (from 1754)

1754   Few brothers were sent to Paramaribo. They initially worked as craftsmen and raised funds for themselves and for further work among the Arawaks.
Because of the negative attitudes toward them both in the plantations and in the city, brothers were not able to devote themselves to missionary work at all.

1776   The first baptism took place and a mission station was set up in **Paramaribo**.

1776 Brothers built the first church and the attitude towards them began to change.

1778 More and more blacks were joining them in the city. The number of plantations that the brothers could visit was increasing.

1785 A great move forward was the possibility for brothers to go to the countryside. They soon established the **Sommelsdyk** station to be closer to black people in the surrounding plantations. The mission expanded even in the city and gained trust in its surroundings.

1793 The Missionary Society was founded by brothers in Zeist, the Netherlands, and it began to significantly support work in Suriname.

1799 The area became an English colony several times during these years. In the end,
1816 however, it remained Dutch.

1821 After a smallpox epidemic and a great fire in Paramaribo, the opportunity to preach the gospel was reopened and brothers could also visit plantations to preach to slaves.

1835 Brothers were allowed to establish more stations, mostly on existing plantations.
1859 This was the origin of **Charlottenburg**, **Salem**, **Beekhuizen**, **Rust en Werk**, **Leliendal**, **Catharina Sofia**, **Heerendijk**, **Bersaba**, **Waterloo** and **Clevia**. Brothers were allowed to preach on ninety plantations.
- Daily Watchwords of the Moravian Church was released for the first time in local Black English and Dutch (1857).

Indigenous settlement in Suriname

PART II

1863 With the abolition of slavery and once the transitional period passed in 1873, black people moved in great numbers to the city. The church in the city soon grew to such an extent that it had to be divided into seven smaller churches.
Some missionaries were trying to bring order and Christian morals to blacks who had lived in illegitimate relationships because of slavery. However, it was not always performed reasonably or with empathy.

1898 Brethren established asylum for lepers.

1907 Suriname became a separate missionary province of the Unity of the Brethren.
Schools began to be built both in the countryside and in the city. Brothers worked on an ecclesiastical constitution and an administration of the church separating spiritual and ecclesial things from the economic and commercial ones.

1930 Brothers established a theological seminary where indigenous clergy were educated. The province had more than sixty different schools and several hospitals.

1963 Surinamese Unity of the Brethren became a separate province within the world-wide Unitas Fratrum.

1975 During this period, there was a mass migration of Surinamese people to Holland for better living conditions. (The number of immigrants professing to be members of the Unity in the Netherlands already exceeds the number of members of the European Continental Province.)

| *Bethesda – a station for the lepers*

SOUTH AFRICA

South Africa was a Dutch colony. The original inhabitants of part of South Africa, called Cape Province, were the Khoikhoi (formerly known as Hottentots) in the west and Xhosa people in the east.

Among the Khoi people (from 1736)

The Khoikhoi were forced out of their country by colonists who did not even consider them human, treated them like cattle and nobody cared for them. The news about it arrived in Herrnhut.

1736 6 February 26-year-old Georg Schmidt embarked on a mission. (He was born in Kunvald, present-day Kunín, in Moravia and secretly went to Herrnhut when he was 17.) His journey first led to the Netherlands where he waited a long time for permission to sail.

1737 9 July Georg Schmidt landed in Cape Town.

1738 Schmidt settled in Bavianskloof (later **Gnadenthal/Genadendal**). He built a house and planted a pear at the place he first preached to the Khoikhoi. It became a memorial tree and later a site of many gatherings.

Schmidt taught Africans to cultivate land, taught children to read and write. He gathered listeners around him every night. He read to them from Zinzendorf's writings and taught them from the Epistle to the Romans. He described

Khoi church in Gnadenthal (Genadendal)

everything in his diary which has been preserved to this day.

1741 After receiving a written ordination certificate from Zinzendorf, he baptized the first Khoikhoi. Soon his church had about fifty people, seven of them were baptized.
- Dutch reformed clergy began to persecute them after receiving a *Pastoral letter** from the leadership of the church which warned against the work of the Unity. There was also a threat of persecution from the colonists who despised the Khoikhoi and treated them like animals, and therefore they could not bear the fact that they were brought the Christian message.

1743 Schmidt was banned from baptizing and working and was called to the Netherlands. There on the island of Texel, at the headquarters of the Reformed Church, he defended his work and also hoped that the ban would be lifted and that he would return. But he waited in vain and his congregation in South Africa was left without a preacher.

1744 Schmidt returned to Germany.

1787 Johann Fr. Reichel, on his return journey from visitation in India, found in the Cape area traces of Schmidt's work and saw that Dutch friends living there longed for the restoration of this work.

1789 The General Synod of the Unity of the Brethren decided to resume the work in South Africa.

1791 Brothers obtained permission from the Dutch East Indian Society to set up a mission in the Cape with the condition that they reported the numbers and names of missionaries beforehand and that they only started work in places where there was no Christian church.

1792 Hendrik Marsvelt, Joh. Daniel Schwin and Joh. Christian Kühnel were sent to South Africa. They were given permission to settle in the place where Schmidt had previously worked. They found not only the remains of his house but also an old indigenous Christian Leena whom Schmidt baptized. As a precious treasure, she still had his gift: the New Testament from which she read to herself and her loved ones. The missionaries began to gather the first cluster of natives and some of them were soon baptized. Africans had a great desire for God's Word and were coming in large crowds.

Georg Schmidt

---

* The church office in Amsterdam sent the letter on 30 October 1738 to all their clergy even in colonies – Suriname, South Africa and East India.

1794 Brothers experienced hardships and persecutions again. However, God peculiarly defended them.

1796 24 March Brothers opened a house of prayer in Genadendal, established craft workshops, and worked in the garden and field. The station flourished in every way.

1808 Another station **Groenekloof** was established at the Governor's request.

1817 The development of African work was also associated with Johannes P. Hallbeck, a theologian from Sweden. He was called on a mission to the Cape and commissioned to lead it until 1840. He was an excellent organizer and he won acclaim of many with his work and nature. In 1836, he was elected a Moravian Bishop.

1823 Brothers founded the first hospital and another station in **Hemelen en Aarde**.

1824 They bought and established station **Elim**.

1838 A school for indigenous collaborators was opened in Genadendal.
- As a result of the abolition of slavery, a large number of the Khoikhoi and blacks came to mission stations. Especially Genadendal grew a lot but this was more of a disadvantage for the church's inner life.

1840 – 1859 At the request of the colonists, brothers founded preaching stations and other mission stations: **Roben Island**, **Wittewater** etc.

Czech missionary František Chleboun among the Khoikhoi

At this time, brothers often faced the problem of alcoholism among the natives.

1884 – 1898 People were moving to big cities so brothers decided to set up stations in **Cape Town** and **Port Elizabeth**.

1906 Forty-nine missionaries worked in Western Cape and they looked after 12,071 people.

In the second half of the twentieth century, an institution for colored mentally handicapped children, the first of its kind, was opened in Elim.

1967 The South African Western Province was declared independent at the General Synod in Potštejn, along with the South African Eastern Province where the mission among the Xhosa people began in the nineteenth century (see p. 126).

Indigenous village in Labrador

PENINSULA (from 1752)

1752 The first exploration was led by experienced captain Johann Ch. Erdhardt. Previously, he had been a ship navigator in the West Indies where he met F. Martin. However, Erdhardt and his five colleagues were killed by the Inuit. The remaining four brothers had difficulties getting back by boat.

1763 Labrador, originally a French colony, became part of Great Britain after the signature of the Treaty of Paris.

1764 Jens Haven set out on a second journey. He had been a missionary in Greenland for four years. His low height and his knowledge of Greenlandic language was a great help in meeting the Inuit.

1765 The third journey was undertaken by Haven, C. L. Draschart – former Danish missionary in Greenland, J. Hilt and A. Schlözer. The conditions were favorable. For two months, brothers were sailing around the coast and making friendly relations with the Inuit.

1769 The King of England gave forty hectares of land to Moravian brothers in Labrador.

1770 – 1771 Under the leadership of Haven, Brethren began to build and the station **Nain**.
Eleven brothers and three sisters worked

there. In the period from November to Easter, brothers devoted themselves to teaching and missionary work. Then most Inuit went hunting far from the stations.

- A ship called Harmony started arriving regularly once a year.

1773 Government Commissioner and First Lieutenant Curtis highly praised the civilization and diligence of the Inuit and was surprised at the changes in their behavior. But the Inuit had no desire to change their religion.

1776 The second station **Okak** was created and the first Inuit Angekok Kingminguse was baptized. The mission continued but with minimal success.

1782 **Hopedale** was founded at the southernmost tip of Labrador.

1790 Tuglavina, the uncrowned ruler of Labrador, famous wizard and killer, converted to Christianity. He had sovereign power. He strongly influenced other Inuit and they were mysteriously dying when he decided they should die. As long as he reigned, the Inuit were afraid to change religion. It all changed after his sincere repentance.

1800 By the end of the year, 110 people were baptized in three stations.

1804 An awakening spread across the Labrador coast and brothers referred to that as Pentecost. In the meantime, brothers discovered that in addition to the wizard Tuglavina, the locals were negatively affected by their sexual perversions over

Inuit children

the past thirty years. When the Inuit gave up these perversions, awakening became an instrument of great spiritual change.

1807 The awakening continued among the children.

1830 Mission station **Hebron** was erected at the northernmost point and the British Bible Society printed the New Testament and Psalms in Inuktitut.

1847
–
1848 Eighty other Inuit, who requested Christian teaching, came to Hebron and many of them received the Gospel.
Brothers established more stations: **Zoar** (1865), **Rama** (1871), **Makkovik** (1896),

Killinek (1904). They also served other immigrants coming from the south. The Gospel was taking roots there.

1865 As a result of a major viral epidemic where many people died in Okak, brothers established an orphanage for abandoned children.

1903 A hospital was built in Okak and it was led by Dr. A. K. Hutton.

1906 Twenty-nine missionaries worked at seven stations and took care of 1,321 people.

The epidemics were a big blow for this work, especially the Spanish flu after the First World War. Almost one third of the Inuit died and some stations disappeared.

1939 Station **Happy Valley** was founded.

1960 Brothers established a new station **North West River**.

1967 Labrador became a separate province at the General Synod in Potstejn.

1980 Labrador had five churches and 2 400 members.

2009 At the Unity Synod in Britain, Labrador was established as a missionary province. Financially, the province is dependent on support from an American missionary organization (so far until 2016) without which they could not accomplish work on Labrador today.

Killinek Mission Station

OTHER MISSION EFFORTS

At a time when the church in Herrnhut was busy with the care of the mission in the West Indies and Greenland, Count Zinzendorf began planning a mission in other areas. The Far Orient became an important direction.

Among the Saami and Samoyedic people (1734–1737)

1734 Andreas Grassman, Daniel Schneider and Johann Nitschmann, Jr., were sent to Lapland. Since the church was already active in the Danish part of Lapland, brothers decided to go further north to the scattered settlements of the nomadic Saami people. They traveled via Stockholm and further by boat until they reached Uleaborg. But many tried to dissuade them from that journey. In spite of that, Grassman went further with a group of Saami people to their home to the Arctic Ocean. He soon returned, however, because of language problems. The brothers then had to leave Uleaborg because of the authorities.

1736 Brothers set out on a journey to another Nordic tribe to the Samoyed (Nenets). They traveled to Archangelsk through Stockholm and Moscow. They wanted to leave with the group of Samoyed who arrived there. But they did not get permission to go further north. When repeatedly applying for passports, local authorities accused them of being spies, revolutionaries, or secret treasure hunters. They were arrested and later taken

Arrested missionaries in Archangelsk

to St. Petersburg where they confessed in front of the War Collegium. They were found innocent but were expelled from the country. One of the reasons was that they traveled officially as craftsmen and not as missionaries. Though their goal failed, Count Zinzendorf realized that for further work of the Unity of Brethren in these areas, it would be necessary first to clarify the relationship of the brothers to the Russian Orthodox Church and to gain understanding or even support from that church.

Among the Jews in Amsterdam (1738–1743)

1738   Theologian Samuel Lieberkühn, originally from Berlin, was sent to Amsterdam as a missionary to the Jews. For two years he lived in the Jewish district inhabited mainly by adherents of the Rabbinism – Talmud*. This meant that he could not speak openly about Jesus Christ. But Lieberkühn became a living testimony to many Jews in his attitude and way of life. He soon won their trust. He went daily to the synagogue, attended their Bible lessons and he did not eat the food they thought was unclean. In short, he became a Jew for them. They called him Rabbi Samuel, liked to listen to him, and a hundred years later, they still told stories of his goodness.

Lieberkühn also published his book Harmony of the Gospels which has been translated many times and became very useful in the mission field. (The last part of it containing the Passion of Jesus is still used in all parts of the Moravian Church.)

Samuel Lieberkühn

However, before his work could bear fruit, he was removed from the place because the way he worked was unfortunately misunderstood by Brethren.

1741 – 1743   Samuel LieberkühnOther servants were summoned to Amsterdam but it was not possible to continue in Lieberkühn's work.

Guinea Coast (1736–1769)
(formerly Gold Coast, modern-day Ghana)

1735   In Copenhagen, Zinzendorf met a Guinean coast native of multiethnic origin, Christian Jacob Protten. He was taken to Denmark against his will in 1727 and he was baptized there.

---

* Jewish interpretation of the way to salvation that God clearly showed in the Old Testament.

Protten was supposed to learn craft in Denmark but eventually he was allowed to study. Protten talked of the conditions in his country and Zinzendorf found him a good helper for missionary work.

1736 Protten was sent along with Henrick Huckoff to the Guinean coast. They sailed from the Netherlands with a letter of recommendation to the governor. Since Protten had come from Guinea and could speak the local language, Zinzendorf hoped for a successful mission. However, before work in Accra (under Dutch rule) could develop, Huckoff died of fever in June 1737. Protten then went to his hometown of Elmina (belonging to Denmark) where he asked for permission to establish a school for indigenous children. He was detained, however, because he was considered a runaway slave. Later, he could return to Europe where brothers offered him another task but he refused it.

1767 At the request of the Guinea society in Denmark, the Moravian Church sent another five men to the area.

1768 In July, brothers arrived in Africa but three of them died by September. At the society's request, three more brothers were sent. It was agreed that they would all go together inland, far from the colonialists, where they would serve the indigenous people. They looked for a place, started building a house. But fever struck them again and, in the end, none of the brothers survived.
Despite repeated requests from the Guinean society, brothers in Herrnhut decided not to send anyone to the area. Brothers made many sacrifices but without results.

Christian Jacob Protten

Algiers (1740)

1734 Abraham E. Richter, a wealthy merchant, joined the Moravian Church after contact with Zinzendorf. For some time, he served as an evangelist in Germany and among the Germans living in London. In Amsterdam, on his way home, he met Admiral Schryver who told him about spiritual needs of Christian slaves in Algiers.

1739 Richter was 50 years old but brothers allowed him to begin this missionary work.

1740 11 February Richter arrived in Algiers. Thanks to letters of recommendation

from the Netherlands, he was appointed teacher of religion among slaves.
- **In March** a plague epidemic broke out but Richter continued to work among the sick.
- **10 July** Richter succumbed to plague himself. Although he worked in Algiers for a very short time, he earned recognition of many people. Two of his English slaves later became members of the Moravian Church thanks to his ministry.

MISSION EFFORTS IN THE ORIENT

1735 David Nitschmann the Syndic was sent to St. Petersburg to get as much information as possible about the countries of the Orient. He returned with many reports on China, Siberia, Tartary*, Kamchatka, and especially Kalmyks. These positive reports caused Zinzendorf to consider sending brothers to Wallachia, Ethiopia, China, Persia and Hindustan. Johann Nitschmann was sent to Reval in former Livonia (modern-day Tallin in Estonia).

There were two ways to the Orient; northern – via Russia, which the brothers had already unsuccessfully tried on their travels to the Samoyedic people, and southern – via Constantinople (modern-day Istanbul).

Constantinople (1740)

1740 Zinzendorf sent Greek scholar Arvid Gradin to Constantinople as a mediator. He hoped to gain favor with the Greek Catholic Patriarch and this could open the door for mission work in the East. Gradin was accepted by the patriarch and gave him the Brethren's History by

Constantinople, modern-day Istanbul

Zinzendorf translated into Greek. Nevertheless, he was accepted with reservations and mistrust. In the end, Gradin did not obtain permission or support for Moravian mission work.

Romanian Wallachia (1740)

When both trips to the Orient failed, brothers decided to set up a settlement in Wallachia, Romania, as a base for further work in the east. Prince of Wallachia was looking for German craftsmen at that time to improve the state of the country and he wrote to brothers in Herrnhut.

1740 In the summer, Andreas Jäschke and Zacharias Hirschel arrived in Bucha-

---
*Part of the Russian empire of the time south of Siberia.

rest to negotiate further terms. They were promised not only land but also religious freedom and fee exemption.
- **In December**, brothers returned home. But the Prince died shortly afterwards and the agreed plans were no longer realized.

Among Kalmyks (1742–1822)

1742 Jäschke and Hirschel set out on a journey again. Conrad Lange joined them; he was to accompany them to the Kalmyks and then go further to China. But as soon as they arrived in St. Petersburg, they were labeled as spies and arrested. Despite their innocence, they were not allowed to continue in their journey and had to return home.

1762 Another journey to Kalmyks was more successful. The door to Russia was opened with Catherine the Great taking over the reign. To improve the quality of life in her country, she invited skilled craftsmen and offered Moravians from Herrnhut to settle there. Brothers were promised that they would be protected and that they could operate freely. But the Russian Church opposed this.

1764 According to the decision of the Moravian Synod, a settlement was established in Astrakhan*, which was very convenient for the missionary work among Kalmyks. The conditions that brothers laid down were accepted in St. Petersburg.

1765 The first five settlers arrived and they moved into new houses on October 11.

Brethren's settlement of Sarepta

* An area between Volgograd and the Caspian Sea

PART II

That was the beginning of the thriving settlement of **Sarepta** on the Volga River. In 1773, 200 people lived there already.

1766 Johann Nitschmann, Jr., later a bishop, began to work in Sarepta. Before that, he had traveled through several Nordic countries. He stayed in Sarepta until his death in 1783.

1769 Brothers established first contacts with the Kalmyks who either robbed or begged in Sarepta. Brothers Neitz, Hamel and Maltsch began to learn their language and then lived with them in their village. Thanks to the medical knowledge, brothers could even participate in a great nomadic campaign.

1770 The first Kalmyk girl who had been brought to Sarepta the year before by her father was baptized.
Brothers Gregor, Neitz, Seiffert and Pfeiffer were officially appointed missionaries. They occasionally visited the Kalmyks but the nomadic way of life made missionary work virtually impossible.

1800 Brothers founded a school for Kalmyk children.

1806 A famine broke out, causing the Kyrgyz to sell their children. The government bought those children to provide them with Christian education. Four girls were also admitted to Sarepta. They were baptized in 1810.

1813 Brothers received financial support from the London Missionary Society for a mission among Kalmyks. All this, however, caused great hostility from Russian priests.

Johann Nitschmann, Jr.

Despite these adversities, brothers managed to establish closer ties with four Kalmyk families who then settled near Sarepta.

1822 Brothers asked the government for a formal concession for missionary work. But it was rejected saying that brothers can give out Bibles but not baptize. Thus the brothers' independent work among the Kalmyks was completely impossible. The twenty-three Kalmyks that brothers won over were then baptized in the Greek Catholic Church.

1852 A superior of Sarepta, H. A. Zwick, wrote Kalmyk – German dictionary and the Grammar of the Western Mongolian or Kalmyk language.

PART II

In the Caucasus among the Tartars

1768 **17 July** Brothers Kučera and Becher left Sarepta for the Caucasus. It was said that the descendants of Czech Brethren still lived in that area. However, the local commanding general did not allow them to cross the mountains because of great danger. He recommended to them to learn Tartar first and then set out on this journey pretending to be merchants for example.

1777 Two other brothers, including Jäschke, were sent to the Astrakhan region to learn the language.

1781 After a ten-month journey they arrived
– in Tiflis (modern-day Tbilisi) but the jour-
1782 ney remained unsuccessful.

Persia – today's Iran (1746–1750)

Zinzendorf met an Armenian merchant in Amsterdam who brought him to the attention of the Cheber tribe (possibly Asian Kaffirs) living in Persia. He thought they might be descendants of the Wise Men. For this reason, Zinzendorf decided to go to them. There was a shortage of doctors in Persia.

1738 It was decided to send Moravian doctor David S. Kriegelstein but the plan did not work out.

1743 Dr. August Eller went on a journey through Astrakhan. But the Russian government did not let him continue and he died on his way home.

Izmir, second biggest city in Persia

1746 Doctor Friedrich W. Hocker and surgeon Johann Rüffer were sent to Persia.

1747 **In November**, they arrived to the city of Isfahan along with a caravan heading from the Syrian Desert to Baghdad. They had a terrible journey; they were injured and they were twice mugged by the Kurds. In Isfahan, brothers were received by the English consul. He informed them that most of the Chebers had been massacred or arrested to recant their faith. Both doctors were eventually forced to leave the country. They traveled home through Egypt where Johann Rüffer died. Friedrich W. Hocker arrived home in February 1750.

Egypt and Ethiopia (1752–1782)

1752 Hocker returned to Egypt with the intention of working among the Copts. He worked in Cairo as a doctor, learning Arabic and waiting for permission to go to Abyssinia (modern Ethiopia) to the Copts. But political confusion caused his intentions to fail.

1755 Hocker returned to Europe.

1756 He set off again, this time with George Pilder, trying to get to Abyssinia.

1758 Until October, they stayed in Egypt. But then their ship was wrecked, they lost medical equipment and had to go back to Cairo for new equipment. Zinzendorf, in one of his last letters, wrote to the Coptic Patriarch in order to obtain permission for brothers to enter Abyssinia. But both got seriously ill. Pilder left immediately and Hocker followed him in 1761.

1769 Hocker arrived in Egypt for the third time. His main co-workers were Johann Danke and John Antes, who was a clockmaker. Because the road to Abyssinia was closed due to riots, brothers worked in Cairo in their fields. And because preaching the gospel to Muslims meant risking the death penalty, they began to translate the Bible. Danke managed to reach the Coptic village of Benesse by boat on the Nile. He found many open doors and worked there until his death in 1772.

The work of brothers in Egypt was unusual. They attended Coptic services, visited their priests and spoke to them

Friedrich Wilhelm Hocker

about matters of faith. They did not preach in public but by their simple ministry and trust to God they showed people that man was not saved by good deeds or rites but by living faith in the crucified Christ.

1779 Brothers were often in danger, Antes was even flogged – one greedy Turkish governor hoped to receive a financial reward for it.

1782 Hocker died. That same year, the Moravian Synod decided that all brothers from Egypt should come back.

MISSION EFFORTS IN EAST INDIA

Count Zinzendorf decided to include East India in the mission plan thanks to his contacts in the Netherlands and with the East and West Indian Company based in Amsterdam.

Ceylon – modern Sri Lanka (1740)

1739 **18 January** August Eller and David Nitschmann the Syndic were sent to the island of Ceylon which was a Dutch possession.

1740 **In January**, brothers reached the island's town of Colombo after a stop in South Africa where they met with Schmidt. *Pastoral letter** had already arrived in Ceylon. Nevertheless, their work was initially successful with the support of the Governor van Imhoff and a clergyman Wetzel.

- Brothers began to build dwellings among the Sinhalese in Mugurugampele.
- **2 April** Brothers moved there and started to establish relationships with the natives and to learn their language.

But they did not limit their work just to them. They had also regularly visited the capital, worked among immigrants, and soon gathered a group of people around them. But after a few months, they had to stop working. The governor died and his successor, under the influence of the *Pastoral letter*, did not agree with brothers continuing their "heretical" activities in the area. Brothers were accused of outrageous interference.

| *Forts Negombo in Ceylon*

* see the footnote in the chapter about South Africa (p. 94)

■ **8 October** They embarked and returned to Amsterdam.

Bay of Bengal and Nicobar Islands (1758–1787)

1758 Count Zinzendorf received an offer from the Royal Danish Court to populate the Nicobar Islands in the Bay of Bengal where the Danish East India Company had its branch. Georg J. Stahlmann was commissioned to make arrangements for brothers. They were granted religious freedom; they were allowed to work among the natives, baptize them and set up congregations. This authorization, however, was valid only for the Nicobar Islands.

But before settling directly on the islands, brothers were given permission to settle in the port city of **Trankebar** (modern Tarangambadi) on the east coast of India which was administered by the Dänisch-Hallesche Mission.

1759 **28 September** The first group of brothers was appointed to prepare for the journey and learn the language.

1760 **2 July** Fourteen brothers headed by Stahlmann arrived at the site. They acquired a house and began to grow rice – the staple food of the country.

1761 **In August,** a second group under the leadership of Jäschke arrived to Trankebar. Sadly, he soon died and his wife as well.

Brothers built a settlement called 'Brethren's Garden'. Thanks to their craft and

| *The port town of Trankebar and its surroundings*

growing skills, the settlement soon became a renowned place.

Brothers waited for the opportunity to relocate to Nicobar but the East India Company closed its branch there due to frequent deaths. There were no ships going in that direction and brothers had been looking for a long time how to reach the islands.

In the meantime, there was great tension growing between Moravian brothers and the mission society. The society did not like brothers and their missionary activities. But the East India Company with the support of the royal court was protective over Moravians.

1768 **In August**, brothers finally had an opportunity to sail. A ship sailing in a similar direction was willing to take brothers and cargo to **Nicobar Islands**. The local governor helped them with preparations and equipment. Brothers also carried with them two dismantled wooden houses that could be easily assembled on site.

Six brothers set out on the journey and anchored on one of the islands called Nancowry. Chiefs of the surrounding villages welcomed them and allowed them to settle near them.

Then the rainy season began. The unhealthy forest environment caused death of three brothers (among them their leader and doctor) by the end of the year. Others had great difficulty supporting themselves.

Ships either consciously avoided the islands or had trouble finding them so brothers were often completely cut off from contacts, messages or other supplies.

Andreas Jäschke from Žilina

1769 –
1773 The branch of the trading company was temporarily reopened on the island, thus ensuring a regular connection with the mainland.

1773 Other reinforcements arrived at the island from Europe – that had been forbidden in previous years.

1774 Brothers were given a two-masted vessel and later even a larger ship allowing them to maintain contact with the mainland. But the operation costs were very expensive.

PART II

1781 Their ship fell into the hands of French pirates. It took three years for another Danish ship to arrive on the island. Brothers were surviving in very poor and unhealthy conditions barely making their own living. Some of them died.

1786 Johann F. Reichel, who came to visit, became convinced of the hopelessness of this work. The authorities have also told him that shipping to the Nicobar Islands is very costly and will no longer be operated.

1787 The last brothers left the islands and this mission effort, which brought no results, was discontinued. Only eight of the twenty-one brothers who originally arrived to the islands returned home.

Bengal – modern-day India (1776–1792)

1776 At the instigation of the Danish East India Company, two brothers, Johannes Grassmann and Karl F. Schmidt, left Trankebar. They went to **Serampur** on the Ganges River near Kolkata, bought some land and soon found work there. Grassmann worked as a gardener and Schmidt was a doctor.

1782 They obtained land in **Kolkata** as a gift from an English friend. Thanks to this land, work could be developed even in Kolkata.

1783 They also moved to **Patna** where there was a Danish settlement. Broth-

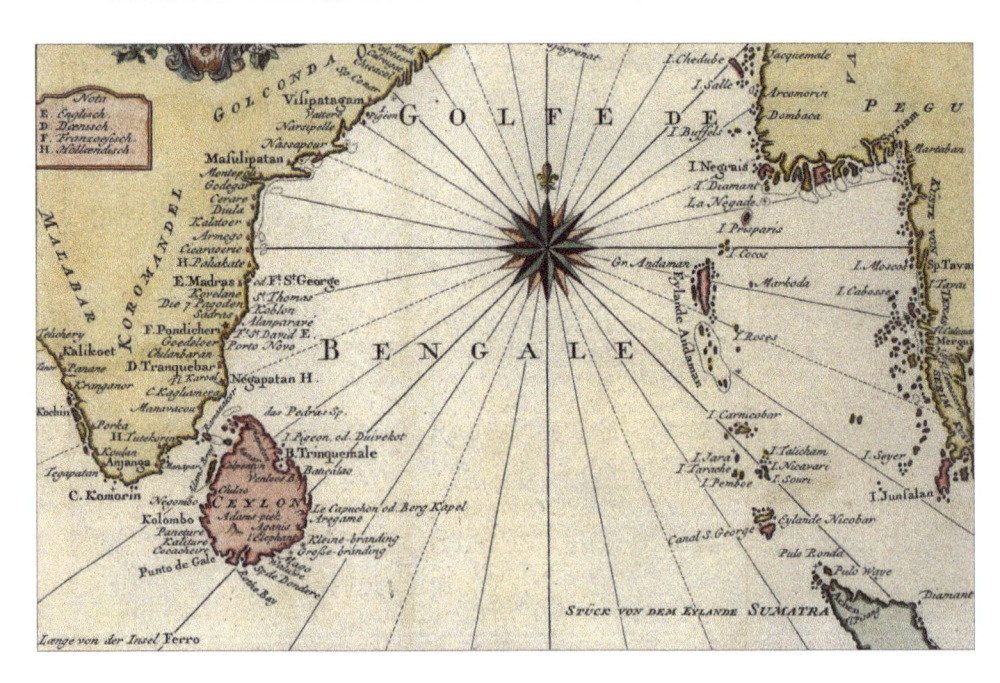

| *Map of Bay of Bengal and Nicobar Islands by J. M. Bellina (1703–1772)*

ers were given permission for another group to settle there. The circumstances seemed very favorable to missionary work, yet brothers encountered almost insurmountable obstacles. For the first time, they had to face a highly important religion in the nation and brothers were not well-equipped for that. Every attempt to get someone for Christianity was causing riots and they ran the risk of being expelled from the country.

1784 Brothers left Kolkata. Three years later, they left Patna as well.

1792 Brothers decided to abolish the settlement in Serampur. Only one slave woman was baptized during their entire work.

In Conclusion

That marked the end of the Moravian colony in Trankebar, which was founded to support the missionary work, when it lost its purpose. Until 1792, the settlement was still getting reinforcements, but there were tensions and disagreements among brothers living there.

In 1795, the Mission Board decided to abolish the 'Brethren's Garden'. The government then allowed brothers to return home and the last of them left the territory of India in 1803.

Early Christians from Moravian mission among different nations (Erstlingsbuild by J. V. Haidt, 1747)

THE UNITY OF BRETHREN IN EUROPE

The work of the Moravian Church was also rapidly developing in Europe. New churches were formed across the whole continent.

1735 13 March Daniel Ernst Jablonski, Bishop of the Polish branch of the Unity of Brethren, consecrated (with the written permission of Bishop Christian Sitkovius) in Berlin the first bishop of the renewed Unitas Fratrum. It was David Nitschmann, originally from Suchdol nad Odrou, one of the first Moravian exiles who came to Herrnhut. During the consecration, two witnesses stood with Nitschmann – Václav Zlatník and brother Janík. David Nitschmann became the sixty-third Bishop of the Unity of the Brethren (see bishop genealogy in Appendix).

1736 6 – 9 December Under the leadership of Count Zinzendorf, the leading brothers met in Marienborn. The most important subject of discussion was the importance of the Moravian bishop's office. Brothers saw an assurance of a clearly defined and independent position of the church in having the office of a bishop. They also discussed new possibilities for the work of the Unity in the Danish colony of Pilgerruh in Holstein, in Heerendijk in the Netherlands, and missions in Suriname and North America.

1737 20 May King Friedrich Wilhelm I gave authority to Bishop Daniel Ernst Jablonski (Reformed priest in Berlin) to consecrate the second Bishop of the Unity of the Brethren, Count Zinzendorf himself. The

Bishop David Nitschmann

consecration took place in the house of Bishop Jablonski. David Nitschmann was present; Bishop Kristian Sitkovius of Leszno sent his consent in a letter. Witnesses were David Nitschmann the Syndic and Matthias Schindler. This consecration was indeed quite unusual at that time since Reformed clergymen consecrated a Lutheran to become a bishop of yet another church.

- J. A. Rothe, Lutheran preacher, left Berthelsdorf and Herrnhut. He had worked there for fifteen years. He played an important role in establishing the Moravian community. Later, however, he lost his enthusiasm for the development of the renewed Unity of the Brethren.

- Fifteen years had passed since the establishment of Herrnhut and the anniversary was duly celebrated in the presence of Zinzendorf with an even deeper prayer life.

1740 **9 July** Polykarp Müller was consecrated a bishop. He was in charge of a theological seminary in Marienborn.

1741 **25 May** Daniel Ernst Jablonski died in Berlin. He was a grandson of John Amos Comenius, bishop of the Polish branch of the Unity of the Brethren, a theologian and a reformer.
- **22 July** Johann Nitschmann, Sr., was consecrated a bishop of the Unity.
- **13 November** Jesus Christ was proclaimed the Chief Elder. Until then, this office had been held by one of the brothers. The Chief Elder in office, Leonhard Dober, could not bear the task anymore in the growing Moravian Church and resigned.

"By this experience, the Moravian Church was saved from a spiritual pontificate. The daily personal communion with the Savior is the essence of understanding spiritual life. Since the first moment of the Moravian denomination, Jesus Christ has been, indeed, its head which ultimately influenced the Brethren's conception of ministry that preachers are the absolute property of Christ and are unjustly sanctified for ministry, and that all forms of work performed for Him and in front of His face are equal and deserve the same respect."[26]

1742 Niesky (formerly Nízký), a Czech exile community, was founded in Upper Lusatia. Shortly thereafter, another group of secret brothers left East Bohemia

Moravian pedagogium in Niesky

and North Moravia (for example, almost the entire village of Dolní Čermná moved out).

1744 **15 June** Martin Dober, Leonhard's older brother, became a Moravian bishop.
- **26 July** Augustus Gottlieb Spangenberg became a Moravian bishop.

1745 Brethren began to meet several times a year at conferences to address necessary issues of the functioning and administration of the church.

1746 **14 June** Friedrich Wenzel Neisser, David Nitschmann the Syndic and Christian Frederick Steinhofer were consecrated as bishops in Zeist.

- **25 September** John Frederick Cammerhof was consecrated a bishop in London.
- A young instructor Johannes M. Langguth was called as secretary of Count Zinzendorf. He was later adopted by Friedrich von Watteville and became Baron von Watteville.

1747 **4 June** Leonhard Dober, Johannes von Watteville (Langguth) and Albert Anthony Vierort were consecrated as bishops.

1748 **10 January** Frederick Martin and Peter Böhler were consecrated Moravian bishops.
- Jan Jeník was born. He was the co-founder of the Brethren's settlement in Rixdorf where he later became a preacher and worked there until his death.
- Bishop Martin Dober died in Herrnag.

Moravian congregations in Silesia

1734 Ernst Julius von Seidlitz, a well-known benefactor of the exiles, moved to the Prussian region of Ober-Peilau. Seven years later, a Moravian settlement called Gnadenfrei was established following the example of Herrnhut.

1739 **9 July** Ernst Julius von Seidlitz was arrested and interrogated in Jawor, Silesia because he protected the exiles despite bans. He was released on 21 December 1740.

1741 **Gnadenfrei** settlement was founded. Local brothers were in lively contact with Herrnhut.

| *Gnadenfrei, present-day Pilawa Górna*

1742 25 December The Prussian government issued a general concession allowing Brethren to settle anywhere in the Prussian countries and Silesia. Moravian Church was thus recognized as an independent church – independent from the state churches.

1743 13 January A Moravian congregation was inaugurated in Gnadenfrei. Becoming a member of this church was not easy at all. Applicants were asked questions which obligated prospective members with obedience and discipline.
- **21 March** Gnadengrei hosted a special gathering with Moravian and Silesian exiles which was thirty-five people at that time. Brothers began a construction of a Moravian colony. The number of members soon increased from 200 to 1,254.
- **27 July** Brothers got a special concession for the establishment of the Moravian settlement **Gnadenfeld** (present-day Pawłowiczki) from the King of Prussia Frederick II. Moravian preacher Michael Lauterbach started to serve there. For many years, however, development was hampered by major obstacles: unwillingness of the local Lutheran church and later the war between Prussia and Austria. Gnadenfeld was being taken care of by brothers from Gnadenfrei. The settlement had not been an independent congregation until 1782.
- Other Moravian settlements **Gnadenberg** and **Gnadeck** (modern Borowe) were established in Silesia. Gnadenberg received a special concession from the king on January 5 and two months later the congregation was inaugurated. By

| *Gnadenberg, present-day Kruszyn*

the end of the year, a Brethren's hall was completed.
- **25 August** Friedrich von Watteville was consecrated a bishop in Gnadeck.
- Ernst Julius von Seidlitz came to **Neusalz** (present-day Nowa Sól) to establish a Moravian settlement. The place was convenient because it was located near the navigable Oder River. In June brothers received a special concession from the King of Prussia Frederick II and immediately began building. They planned to build a house of prayer, orphanage, pharmacy, printer house and manufactory for striped canvas. Some locals were not pleased with it which resulted in Brethren not acquiring city rights for this place until October 1743.

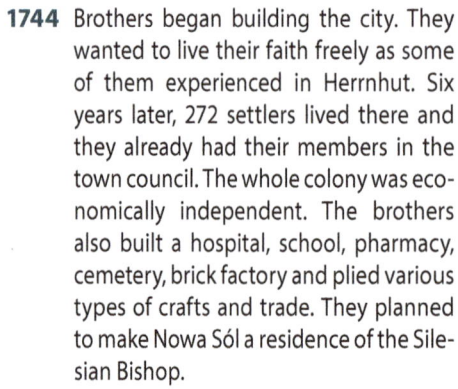

1744 Brothers began building the city. They wanted to live their faith freely as some of them experienced in Herrnhut. Six years later, 272 settlers lived there and they already had their members in the town council. The whole colony was economically independent. The brothers also built a hospital, school, pharmacy, cemetery, brick factory and plied various types of crafts and trade. They planned to make Nowa Sól a residence of the Silesian Bishop.
- Bishop Polykarp Müller immigrated to Silesia with the intention of setting up a Moravian seminary in Nowa Sól but he did not manage to do it in time.

1747 **17 June** Bishop Polykarp Müller died.

1759 **24 September** In the Third Silesian War, a Russian army invaded Nowa Sól. The soldiers were extremely cruel and they completely destroyed and burned the town.

Nowa Sól

1763 Brothers began to return to Nowa Sól to rebuild the city.

1766 Ernst Julius von Sedlitz died.

1769 They inaugurated a new house of prayer in Nowa Sól. The Prussian king Frederick II tried to accelerate the economic development of the town and brothers met his expectations. Despite its specific internal coherence, the Moravian community was open to other local merchants and brothers were willing to participate in public life. They gave the whole city and its neighborhood an example of healthy economic development and overall order in the city. The work was discontinued in 1945.

No other emigrants came to Moravian settlements after the Patent of Toleration was issued in 1781.

Further development of ministry

The beginnings of work in the United Kingdom were closely linked with missionary work. Zinzendorf originally did not intend to establish the Unity of Brethren there. London, however, served as a stopover for missionaries on their way overseas.

1739 At the instigation of Bishop Petr Böhler in London, a **Fetter Lane** Society was founded where John Wesley (founder of Methodism) later experienced a spiritual renewal.

1742 In October, the Fetter Lane Chapel, registered according to the Toleration Act, became the first (city) congregation of the Moravian Church in the British Isles which became a base for further activities.

In 1749, the Unity of Brethren was recognized by the British Parliament as an independent Protestant Episcopal Church, a legitimate successor of old Brethren.

John Cennick, who was ordained in 1749 and worked for some time as a traveling preacher, was also a significant person. Thanks to his work, many groups (societies) were formed.

Establishment of Moravian communities/congregations did not take place in England and Ireland with the support of the nobility, but grew thanks to awakened groups mostly in places that were not adequately served by the Church of England.

1750 Moravian village of **Ockbrook** was founded by the decision of Bishop

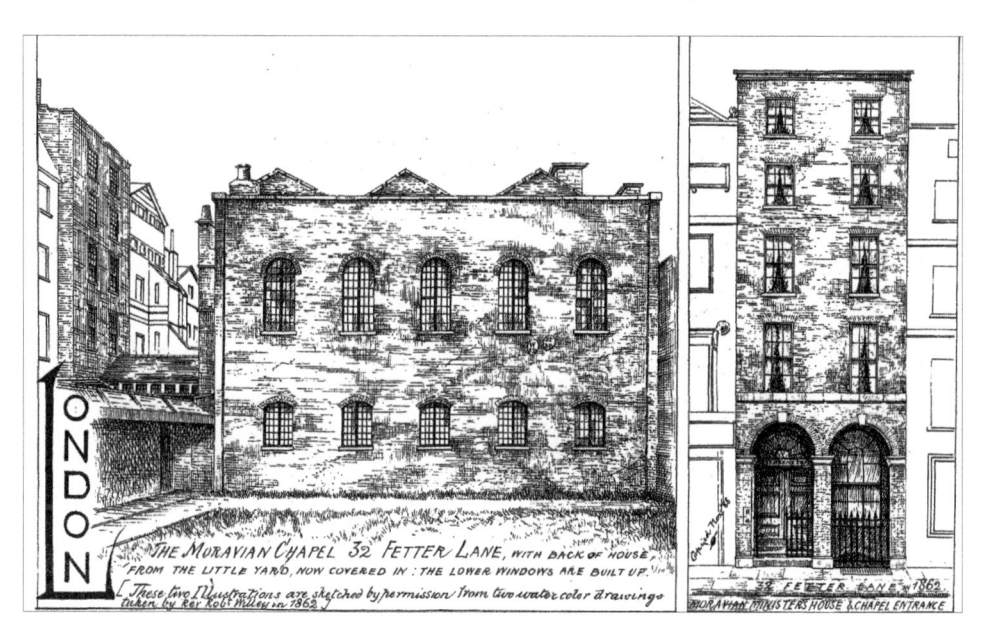

Fetter Lane building in London

Böhler. Another settlement, **Gracehill**, was founded (1763) and thanks to the work of Benjamin Latrobe, a leading minister of the British Moravian Church, it was decided to build the Moravian community of **Fairfeld** (1783).

Around 1750, the renewed Unitas Fratrum was recognized not only in Britain but also in other European Protestant countries as an independent evangelical church with its own bishop's office and its own world mission (the church was also known as the Moravian Church).

1750 6 December Johann Georg Waiblinger, who served in Silesian congregations, was consecrated a bishop in Herrnhut.

1751 3 February Christian David, a carpenter and co-founder of Herrnhut, died.
- **24 September** Matthew Hehl became a bishop in London.
- Bishop John F. Cammerhof died.

1754 14 November John Gambolt became a Bishop in London.

1756 1 March The so-called Czech village Rixdorf was founded on the southern outskirts of Berlin. Saxony refused to accept other exiles from Moravia and Bohemia so Czech brothers (especially from the area of Horní Čermná) found their new refuge in Rixdorf.
More than twenty years after the establishment of Herrnhut, more Brethren's settlements were growing in other parts of Germany as well as in Holland and

Pohled na „Český Rixdorf" u Berlína v roku 1755.
(Bratrský dum.)

| Rixdorf – Czech village, today is a part of Berlin

Denmark (Herendijk 1732, Pilgerruh 1737, Herrnhaag 1738, Neudietendorf 1742, Zeist 1746, Neuwied 1750, Kleinwelka 1751, Gnadau 1761, Christiansfeld 1772, Königsfeld 1807).

- **25 April** The General Conference of the Moravian Church was initiated and Count Zinzendorf formulated the definition of a "Moravian Brother": *"Who can prove that he or any of his ancestors left everything to enjoy the happiness and freedom of the people of God, who will therefore give up everything that the Saviour asks from him, except life."*[27]
- **5 July** Andreas Grassmann became a Moravian Bishop.

1758 **12 May** Johann Nitschmann, Jr., and Nathanael Seidel were consecrated bishops.

1760 **9 May** Count Nicholas Louis Zinzendorf, the sixty-fourth bishop, died. At that time, the renewed Unitas Fratrum had a total of twenty-two bishops, six of them were born Moravians.

1762 **2 August** Jan Raschke, co-founder of the Moravian settlement in Nízký, died.

1764 **2 July** The first constitutional General Synod of the renewed Unitas Fratrum was held in Marienborn (see page 154).

1766 **1 April** Jan Leonhard Dober died. He was the first Moravian missionary and the seventy-fifth Bishop of the Moravian Church.

- Johann Nitschmann, Jr., left for a new colony in Old Sarepta. He had worked there among Kalmyks for eighteen

Graves of Count Zinzendorf and his closest ones in Herrnhut God's Acre

PART II

years. He was also buried in Old Sarepta.

1769 The second constitutional General Synod took place in Marienborn under the leadership of August G. Spangenberg.

1772 In May Johann Nitschmann, Sr., died in Zeist, the Netherlands.
- **In October** David Nitschmann died in Bethlehem. They both were Moravian missionaries and bishops, born in Moravia (today part of the Czech Republic).

1773 7 October Karel August Pácalt, later a Moravian missionary and a follower of the missionary work among the Khoi people in South Africa, was born. He died at the age of 45.

1775 The third constitutional General Synod took place in Barby.

1777 Friedrich Wenzel Neisser, born in Moravia, a very humble man and Bishop, died in Barby.
- **24 April** Bishop Friedrich von Watteville died in Herrnhut. He was Zinzendorf's friend since his youth and from the very beginning he was eager for the work of the Moravian Church. He was an excellent preacher, powerful in word and love.

1779 29 March David Nitschmann the Syndic, Bishop, member of the Directory and archivist of the Moravian Church, died in Zeist, the Netherlands.
- The doctrine of the renewed Moravian Church by Spangenberg, entitled *Idea fidei fratrum* (Exposition of Christian Doctrine), was published. Jan Jeník translated it into Czech.

Andreas Grassmann

1781 Melchior Zeisberger, who served primarily in northern Europe, died.

1783 In March Bishop Andreas Grassman passed away.

1785 2 August Moravian missionary Georg Schmidt died. He began missionary work in South Africa among the Khoi people. He is buried in Niesky.

1786 Johann Friedrich Köber, an excellent lawyer, a friend of Count Zinzendorf and an important Spangenberg's assistant, died. He had been a member of the Moravian Church since 1747 and, especially at the end of Zinzendorf's life, was able to restrain Count Zinzendorf's idealistic plans in a healthy way. He made a significant legal contribution to the first three constitutional synods. He thus helped the new emerging structure of the renewed Moravian Church.

1788 Bishop Johannes von Watteville died in Gnadenfrei. He had served in the church for nearly fifty years.

1792 **18 September** Bishop August Gottlieb Spangenberg died in Berthelsdorf. After Zinzendorf's death, Spangenberg became his successor. Thanks to his 30-year ministry in Herrnhut, the church developed a structure, stabilized and consolidated its position especially on missions. He directed the renewed Moravian Church until his 88 years with great inner authority and clear vision.

Diaspora in Livonia

Christianity in Livonia (modern Latvia and Estonia) can be traced back to the German knights. Nevertheless, locals secretly sacrificed to natural gods and practiced witchcraft and even the reformation in 1521 could not change these practices.

1721 After the Great Northern War, which was concluded with the Treaty of Nystad, Livonia became a Russian province for a long time. But the Russians did not settle in the country and therefore the Baltic German nobility maintained their power and identity.

The clergy who studied theology in Germany brought the Halle Pietism back to Livonia. Pietism thus gained supporters even among the nobility. Influenced by pietistic ideas, people became interested in the social and spiritual situation of local peasants, building schools in rural areas and revision of Bible translations (first translation to Latvian in 1689, New Testament to Estonian in 1676). From the beginning, the pietistic aristocracy sought to establish contact with the emerging Moravian Church and Count Zinzendorf. Brethren were, therefore, warmly awaited and welcomed in Livonia.

1729 Christian David and Timotheus Fiedler visited Livonia. They settled in Riga for some time and they worked as craftsmen. They became close with local farmers and learned a lot about their situation.

August Gottlieb Spangenberg

Christian David was the first to learn Latvian. Brothers also visited Wollmar and Reval (modern Tallinn). This was the beginning of the greatest diaspora work of the Moravian Church at the time. Fiedler continued on a mission to India in 1733.

1736 Count Zinzendorf arrived in Livonia. He visited Riga, Wollmar and Reval. He preached in many crowded churches. His person and message were enthusiastically received not only by the nobility, but also by clergy and burghers. This opened the door for further work of Brethren. Zinzendorf developed a so-called "Livonian Plan" which sought to send brothers to help the overburdened Lutheran clergy when they would ask for it. Their ministry was mainly in Bible lessons, practical work and leading church members in groups to work actively for the church. In pastoral care, brothers were supposed to be replaced by local believers soon.

1738 A teacher seminary was founded in Wollmarshof with the support of Moravians. It was led by theologian Magnus F. Buntebart.

1738 – 1741 Christian David worked in Livonia again. He also helped to build Moravian centers like in Herrnhut or Greenland. Brothers who came from Herrnhut (about fifty by 1740) preached all over the country. Their sermons prompted a revival that spread rapidly throughout Livonia.

In the north of Estonia and on the island of Ösel (present-day Saaremaa), the revival touched all the population including the nobility and German burghers.

Reval, modern-day Tallinn (Estonia)

The taverns were deserted; working morale improved the relationship between landowners and their subjects. Rooms and premises were soon too small to accommodate the believers so gatherings were held in the woods in the open air. After the turbulent beginnings, Brethren began to build a solid structure and local believers gradually took over the leadership of individual churches. In some places, Moravians established churches according to the Herrnhut model.

All this understandably caused tensions with the Lutheran Church.

Moravians worked as doctors, teachers or craftsmen and also looked after the awakened Latvians and Estonians in individual church districts. They won the hearts of local farmers with preaching in their language and kindness. This breached the walls of hatred the population had towards everything German which was caused by the cruel rule of the German nobility.

A pastoral and liberation service from demonic ties to old pagan customs meant a great breakthrough. After that, people were approaching their masters and returning what they had stolen from them. And the locals were destroying places of pagan sacrifices and sacred groves themselves.

1739 About 5,000 people gathered regularly in congregations.

1740 More brothers came to Livonia, Johann Nitschmann, Jr., among them.

Livonia 1573–1578

1742 David Sigmund Kriegelstein, a physician and a theologian, was sent from Herrnhut to take over the management of the Livonian work.
- By the end of the year, Moravians worked among 14,000 to 15,000 local believers.

1743 **16 April** Russian Empress Elizabeth issued a decree which banned all activities of the Moravian Church in the Russian Empire. But the Moravian Church continued to work there and experienced a persecution.

At that time brothers were arrested in Saint Petersburg on their way to Kalmyks. Other brothers from Livonia were also imprisoned and some of them were martyred. Work in the diaspora did not stop but it was experiencing a time of suffering.

1747 David Sigmund Kriegelstein was arrested. After twelve years of imprisonment, he was released and sent into exile to Kazan where died in 1760.

1764 The work in the diaspora developed again.

1801 Alexander I, who was very open to European Christianity and even supported the Moravian Church, became a Russian Tsar.

The work of the Moravian Church grew until the mid-nineteenth century. Brothers were building wooden houses of prayer. According to the existing list, there were 253 of them by 1840. By 1854, the number of houses of prayer rose to 276 with 83,272 members.

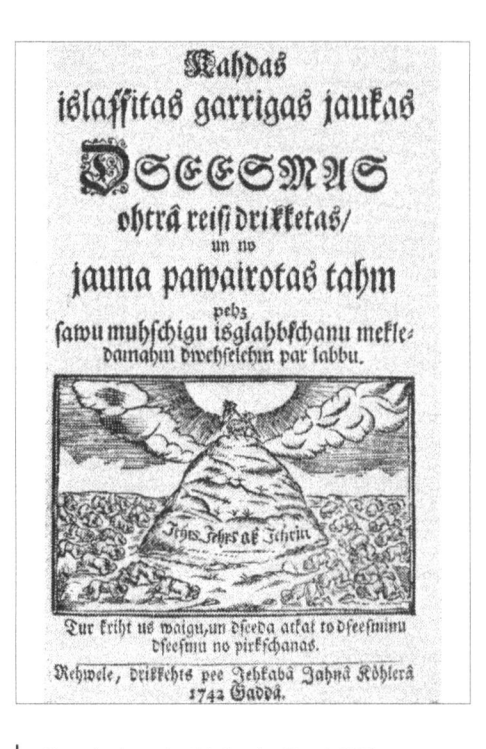

Moravian hymn book in Latvian (Reval, 1742)

The Moravian Church had a relatively large impact on social and economic life of the country. And Moravian-oriented nobility opened up to the Estonian and Latvian way of life and supported the national awakening of the people.

1857 The General Synod decided to change the structure of the work in Livonia. The Synod abolished the specific Herrnhutian character the locals were used to. This decision disrupted the spiritual life of the local members and many of them left the Moravian Church. The communities were shrinking. Many prayer rooms became empty and were sold or handed over to the local Lutheran Church. With the increasing adaptation to the local church, the work in the diaspora suffered a great damage. The church welcomed it, but the mission lost the feature of spiritual awakening it had gained through the specific Herrnhutian ministry.

1903 There were only a few brothers left who could act freely. But the Moravian Church had virtually no influence on religious or public life that would be comparable to the past.

The war of 1914 and the revolution of 1918 completely changed the overall situation and forced the Moravian Church to abandon this area completely.

In conclusion

In the eighteenth century, Moravian missionaries visited twenty-four countries and nations in total and, by the end of the century, they had helped nearly 15,000 people to turn to Christ. This is definitely a large number and today, we can certainly be grateful for the work of the Moravian Brethren. Looking at the current map of the congregations of the Unitas Fratrum in the world, one can state, as William Carey did: *"Look what these Moravians achieved!"* It can be said that the Moravian Church in the eighteenth century brought to pagans above all the message of Christ crucified, of His suffering and redemption from people's sins.

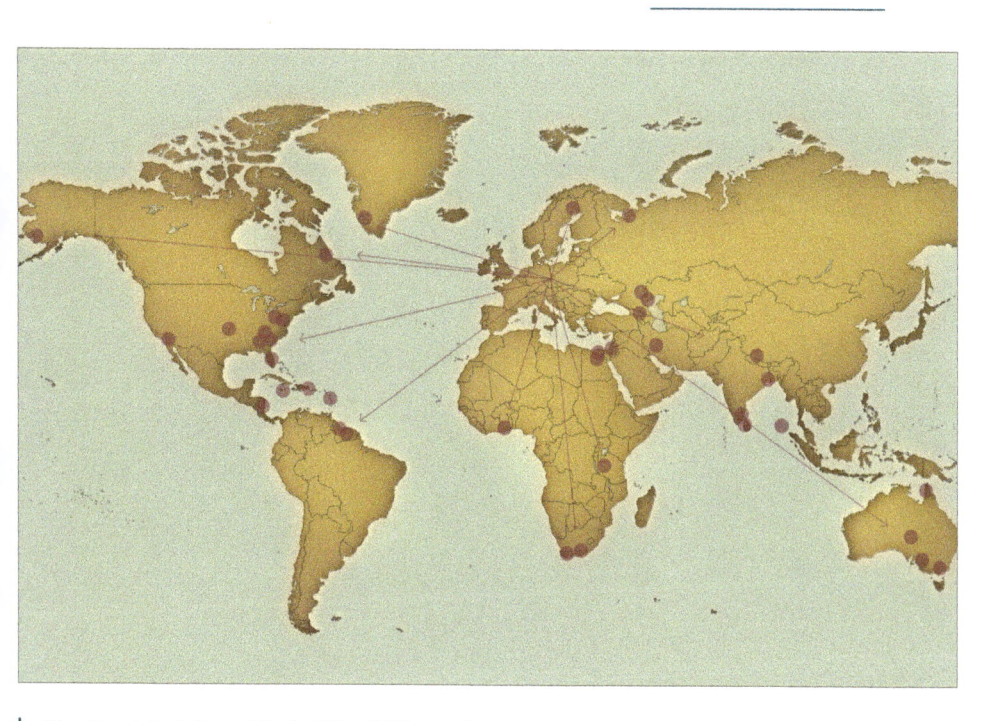

Moravian mission in the world in the 18th and 19th centuries

NINETEENTH CENTURY MISSIONS

In the eighteenth century, the Moravian Church was virtually the only one to develop missions among the pagans. From the beginning of the nineteenth century, other groups began these missions as well. They were mainly English missionary companies. The Moravian Church thus gained experience from others and it also led to even greater zeal in this activity.

Results of these missions were stirring up interest in Europe and the Moravian Church received more donations and additional support. Although the church was growing spiritually in this ministry, it did not leave its original way of working. It was not a mass Christianization of entire territories and nations, but it focused on the heart of an individual and led everyone to a personal relationship with Christ.

In some places, the mission was transformed into independent work, some areas had to be abandoned by brothers completely, and, in other places, work is still being born.

SOUTH AFRICA

The Xhosa people lived in the eastern region of South Africa; their territory bordered the Khoikhoi (see p. 93)

Among the Xhosa people (from 1818)

1818 The **Enon** station was founded. It was more of a preparation for the mission

Xhosa women at work

among the Xhosa people because in this area lived mostly the Khoikhoi.

Missionary work began slowly because of the repeated war of Xhosa people with the English. These battles were often very cruel and bloody.

1827 Chief Da Bauan invited Moravians because he wanted them to work as missionaries among his people. The meeting was attended by brothers Hans P. Hallbeck and Fritsch.

1828 Brethren founded the first station **Silo**. In addition to the Xhosa people, the Khoi people started to come as well which brought tensions. For a long time, it was necessary to hold two different church services.

1850 **Goshen** station was established. However, a war broke out a year later, brothers had to flee and both stations were destroyed. After a few years, work continued once again and besides the mission houses, schools were built there as well.

1859 Brothers founded a station **Engotini**. Other stations were being established in the **Tembuland** area where missionary Heinrich Meyer worked with the support of Chief Zibi.

In following years, the work also spread to the cities of **Queenstown** and **East London**.

1875– Brothers opened stations **Elukolweni**, **Tinana**, **Bethesda** and more.

1905 František Chleboun, a Czech missionary who worked mainly in the Enon station in 1894–1913, also devoted his missionary work to the Xhosa people.

A missionary among the Xhosa people

1901 A teaching and missionary seminar for indigenous teachers and collaborators was opened. The local collaborators were firm in faith and a great help to brothers in day-to-day ministry. The Xhosa people, who had lost their political independence and had to submit to life in colonies, saw missionaries as political agents rather than true friends and that is why the work continued slowly.

1906 Ninety-eight evangelists, thirty-five missionaries and seven natives worked in the area. They took care of 8,771 people.

1930 The Moravian Church had 126 teachers at sixty-one elementary schools in this part of South Africa. In addition, three vocational secondary schools were established.

Both South African provinces, Western and Eastern, worked separately and independently. While the division of the work was legitimate, it caused deep long-term problems of alienation, separate structures and suspicion.

1976 The Unity Synod in Jamaica decided to join the two provinces into one.
- That was a long process. The whole situation was made worse by the great problem of that time – South African apartheid which strictly favored the rights of white people and incited racial discrimination.

1980 There were over 90,000 members and about seventy-five churches in South Africa.

1986 A commission was set up to work on the unification of the two provinces.

* today's Guyana

Sunday at Moravian mission station in South Africa

1998 A new constitution has been adopted and since then, the Moravian Church has been operating in South Africa as one province.

SOUTH AMERICA – British Guiana* (from 1835)

The area near the Essequibo, Demerara and Berbice Rivers was originally under the rule of the Dutch where missionaries served among the Arawaks (see page 88). After various changes of governments, it ended in the hands of the British.

1835 A mission was started among black peo-
– ple. The family of Colemans and later the
1838 Hamanns served there but the work was

discontinued due to lack of interest and considerable difficulties.

1878 At the invitation of a plantation owner, three native Moravian missionaries – Henry Moor, A. Pilgrim, and teacher Robert E. Potter arrived from Barbados. They began working among the blacks and mixed-race people. Most of them were already Christians, some of them even members of the Moravian Church from other regions. (After the abolition of slavery, the blacks moved to different places for work.) Together with the care for individual groups, brothers also took care of education and built schools.

New stations or congregations were gradually built at the mouth of the Demerara and Berbice rivers: **Graham's Hall** (1878), **Beterverwagting** called Tabernacle (1883), **Queenstown** (1902) and others. Native worker John Dingwall took over the management after Henry Moor and contributed the most to this development. Dingwall worked there until 1944.

1907 Guyana became an independent missionary province of the Moravian Church with its own orders.

Missionaries also began working among a polytheistic tribe of Indian descent. However, this work could not fully develop due to lack of co-workers and financial resources.
The number of groups of black people that brothers served to was increasing. This period was the most fruitful

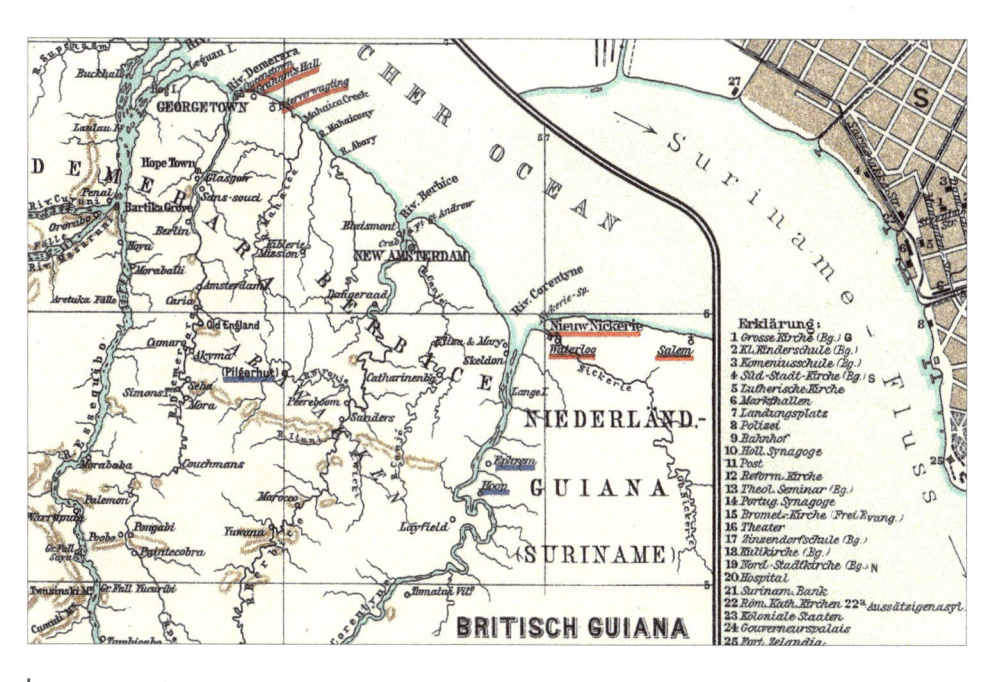

Mission map of British Guiana

for Guyana. Brothers founded in total ten mission stations attended by 3,600 members and three schools with 950 children and 600 Sunday school pupils. In the capital of Queenstown, Dingwall founded J. A. Comenius High School which taught about 1,000 pupils.

1966 After Guyana gained independence, all local schools were nationalized.

Guyana has remained a province of the Moravian Church.

CENTRAL AMERICA – Nicaragua (from 1849)

In 1848, the General Synod of the Moravian Church decided to send missionaries to the Mosquito Coast* after hearing about the difficult conditions of Miskito people living there.

Village in Nicaragua

1849 14 March Heinrich Gottlob Pfeiffer with his wife, Johannes Eugen Lundberg and Ernst Kandler arrived in the capital **Bluefields**. With the approval of the British consul and the Indian chief, they began to work there. Pfeiffer was visiting people and preached, Lundberg devoted himself to teaching and soon opened a school. They first took care of English-speaking population and established the first station.

1856 Gustav Feurig, former missionary in Jamaica, was called to Pfeiffer's place after a visit from the Mission Board. The goal of this change was to focus primarily on work among the indigenous peoples. Other helpers, such as Peter Blair, a black teacher from Jamaica, Eduard Grunewald, August Martin and others, were coming here. Both Blair and. Grunewald learned the Miskito language really fast. Brothers visited Miskito villages along the coast and began to build new mission stations **Magdala – Perl Lagoon** (1855), **Rama Cay** (1858), **Ephrata** (1860) and **Karata** (1875).

1865 A great hurricane hit the coast. The sea flooded the crops and degraded the land for a long time. Many houses were damaged and there was a threat of famine. Yet brothers endured, restored houses and churches and continued working.

* Eastern coast of present-day Nicaragua and Honduras. The area is called after the Miskito Kingdom.

1881 A spiritual awakening began and soon spread throughout the coast. Most residents, regardless of race, were clearly and fearfully aware of their sins. People were eventually filled with peace, joy, and the certainty of forgiveness. They themselves sought out missionaries asking for baptism and Bible teaching. They came in crowds, even from the most remote places. The seven missionaries who lived there at that time served all day long.

Other mission stations quickly emerged – **Quamwatla** and **Yulu** (1884), **Sharon** and **Twappi** (1886), three stations north of the border in Honduras – **Dakura** (1893), **Sandy Bay** and **Wasla** (1896), and others (by 1906 there were sixteen stations).

1899 – 1914 Nicaragua was undergoing political and economic difficulties which greatly affected the mission. The local government also decided that Spanish would be an official language and introduced a new school system. This led to the closure of all sixteen Moravian schools that were still operating.

The mission continued, brothers managed to penetrate deeper inland, and instead of other mission stations they established preaching stations (there were sixty-eight of those by 1912). The missionaries became mainly traveling preachers.

In the meantime, another revolution took place which once again guaranteed freedom for churches and schools. But this also meant more intense pressure from the growing Catholic Church. On top of that, the 1909 General Synod decided to reduce all missions in general. Some brothers were removed from the mission; some already fell ill or died due to the climate. It was necessary to find local helpers on their places.

Local fishermen

1914 Guido Grossmann took over the mission work. Despite the lack of missionaries, forty-six local evangelists and ten helpers entered service. Brothers worked, taught and served as traveling preachers.

They also managed to reach the Mayangna who lived in their smaller territory. In 1912–1913, the first Mayangna were baptized, although contact with missionaries remained occasional as they often moved along the river.

1919 Herbert Cruickshank was called from America to supervise local Moravian schools. After being forcibly closed down in 1900, the schools gradually managed to reopen in many places. However, both resources and teachers were missing. Cruickshank also managed to convince the government that Moravian schools would benefit the country so their numbers grew again.

Brethren were also experienced medical workers and in times of epidemics they were very helpful to all those in need.

1923 Another station **Bilwi** was established meaning that there was no village on the coast without a Moravian mission.
- The **Musafas** station was founded and became a solid base for working among the Mayangna.

Brothers continued to concentrate on a mission inland where they were well received. Missionaries divided the territory between themselves and each of them took care of their area as a traveling preacher. This created a network of preaching stations.

By 1929, they had foundations of Christian congregations in all but one village in the Wangks River basin.

Another direction where the mission could move was the north, Honduras. The Miskito people lived there as well (see p. 147).

1925 The Directory in Bethlehem took over leadership and administration of the mission in Nicaragua. Until then, it had been administered from Herrnhut.
- G. R. Heath revised and reissued the New Testament in Miskito. The Bible was translated step by step; the first parts of the New Testament were published in 1889.

Students of Wasla mission school

1926 G. R. Heath compiled and published a Miskito grammar and dictionary. The first mission school was opened.

1930 There were already twenty-two day schools with 1,218 pupils and forty-nine Sunday schools with 6,005 pupils.

Ten missionaries and twenty-two local evangelists worked at forty-three stations and nineteen preaching places. There were about one third of the Creoles who spoke English and two thirds of the natives with various Miskito dialects. In some places brothers also preached in Spanish.

1931 The Daily Watchwords for local churches were printed for the first time.

A high school Colegio Moravo was opened in Bluefields. By 1950, it had over 600 pupils. To this day, the Moravian Church is present mainly on the east coast of Nicaragua where the hospitals in Bilwaskarma and Puerto Cabezas were built. Theological seminaries and schools were set up in these villages as well.

1974 Nicaragua became a separate province of the Moravian Church with 80,000 members.

MISSION EFFORTS IN AUSTRALIA

Victoria Colony (1850–1907)

In Melbourne, there were about 14,000 immigrants in 1835 and about 15,000 Aborigines, often cannibals, around the village. Despite their predominance, the colonists treated the natives as annoying, dangerous and harmful game, and tried to exterminate them. The Australian government later passed a law to protect Aborigines but it only applied to those who lived in reservations.

1848 The Synod decided to launch a mission among indigenous Australians. The Governor of the Australian Colony of Victoria was Charles Joseph La Trobe, a member of the Moravian Church and brother of the secretary of the London Moravian Missionary Society.

1850 **26 February** Missionaries Andreas Täger from Niesky and Friedrich Spiesecke from Gnadenberg landed in Melbourne.

Mission station in Bluefields

1851 – Brothers tried to work by the Lake Boga on the Murray River (about 300 km north of Melbourne). They were often on the road, looking for indigenous peoples, learning their language, but with no results. It took a long time to get permission to settle on the land, which they soon lost again. Further difficulties and dangers to which they were exposed led the brothers to give up this work and return home without telling anyone in Herrnhut.

1857 The General Synod encouraged resumption of the mission and sent F. W. Spiesecke and F. Hagenauer to Australia.

1858 Brothers settled in a government-recommended location in the Wimmera region (northwest of Melbourne).

1859 They founded **Ebenezer** station, learned a language, and opened a school for the natives. They were gradually gaining their hearts.

1860 The first of the Aborigines was baptized: a boy called Pepper. The natives were giving up their original lifestyle very slowly. Little by little, they settled down, learned to farm, grow vegetables and cultivate land.

1863 The **Ramahyuk** station was established. But one thing the brothers could not stop. The Aborigines were dying very young. The few babies who were born were weak and sick.

1903 –
1907 Both stations were closed and the rest of the natives were transferred to other places. In 1906, the Hagenauer fam-

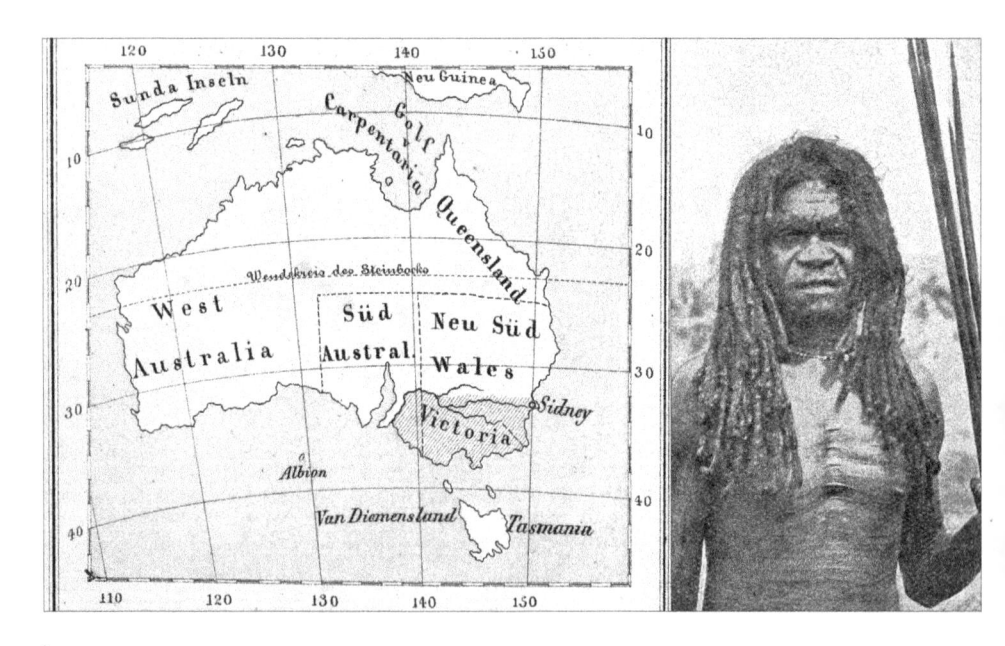

| *Mission areas Victoria and Queensland; Australian Aborigine*

ily worked in the area and cared for twenty-one baptized natives.

Queensland (1891–1919)

1891 In Queensland, Northern Australia, a new ministry was established with the support of the Australian Presbyterian Church. The Mission Board sent James Ward with his wife and Nicolaus Hey. They founded **Mapoon** station on the Cape York Peninsula. Unhealthy climate, drought, barren land, adversity of white people – missionaries had to face all of this. However, the Aborigines soon became their friends.

1895 Ward died but his wife continued the work, especially at school. The locals called her 'mom'.

- They built a church, parsonage, school, craft workshops, farm buildings and thirty houses for indigenous people. Their numbers were gradually growing.

1896 The first baptism took place and other stations **Weipa** and later **Aurukun** (1904) were built.
Brothers also provided health care and the Aborigines were no longer dying prematurely. Even though some of them returned to their nomadic and pagan way of life, the work in mission stations was growing.

1907 Fifty-one natives were baptized in Mapoon and twenty in Weipa.

1919 The ministry was handed over to the Presbyterian Church of Australia and

Mission house in Mapoon – North Queensland

Tasmania which supported the mission financially.

LADAKH AND SOUTH ASIA (from 1856)

1850 At the Conference of the Moravian Church in Herrnhut, brothers decided to undertake a mission among Mongolians in Central Asia. Johannes E. Pagell and August W. Heyde were called to do so. They began to learn Mongolian and also collected medical and surgical knowledge. Since Russian authorities made it impossible to travel through Russia, brothers chose to travel across India.

1853 – 1856 Brothers set out on a hard and painful journey. First, they arrived to Calcutta and then they traveled northwest across mountain passes to the Western Himalayas (present-day Kashmir). They tried to cross the Chinese border in three places but they were always expelled. In the end, they decided to set up a mission station as close to the border as possible if the situation changed. However, the Ladakh area was dangerous, so they chose the Lahul area where Mongolian residents also lived.

Kyelang

1856 Brothers founded a station in **Kyelang** where they bought land and built a house.

1857 The third missionary, Heinrich A. Jäschke, arrived. He had the task of translating the Bible into Tibetan. In addition to biblical stories, he also translated various treatises and textbooks that brothers could print on a lithographic printing press. Brethren began to preach the gospel in the surrounding villages and areas. When they were faced with disinterest and constraint, they at least distributed prints to those who wanted to learn to read. Brethren established a school in Kyelang, provided health care, helped to develop the economy. Their wives worked among women and, beside other things, they taught them to knit woollen socks which has remained a local tradition to this day.

Monastery in Kyelang

1865 The first two men were baptized. More servants came to the Lahul area. A. W. Heyde worked on revision of the Tibetan New Testament. People who had to escape from Ladakh and who were planning to go back often converted in Kyelang. But tensions grew between the Ladakh people and the indigenous population.

During the World War I, missionaries left the area but one native evangelist continued working there. After the war, the missionaries returned and worked there until 1940. But because of World War II, they had to leave the country and the work in Keylang was later cancelled. Only a church with a cemetery and the family of Phuntsog remained there.

Pooh

1865 A new station was established in **Pooh**. The village was on a trade route, two days away from Tibet. The station was led by Eduard Pagell and his wife. At first, people did not accept them. But Pagell was also a good medic and thus became known for that. About 40–50 people were gathering in Pooh but only few were baptized.

1883 The Pagells died of typhoid fever and the mission nearly disappeared. There was a problem of great poverty and lack of food in the area. Many debtors had to sell themselves for forced labor. There was a danger that people would come for food and gifts only and become so-called Rice Christians. The arrival of missionary Theodor Schreve changed the situation. He founded a wool factory, arranged cheap seeds for the poorest and reopened the school. Nevertheless, pastoral care was very difficult. New Christians were mostly members of the lower classes which

Mission station in Pooh

gave the impression that Christianity was only for the poor, and the upper classes looked at them with disrespect. In 1924, the mission work in Pooh was completed.

Ladakh – Leh

1885 The third mission station was established in the Ladakh region by the town of **Leh**. The mission buildings and the church belonged to the government and brothers paid rent (foreigners were not allowed to own anything). It was a strategic place, the capital of the Ladakh region.

1887 Brothers opened a school and also a medical practice and later a health centre led by Doctor Karl Marx. Four years later, however, he died of typhoid fever. It was not possible to replace him for a long time.

1897 Dr. F. Ernest Shawe arrived and the hospital and school were reopened and work continued again. However, during the World War I German missionaries were sent to an internment camp. After the war, the Swiss and the British took turns as doctors.

1897 – 1900 **Simla**, **Chini** and **Khalatse** stations were established. With the exception of Khalatse, the work in the stations ceased to exist within a few years. Missionaries encountered a lack of workers or a problem with language differences.

1906 Ten men and thirteen women worked in five locations across the area. They took care of 150 people.
Gospel Inn caravan shelters have been gradually established in Keylang and Leh. But the work there was extremely hard.

Bishop Friedrich Eugen Peter

1920 Bishop A. Ward of London visited Leh and also ordained the first servants – Joseph Gergan and Dewazung Dana.

1927 Friedrich Eugen Peter, the first and only bishop of the West Himalayan province, was consecrated. He served there until 1936.

Even though local evangelists and assistants worked independently in Ladakh for quite some time, the Mission Board did not want to leave the competences to the locals. This had a bad impact on the church's life.

1945 The mission finally became independent.

Eliyah Thsetan Phuntsog, originally from Keylang, worked there for many years. He studied theology and later participated in the revision of the New Testament in Tibetan.

After World War II, the country experienced economic hardship and the Indo-Pakistani War of Kashmir began in 1947. Many towns were occupied by Pakistan. Missionaries suffered during the war and they were often arrested. The Kashmir dispute has been dragging on until today.

1967 At the Unity Synod, the mission field received the status of Unity Undertaking and was financially supported by all provinces.

1980 Moravian Church had three churches in Ladakh: Leh, Khalatse and Shey. Today, this work has the status of Missionary Area of the Moravian Church – South Asia and it is supervised by the British Province.

Raipur in India

In the 1950s, Tibet was occupied by Chinese Communists which caused an exodus of Tibetans to India. Part of them settled in Mussoorie at the foot of the Himalayas where E. T. Phuntsog was completing the revision of the New Testament in Tibetan. He decided to start working with two hundred Tibetan families. Thus, unexpectedly, a new mission of the Moravian Church began in India.

1957 In Raipur, near Dhaka (East India), an institute for the children of Tibetan refugees was established and it later became a boarding school.

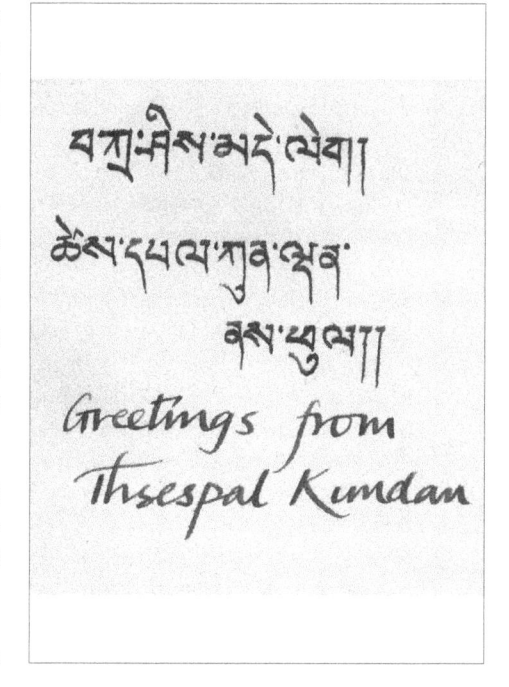

Sample of Tibetan script

1961 Brothers opened a production of small houses for refugees and they also helped with the construction.

1963 Missionaries also opened an open air school in Raipur which has grown into the current Moravian Institute – **Zhan-phan-ling** (it means "a place good for others" in Tibetan). E. T. Phuntsog became the institute's director and worked there until 1971. Since 1980, his grandson Thsespal Kundan has been the director of the Institute.

1995 The Moravian Institute was attended by 228 Muslim and Hindu children.

ALASKA (from 1885)

1884 The Moravians were approached by a school supervisor for Alaska and a former missionary, Dr. Sheldon Jackson, and they were invited to send two brothers from the North American Moravian Church to explore the area.

1885 Brothers William Weinland and John Kilbuck founded **Bethel** station and they built a house with great effort. They began to learn the language of the locals but so far they preached in English with the help of a translator. The following year they founded a school which was soon well established. Thanks to the influence of missionaries, the locals were gradually leaving their igloos, building wooden houses, and learning to grow vegetables.

Weinland could not endure the severe climate and had to leave Alaska after two years. Kilbuck was left alone and had to be preacher, teacher, doctor, hunter, fisherman and carpenter at the same time. His wife, besides the family, took care of seventeen local children who lived with them for upbringing. This laid the foundation for the first children's home.

1887 Kilbuck began to preach to the natives in their language. They gladly received the news of Christ's sacrifice and God's love, and as a result the audience grew. A year later, the first eight natives were admitted to the church. Kilbuck found that they had already been baptized by a Greek Catholic priest at a time when the country still belonged to Russia.

- **A Carmel** station was established – but the work did not bring any results, and so the station was abandoned again.

Alaskans live mainly on fish

The ministry encountered many difficulties. At first the mission came under the American Province of the Moravian Church, later it was taken over by the Mission Board in Germany and after World War II returned to the American province. Other workers were also coming to the area, but they were often changed and there was no stable team.

1892 A new station **Ogavik** was founded north of Bethel, but after 1908 it was no longer occupied.

1901 Brothers opened the first orphanage in Bethel and later a school of finance and industry which was recognized even by the colonists and the government. A small sawmill that was originally set up to build the station and reindeer farm was also generating profit. The station received the first herds from the government (1 046 animals) and 1/3 became the property of the mission. The herding was mainly taken care of by the natives.

1903 The **Quinhagak** station has become another centre for the Yup'ik living in many villages nearby. The tower of church, built by the missionaries, had long served as a lighthouse for the nearby harbor.

1909 More and more people (gold prospectors) were arriving to Alaska. Bethel became a significant place and missionaries began to work among newcomers.

1915 Another station, **Kwigillingok**, was established.

1925 Station **Nunapitsinghak**, where the brothers focused mainly on children, was built. They built an orphanage and a school. By 1930, they had thirty-three children. Women were also involved in the work as a teacher and a nurse. The Yup'ik people were very happy about this, because so far orphaned children had had a very sad lot.

John Hinz worked on translations into the Yup'ik language. He translated and published a hymn book, the gospel of Matthew and other texts.

1927 The whole New Testament was translated.

Over the years, other stations have also been established. Some did not last long, but some still work today. These

Mission station Bethel where missionaries engaged in reindeer husbandry

are **Kwethluk** (1955), **Dillingham** (1956) and **Anchorage** (1962) and others.

Later, Alaska became an independent province of the Moravian Church.

The translation of the entire Bible in Yup'ik was successfully completed and published in the nineties.

EAST AFRICA
later Tanzania (from 1891)

Tanzania was established by the unification of the states of Tanganyika and Zanzibar

1885 After the division of the African continent by European powers, this area became a German colony called German East Africa (until 1919). Moravian missionaries began working in two areas.

Nyasa – Southern Tanganyika Mountains

1891 In the south-western part of the colony, north of Lake Nyasa (also called Lake Malawi), four missionaries established the **Rungwe** station. They taught the indigenous tribe agricultural work and gained their trust.

1894 – 1900 New stations were established: **Ipyana**, **Rutenganio**, **Utengule**, **Isoko**, **Mbozi** and hundreds of natives were coming. From the beginning, young Christians were taught to support the work financially.

1903 Brothers founded a school for helpers in Rungwe where they educated new

Rungwe Mission Station

teachers and evangelists to serve those who were coming to the mission.

Brothers began working on translating the Gospels into the Nyakyusa language.

1904 Missionaries also established settlements for the sick with leprosy.
The ministry was growing with more stations and schools.

1906 Thirty-two missionaries worked in the area. They had thirty-five schools with 4,198 pupils and eighty-one teachers; nine main mission stations, hundreds of preaching stations, and 1,291 people to look after.

1910 In Utengule, indigenous Christians drove out those who still secretly practiced witchcraft. They burned amulets and witchcraft tools. As a result, this area experienced a new awakening.

1912 The translation of the New Testament to Nyika language was completed.

During the World War I, the English occupied the area and all German missionaries were interned. The mission was taken over by the Free Church of Scotland and only in 1926 German missionaries could take over the work again. Work has suffered many damages during the war, but it has grown to 5,000 members.

Education and schools continued to develop, and the numbers of educated teachers increased. They taught in Swahili – colloquial language of Central Africa.

Great Council in East Africa

Unyamwezi – West Tanganyika

1897 After Germany established its colony in the region, German brothers took over **Urambo** station after the London Mission Society; the station was located in the northwest of the colony. The Mission Society worked there patiently for twenty years but without significant success. Brothers sought new possibilities and founded more stations on the south to try to get in touch with work in Nyasa.

1901 – 1907 Stations **Kitunda**, **Sikonge**, **Ipole**, **Kipenbabwe** and **Usoke** were established. However, brothers sometimes encountered obstacles from the colonial rule. A small church was formed in Kitunda station and the first natives were baptized. There was also a school and a boarding house for young men.

1912 Brothers started work in **Tabora**. The city was then connected to the coast by rail which made the work easier.
The number of schools in the area increased to twenty-four with 1,000 students.
Brothers were also developing health care. They taught the natives to grow crops, handle wood, and began to make bricks for building houses.
During World War I, two missionary couples, the Gaardes and the Spelligs, could remain in the Tabora area (with limited movement). Others were interned to France. The Gaardes (originally from Denmark) could stay there even after the war and continue working.

After World War II, the area was visited by brothers from Britain, Denmark, Switzer-

In Unyamwezi

land and they wanted to find where the future work in the country would develop.

1967 Provinces of southern and western Tanzania were established as separate provinces of Unitas Fratrum at the Unity Synod.

Due to the rapid growth, Tanzania's southern province was split into two provinces in 1976, and the same happened with western Tanzania in 1986.

There are currently seven provinces: Eastern Tanzania, Lake Tanganyika, Northern Tanzania, Rukwa, Southern, South West and Western Tanzania. Zanzibar has the status of a mission area and is under the care of the Eastern Province of Tanzania.

Moravian Church in Tanzania continues to grow with new members coming to the church.

EUROPE – CRISIS AND RECOVERY

1803 – 1815 In the first two decades of the nineteenth century, the European Moravian Church went through a crisis even though the work in missions developed well.

The Napoleonic wars swept through Europe, and many of Unitas Fratrum's economic resources, designed primarily to support the mission, suffered financial losses. A whole new generation of servants emerged in the Moravian Church seeking a way out of the crisis: Johann Baptist von Albertini, Friedrich Ludwig Kölbing and Christlieb Reichel.

1814 **24 August** Johann Baptist von Albertini was consecrated a bishop.

1818 The General Synod sought answers to various questions, such as: Why does the Lord have us here? Brothers found some of the answers in archival documents and during the preparation of the centenary of the establishment of Herrnhut. Brothers were gradually rediscovering the purpose of their mission and the Moravian Church experienced another inner renewal from the spiritual faintness and rigidity of past years.

1822 **17 June** The church celebrated the centenary of the foundation of Herrnhut. In 1820, F. L. Kölbing wrote a treatise on *The Memorial Days of the Renewed Unity of Brethren* which was read during the celebration. It helped the Moravian Church to emerge from its internal crisis.

| *A memorial at the place where the first tree was cut down on June 17, 1722 for the construction of Herrnhut*

1824 Bishop von Albertini became a chairman of the Unity's Elders' Conference (see p. 154); he had been a member since 1820.

1831 6 December Bishop von Albertini died. He had a great influence especially on teachers and the young generation. One of his listeners who became zealous for Jesus was Friedrich E. Kleinschmidt (see p. 174).

1832 The Moravian Church celebrated its centenary of the founding of mission. For this occasion, F. L. Kölbing wrote a book *Overview of Mission History* which acquainted all members of the Moravian Church with a century of mission history. This celebration filled the whole church with joy and desire to continue the mission.

1835 13 March F. L. Kölbing was consecrated a bishop.

1840 13 December Bishop Kölbing, a great friend and collaborator of Bishop von Albertini, died. He was a member of the Unity's Elders' Conference from 1818 and its chairman from 1832.

1841 29 July Johann Plitt died. He contributed to the renewal of the Theological College and thus greatly helped to prepare a new generation of preachers. He worked as a Unity archivist from 1836, wrote about the history of the Moravian Church and created a fourteen-volume manuscript *Memorable Occurrences from the History of the Brethren's Unity* on which he worked from 1828 until his death.

Johann Baptist von Albertini

1848 The General Synod held in Herrnhut once again paid great attention to the mission.
The crisis and restoration helped the Moravian Church not to stagnate in its original structure, but to seek a way towards gradual development and independence of the individual mission areas.

A further examination of the church's cohesion was the General Synod of 1857 which approved the division of the work of the Moravian Church into three separate provinces (see p. 159). At the same time, a desire was growing in the whole church to respond to the yet unanswered prayer of Bishop Comenius and to return to the land of the forefathers, that is Bohemia and Moravia.

EXTENSION OF WORK IN THE TWENTIETH CENTURY

The whole church rejoiced at the development of the work in Bohemia and Moravia where brothers could return at the end of nineteenth century (see Chapter IV for more).

The mission work also expanded, and new mission areas emerged. In the second half of the twentieth century, some missions eventually gave rise to other independent provinces.

CENTRAL AMERICA
HONDURAS (from 1930)

Honduras is located north of Nicaragua and was inhabited by natives and descendants of Spanish and indigenous parents.

1914 The leader of mission in Nicaragua, T. Reinke, visited villages along the border with Honduras and he was warmly received by the local Miskitos. However, the intention to establish mission stations was made impossible by the World War I.

1929 Bishop Guido Grossmann went on an inspection. He had obtained a permission to continue with the intended mission in an audience with the President of the country.

1930 Georg Heart, a missionary who had worked in Nicaragua for twenty years, and his wife took on the job. He established the first station in **Kaukira**. Missionaries continued to work closely with Nicaragua.

Missionary work on the Mosquito Coast

1933 The first native of the Miskito tribe, Dannery Downs, was ordained.

1934 **Brus** station was established, then **Butuk-Ahuas** (1937) and **Cocobila** (1938).

1934 The work was hampered, however, by ongoing disputes between Nicaragua and Honduras.

1937 Dannery Downs was imprisoned on suspicion of collaborating with the enemy because of these disputes.

1938 Because of these problems, the work in Honduras became completely independent and was separated from Nicaragua, even though the two countries were predominantly inhabited by the same tribe.

1947 A clinic was built in Butuk-Ahuas.

1978 A secondary school was opened in Brus Laguna. By that year, the vast majority of responsibility for the spiritual leadership of the province was already in the hands of the domestic brothers.

1995 Honduras was accepted as an independent province of the Unitas Fratrum at the Unity Synod in Tanzania.

The work was growing wonderfully over the last few decades. However, tensions between the individual congregations gradually arose and it escalated into an open conflict in 1999, and the church split into two parts.
Today, the province of Honduras has about 35,000 members. It runs church schools, which, for many children, are the only option of higher education.

In Belize, north of Honduras, new mission work has been developing promisingly lately.

2009 The minority part of the Moravian Church in Honduras was first accepted as a Unity Undertaking at the Unity Synod in Britain, then it transformed into a Mission Province of the Unitas Fratrum. There is a very complicated process between the two parts of the Moravian Church in Honduras with the aim of reconciliation.

CENTRAL AMERICA
COSTA RICA (from 1968)

1968 At the Caribbean Regional Conference of the Moravian Church met in Paramaribo (Suriname), all six surrounding provinces agreed on a joint missionary

| *Brother Sam Marx and Miskito Brothers S. Goff with M. Bentles in Ahuas (Honduras)*

work in Costa Rica. In the following period, some families, especially from Nicaragua, moved to the area. Within fifteen years, four congregations had sprung up and another one began to form.

1981 The Unity Synod recognized Costa Rica as a new mission work, and the Unitas Fratrum's offering from that year was dedicated to expanding the work there.

1983 **25 – 27 February** The annual meeting of the staff of the Moravian Church was held in **San José**. Brothers adopted a vision here to establish a new congregation each year.

- **11 March** The Moravian Church in Costa Rica was officially recognized as a separate church under the name *Iglesia Morava en Costa Rica*.

Costa Rica has recently focused mainly on three tasks: developing Sunday schools, working with young people and educating lay people. Work with young and also lay people is focused on educating towards discipleship. The program seeks to motivate members for mission and develop their knowledge and skills. The church hopes that through this work they will be able to grow both in numbers and spiritually.

2009 At the Unity Synod in Britain, the province was accepted as a Unity Province.

Mission efforts and the establishment of other provinces of the Moravian Church in individual regions of the world continue to this day.

Bishop Samuel Gray and President of the Province of Costa Rica, Leopold Pixley

PART III

PART III

From awakening in Herrnhut and subsequent missionary movement to a church

THE LIFE AND DEVELOPMENT OF THE UNITAS FRATRUM IN THE WORLD

It seemed at first that the spiritual awakening in Herrnhut would be just one of the many movements that had emerged and vanished in various places in Europe. However, by God's direction, this revival in Herrnhut gradually gave birth to a church with a clearly defined structure, ideas and focus on mission.

1727 **In May**, the congregation in Herrnhut elected twelve elders to oversee the life in the Brethren village. Four of them were chosen by lot as chief elders as was customary in the Ancient Unity; these were Christian David, Georg and Melchior Nitschmann, and Christoph Hoffmann.
Brethren's meetings were called the **Elders Conference**. The members of the conference varied throughout the years.

Although the Brethren made decisions about their matters themselves, they officially belonged to the Evangelical Lutheran Church which could perform sacraments. That is why they attended a church in Berthelsdorf led by a Lutheran preacher J. A. Rothe.

In the following years, Herrnhut continued to seek the form and structure of leadership and there were frequent changes.

1730 By the end of that year, there was only one chief elder, Martin Linner, and his deputy Augustin Neisser. Count Zinzendorf retained some powers as the owner of the lands.

Church in Berthelsdorf

1733 Martin Linner died at the beginning of the year.
- **26 March** Leonhard Dober was chosen by lot to become a chief elder. At that time, Dober was on mission with David Nitschmann on the island of Saint Thomas.

1735 **5 February** Dober returned to Herrnhut to assume office.
- **12 February** Dober was inducted in the office.
He carried out his duties conscientiously and thoroughly. The office, however, was becoming a very difficult and arduous task for one person because of another growth of mission work in the world and development of congrega-

tions all around Europe. Dober was the chief elder not only in Herrnhut, but in the whole Moravian Church. During his tenure, congregations were formed and mission work was growing in the West Indies and in Greenland, as well as in South Carolina, Georgia, Suriname, Guinea, South Africa etc. In Europe the work developed in Germany, the Netherlands, Britain, France, Switzerland, Denmark, Sweden and Livonia (part of modern Latvia and Estonia).

Jesus Christ, the Chief Elder of the Moravian Church

Apart from the Elders Conference, Count Zinzendorf sometimes called together a wider circle of leading church servants – **Synodal Conference** (synodus).

1740 **5–31 December** Synodal Conference took place in Marienborn (present-day Germany). Leonhard Dober requested exemption from the office of chief elder due to overburdening and excessive responsibility of such a mission. His request was not accepted.

1741 After a quarrel in the congregation of Pilgerruhe in Holstein, Dober requested exemption from his office again.
- **11–23 September** Synodal Conference was held in London. On September 16, the Conference resolved that Jesus Christ would be the Chief Elder of the renewed Moravian Church. This decision was circulated to the whole church.
- **13 November** The decision was solemnly read out in all congregations of the Unity.

Count N. L. Zinzendorf

The administration of the church was thereafter led by the so-called **General Conference**.

1742 The Prussian king Frederick II the Great issued a general concession* allowing the foundation of Moravian congregations formed by emigrants. The concession was valid in Silesia as well as in all other Prussian lands. The General Conference thus decided to establish new congregations in Silesia: Gnadenfrei, Gnadenberg and Neusalz (see also p. 114). These Moravian colonies, which were under the authority of bishop from Moravia, were granted total independence on evangelical Lutheran consistory. This way, the Moravian Church

* The permission was issued on 25 December 1742.

was recognized in Prussia as an independent church with Episcopal system and it was expanding with new congregations.

1743 In April after his return from America, Zinzendorf disapproved of the Conference's decisions and dissolved the Conference for some time.

1745 Gradually the structure of synodal conferences was established. These conferences were still held during the Count's lifetime.
–
1756

1760 After Zinzendorf's death, the synodal conferences transformed into proper synods (called **General Synods**) thanks to bishop August G. Spangenberg and lawyer Johann F. Köber from Gersdorf.

Constitutional Synods

1764 The General Synod took place in Marienborn. For the first time, all congregations were represented by delegates who were authorized to comment on every resolution and regulation of the Synod that concerned the life of individual congregations as well as the whole church. It applied to the administration of spiritual, economic, civil and church-related issues. The Synod was chaired by highly regarded fathers of the church of that time – Johannes von Watteville, August G. Spangenberg, Leonhard Dober, Friedrich von Watteville. The Synod decided that: all legislative power belonged to the Synod, the members of the Synod were to be elected by the individual congregations and during an inter-synodal

Synodal Conference in 1750

period the management of the church would be in the hands of the so-called **Directory** that would be accountable for its decisions to the following Synod. The Directory was elected by the Synod and consisted of nine members.

1769 The General Synod was held in Marienborn again. The Synod changed some clauses agreed on the previous Synod that had not proved successful. These were mainly economic affairs and debts of the Unity. The Directory transformed into **The Unity's Elders' Conference** (UEC). The Conference continued to have the role of supervision over the Unity and it managed the church in the period between General

Synods. The Synod also decided that all the congregations would become organizationally and economically independent. In the internal affairs of congregations, the UEC acted only as an advisor.

1775 The General Synod in Barby (seat of UEC near Magdeburg, modern-day Germany) reflected on all previous decisions since 1764 and specified them so that the church would thrive spiritually as well as economically. The fathers of the church with their inner authority helped a lot while visiting congregations where they were explaining synodal decisions and encouraging the church to selflessness, togetherness and trust in Jesus Christ as the Chief Elder of the Unity.

The Synod also dealt with the teachings of the Unity. After much thought and consideration, it was agreed to hold on to the decision of 1734: *"The reconciliation of a sinner with God is through the blood of Jesus Christ. The assurance of salvation rests generally on the revealed word of the cross and personally, on the personal heartfelt belief in the crucified Saviour."*[28]

The members of the UEC often visited congregations and helped to unite the church. Just as bishops, they assisted with strengthening of the unification and subsequently with the supervision of individual congregations. Unlike in the Ancient Unity, bishops had only pastoral and prayer role which was even embedded in the constitution. They were held

Barby – the administrative seat of the Unitas Fratrum and the Unity's Elders' Conference

in high esteem in the renewed Unity; all congregations had great respect for them and took their advice seriously. Bishops were authorized to ordain and consecrate within the whole Unitas Fratrum. They also helped with the church administration and often held honorary positions.

Following General Synods

The UEC moved to Herrnhut and Synods were summoned there until 1931.

1782 The General Synod met in Berthelsdorf at a manor formerly belonging to Zinzendorf. For the first time, the Synod was attended by representatives from British and American congregations.

1789 The General Synod in Herrnhut abandoned the use of a lot in external matters, for example selling or buying property. In other cases, the use of lot was retained. Synod also initiated the foundation of mission department which later transformed into the Mission Board.
Both Synods expressed joy at the continuing mission work, schools and the diaspora.

1801 **1 June – 31 August** The mistake of this General Synod was that there were almost no laymen. The delegates elected from the congregations were primarily workers paid by the church. Only Herrnhut was represented by two non-clerical workers. The Synod reflected on the deep crisis in the church because the worldly lifestyle penetrat-

Berthelsdorf, N. L. Zinzendorf's manor

ed into the church and the youth was growing away from the church. The Synod, however, did not make any decision that would help to change the spiritual decline. The fathers of the church had died by the end of the previous century and the church was losing its identity.

1818 from 1 June The General Synod was attended by the younger generation. The only witness of the previous era was Moravian Bishop J. G. Cunow who remained the chairman of the Synod. Other delegates were mainly those who did not remember their spiritual fathers and they had idealistic ideas about the beginnings of the Herrnhut awakening. Members of the Synod addressed the difficult situation of the church with great zeal and responsibility; they did not, however, have much experience. They did not complain about difficult circumstances as their predecessors did. On the contrary, they asked themselves fundamental questions whether the Unitas Fratrum is still a church of Jesus Christ.

1825 from 30 May The General Synod brought a completely different picture about the state of the Unity. This was facilitated by the centenary of the founding of Herrnhut when Christian David felled the first tree for the construction (June 17, 1722). The church was well prepared for the celebration which lasted several days. On the occasion of the anniversary, Friedrich Ludwig Kölbing published his book *The Memorial Days*

Christian David fells the first tree for the new settlement of Herrnhut on June 17, 1722

of the Renewed Unity of Brethren (printed in 1821). The book was written from archival sources; it helped young generation to comprehend the identity of the Unity and the church experienced an internal revival. Consequently, the delegates of the Synod were able to get the gist of the church in depth, understand why God called it to life and what other pressing decisions it needed for its life and mission. The Synod was chaired by the great authority of F. L. Kölbing (later a bishop).

1836 30 May – 3 September The General Synod discussed a reaction to two movements heavily influencing some of the Moravian congregations. The ultra-radical movement demanded greater congregationalism, full independence when founding individual congregations, and separation from all particularities.* The moderate movement wanted democratization in a way that all decisions and reports of the Synod would be printed and published. Their motives, however, were hypocritical.

Nevertheless, none of the delegates shared these opinions. On the contrary, the Moravian Church united at the Synod and expressed for the first time the importance of the day of November 13, 1741. The church also declared that by calling Jesus as the Chief Elder, it does not claim any superiority over other evangelical churches. A summary of the synodal report was finally printed in 1838 and brought to the attention of congregations and communities.

The Synod was also attended by representatives from missions in South Africa, Jamaica and West Indies. From

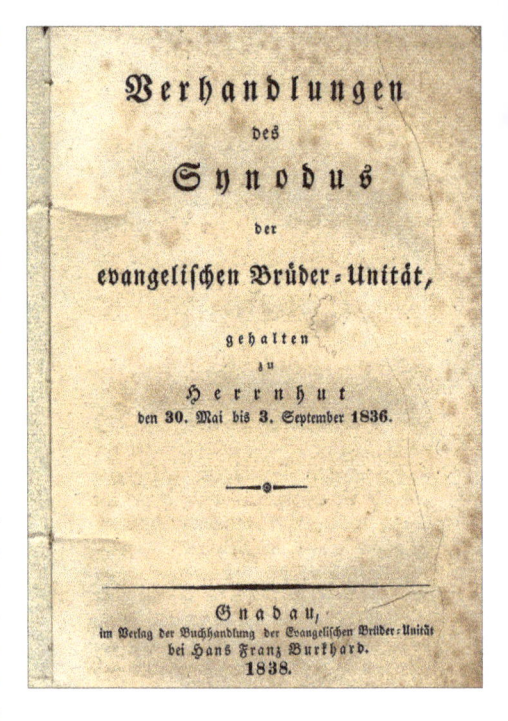

Minutes of the 1836 General Synod printed in 1838

1818 to 1836, the General Synods addressed economic issues of the Unity which had been indebted since the crisis at the turn of the century. They also dealt with the question of the use of a lot and the question of membership – especially with regard to congregation members and inhabitants of the Moravian villages.

1848 29 May – 5 September The General Synod was public for the first time. That helped to further connect the Synod with the church. The UEC also appealed to congregations to choose their representatives among laymen as well. This Synod discussed closer ecumenical cooperation with evangelical churches,

---
*Like celebrating Jesus Christ as the Chief Elder of the Moravian Church.

question of baptism and confirmation of children, founding of new subsidiary congregations and also theological education of future workers. The delegates welcomed a report about the improvement of the church finances. They also organized mission activities which had expanded into new places. This Synod also noted that the Moravian Church reached an internal spiritual transformation that began in 1818.

The Moravian Church formed into regional units, provinces, with provincial synods dealing with local issues.

1857 **8 June – 1 September** The General Synod met in Herrnhut. It was preceded by a complex structural crisis. After civil wars and upheavals in North America, the local congregations longed for complete independence. Similar desire was growing in British congregations at the beginning of the century. Both territories had only minimal representation at Synods. The members of UEC were also mostly German. Therefore, the American Provincial Synod proposed full independence of individual provinces. In Germany, this proposal caused a stir and outrage but thanks to internal spiritual renewal in the Moravian Church and thanks to the ability to reach an agreement, the Synod eventually established three provinces: German, British and American.* The General Synod remained the supreme body to be summoned every ten years. This period was not always kept.

Herrnhut

*North American province was later on divided in two – North and South (see p. 88).

This Synod also resolved that the Moravian Church would hold the Latin name Unitas Fratrum wherever it serves.

Back to the land of forefathers

The nineteenth century saw a growth in mission as well as in desire to restore the work in the land of forefathers – in Bohemia and Moravia (modern-day Czech Republic). The following overview of synods and conferences demonstrates this development and also the formation of new provinces.

1862 Bohemian-Moravian Committee began work within the German province and it was preparing the establishment of the work under the name Bohemian-Moravian Mission (see also p. 173).

1869 **24 May – 8 July** The General Synod took place in Herrnhut. Its chairman, Levin Theodor Reichel, talked about the past hundred years of life and work of the Moravian Church since the first constitutional synod with gratitude.
This Synod newly defined which competences would fall under the Unitas Fratrum and which would belong to the individual provinces and their respective synods. The Synod also divided orders into three groups: 1) general principles of teaching and life, 2) common UF constitution, 3) collective work of the UF in the non-Christian world – the mission.
The German Province was renamed the European Continental Province (ECP*).
The Synod also prepared and approved a fundamental change in the organization and function of the undertaking in Bohemia and Moravia. *"Apart from diverse work for God's Kingdom in all three provinces, the Moravian Church also holds a joint undertaking in the lands of our forefathers, in Bohemia and Moravia. Our work there can take place on more levels – partly on the basis of the diaspora, partly in a mission of locals, God willing."*[29] (see more on p. 175)

1879 **26 May – 3 July** The General Synod attended to the individual places and workers in missions on other continents, their responsibilities and financial situation. Among the participants of the Synod were representatives from South Africa, islands of St. Thomas and St. John, Suriname and Nicaragua (Mosquito Coast).

| *Levin Theodor Reichel*

---

* ECP included Germany, Switzerland, the Netherlands and later congregations in Denmark and Sweden.

Regarding the Bohemian-Moravian Mission, it was decided that it would continue under the administration of the Unity's Elders' Conference (see p. 177).

1889 **27 May – 1 July** The General Synod redefined its understanding of the terms: church, congregation and Unity. Church should not strive for its independence in the first place, but also for inner understanding and its role to be a fellowship (congregation) and a Unity.

The Synod also approved the much needed broadening in the field of mission. The work of Bohemian-Moravian Committee was positively appraised and all those present were grateful to God that the mission in Austria was recognized as an independent church in 1880 under the name of Evangelical Church of the Brethren (see also p. 177).

1899 **16 May – 30 June** The General Synod met in Herrnhut again and reworked and rearranged Church Orders. It also defined its mission course, the question of missionaries and financial security of individual mission fields.

The Synod also approved practical decisions and individual steps of development and work of the Bohemian-Moravian Committee (see also p. 183).

1909 **18 May – 3 July** The General Synod in Herrnhut worked on principles and orders: some of them were reaffirmed and some redefined. The Synod recognized another two provinces as transitional provinces. These were Jamaica and Eastern West Indies.

The Synod terminated the work of the Unity's Elders' Conference, that had

General Synod in Herrnhut in 1899

been the administrative authority until then, and it was replaced by the **Unity Directory**. The Directory together with the Bohemian-Moravian Committee supervised the Bohemian-Moravian Mission (see p. 184).

1914 **16 May – 13 June** The General Synod in Herrnhut worked once more on modification of principles and orders of the Unity so that they were functional and relevant for the following period. The Synod called on provinces to support the Bohemian-Moravian Mission and elected a new Bohemian-Moravian Committee (see more on p. 185).

- All events were interrupted by the World War I.

PART III

1918 The Unity Directory board met right after the end of the World War I. It declared that the UF was still connected by spiritual unanimity. This was confirmed by the Unity conference in Zeist, the Netherlands, in the summer of 1919. Many UF members from different countries involved in the World War I came together for that conference.

1922 11–21 August The German Province conference in Herrnhut needed to change Church Orders after the dissolution of Austria-Hungary into independent states: Czechoslovakia, Austria, Italy, Yugoslavia and Poland. The conference also discussed new structure of the Bohemian-Moravian Mission in the new Czechoslovak Republic (see p. 187).

1931 28 May – 22 June The General Synod met in Herrnhut again. Concerning the work in Bohemia and Moravia, the Synod took a decision to involve actively all members of the Moravian Church and prepare them for future establishment of the Czechoslovak Province.
"It was declared with joy that the Moravian Church is truly a unity of brothers and sisters. We are to work side by side with brothers and sisters from big and small nations for the God's Kingdom."[30]

1946 3–7 July The General Conference met in Montmirail, Switzerland. In a way, the Conference substituted for the General Synod and it charted the post-war situation of the UF. From the European Continental Province, Germany was most ravaged both economically and socially. Exiles from Silesia (present-day Poland) were moving to borders with the Netherlands where they started building new settlements in tough conditions. Businesses in Silesia (Neusalz, Gnadenfrei and Gnadenfeld) were destroyed.
The General Conference approved a resolution calling for help with a burnt-out house of prayer in Herrnhut.
The Conference was also informed about events in British and American Provinces and the situation in Czechoslovakia.
Other resolutions concerned the work in Jerusalem, Suriname, South Africa. Some of the German missionaries seriously harmed the image of the church with their Nazi attitudes and therefore the prevailing view outside Germany was that German participation on missions was impossible at that time.

Montmirail Chateau – a venue for the General Conference of 1946

1957 13 August – 10 September The General Synod met overseas for the first time. Twenty six years after the previous meeting, the delegates gathered in Bethlehem, Pennsylvania.

The Synod made the following decisions:
- The mission in Czechoslovakia became the fifth independent province – the Moravian Church in the land of forefathers.
- The Ground of Unity was reformulated.
- Provinces were newly classified: *Unity Province* (formerly *home province*), *Synodal Province* (formerly *province in a state of transition*), and *Associate Province* (formerly *mission field*).
- Twenty-six bishops submitted an appeal to renew the prayer watch that had started in August, 1727 and continued for at least one hundred years.

Unity Synods

1967 6 July – 13 August The General Synod* met in Potštejn (present-day Czech Republic). It was the first synod of the Unity in the land of the forefathers with delegates from 18 regions (see p. 165) where the Unity worked. Every province reported on its activities.

The Synod agreed on many subjects including:
- key and fundamental decisions about the future as well as the circumstances of the divided world;
- new Church Order of the Unitas Fratrum (COUF) – it was a revolutionary step that gave equal rights to existing provinces;

Moravian bishops at the General Synod in Potštejn in 1967

* *The term General Synod was gradually replaced by Unity Synod (synod of the world-wide Unitas Fratrum).*

PART III

T. Kisanji, P. Misigalo and T. F. Mbangulla – representatives of Tanzanian provinces at the General Synod in Potštejn in 1967

- regulations concerning Moravian bishops;
- a decision that younger provinces could manifest their spiritual independence and older provinces would no longer have responsibility for mission efforts in those new provinces;
- a resolution that the Unity Synod would meet every seven years given the growing work of the church in regions.

1974 23 June – 10 July The Unity Synod held a meeting for the first time outside Europe or North America in Kingston, Jamaica. The Synod was summoned by the Unity Board (UB)* which met in inter-synodal period and supervised the fulfillment of synodal decisions. (Over the course of the twentieth century, the Unity Board became an executive body accountable to the Unity Synod.) Synodal delegates included representatives

List of provinces in 1967

	Unity Provinces	**Congregations**	**Ministers**
1.	America, South	46	55
2.	America, North	114	103
3.	Great Britain	40	40
4.	Czechoslovakia	18	19
5.	European Continental	18	65
6.	South Africa, West	25	35
7.	Suriname	55	30
	Synodal Provinces	**Congregations**	**Ministers**
8.	Jamaica	38	15
9.	South Africa, East	21	16
10.	Nicaragua	17	22
11.	Tanzania, Southern Highlands	33	32
12.	Tanzania, Unyamwezi	13	14
13.	Eastern West Indies	44	25
	Associate Provinces	**Congregations**	**Ministers**
14.	Alaska	19	8
15.	British Guiana	11	4
16.	Himalayas	1	1
17.	Honduras	19	5
18.	Labrador	5	4
	Total 302 593 members	537	493

*The board of the UF consisting of representatives of individual provinces.

not only from Unity and Synodal Provinces, but also from Associate Provinces and missions.

The Synod stated that:
- the UF exists in the midst of divided world both geopolitically and economically;
- all provinces have to deal with many specific questions in their respective regions; and
- there is a diversity in political, cultural and social opinions among provinces.

The Synod nevertheless confirmed the continuation of the direction set by the Synod in Potštejn in 1967 that all provinces should strive for equality.

1981 29 August – 13 September The Unity Synod was summoned to Herrnhut, then East Germany. The delegates worked in committees and in plenum and adopted 46 resolutions in total. One of them was:

The Moravian Church recognizes the Word of the Cross as the centre of the Holy Scripture and of all preaching of the Gospel and it sees its primary mission, and its reason for being, to consist in bearing witness to the joyful message.

The Synod further:
- decided that a Unity Board comprising chairmen of individual provinces would meet at least once in inter-synodal period;
- recommended that the three existing Tanzanian Provinces seek a new form of structure in the UF because of growing work;
- invited the UF to permanently reinstate a prayer watch and prepare its schedule in 1982 on the occasion of 250th anniversary of Moravian mission;

General Synod in Herrnhut in 1981

- decided that a new work arising in Costa Rica would be cared for by the Nicaraguan Province and the Labrador Province would fall under the US provinces.

1988 3–16 July The Unity Synod met in Antigua, West Indies.

The Synod discussed:
- the service of Moravian bishops. It was deemed necessary to reformulate their mission and service. The Synod proposed to prepare the Bishops Handbook. It was created in 1992 at the first world-wide conference of Moravian bishops held in Czechoslovakia on the occasion of 400th anniversary of the birth of John Amos

Comenius. The handbook was then presented to the Unity Board for consideration and approval.
- a proposition for individual provinces to consider appropriate pastoral approach to the problem of so-called rebaptism.

1995 13–25 August The Unity Synod held a meeting in Dar es Salaam, Tanzania.

At the meeting, the Synod:
- attended to the topic of Moravian bishops in detail and adjusted the proposed Bishops Handbook. Some changes concerning the service of Moravian bishops were then integrated into the Church Order of the Unitas Fratrum.
- granted Honduras the status of a Unity Province.

List of provinces in 1995

	Provinces	Congregations	Stations	Ministers
1.	Alaska	23	1	13
2.	America, South	56	5	65
3.	America, North	106	0	134
4.	Great Britain	37	2	28
5.	Czech Province	21	24	18
6.	Dominican Republic	37		30
7.	European Continental	26	6	57
8.	Guyana	8		2
9.	Honduras	77	12	13
10.	India	4	7	5
11.	Jamaica	56	2	21
12.	South Africa	91	186	66
13.	Costa Rica	5	2	4
14.	Labrador	5	2	3
15.	Nicaragua	176	135	46
16.	Suriname	55		40
17.	Tanzania, South Western	103		80
18.	Tanzania, South	102		88
19.	Tanzania, Rukwa	22	300	33
20.	Tanzania, Western	41	181	61
21.	Eastern West Indies	48	4	33
	Total 622 219 members	1 099	869	840

- assigned Unity Board to address a new concept of UF structure in the context of development and administration of the church.
- formulated current mission statement of the UF called *New World Witness*:
  · Mission amongst unreached people of different cultures (Chukchi or Garifuna people and others)
  · Mission in countries where other churches work but not the UF (for example Zambia, Malawi, Democratic Republic of the Congo – then Zaire)
  · Mission through the media or urban mission (among the homeless, students etc.)
- accepted mission activities in Albania, French Guiana, Zambia, Malawi, India and Asia as such according to a definition of mission in the UF.
- decided that the Unity Archives in Herrnhut is a collective work of the Unity and would be provided for financially.
- dedicated a great part to the issue of rebaptism which emerged in the world as a new phenomenon. The Synod then decided that rebaptism would not be generally accepted but that provinces can institute ceremonial confirmations of baptism.

2002 8–9 August The Unity Synod met in Bethlehem, Pennsylvania.
The main issues discussed at the Synod were:
- the Moravian Church's attitude towards new spiritual trends.
- the church's stance on homosexuality (potential ordinations of practicing homosexuals and marrying same-sex couples). Given that the UF is present in a multicultural world and on different continents with diverse political and social conditions, the Synod imposed a moratorium on that matter so that provinces would not take any action.

Unity Synod 2009 in England

2009 27 July – 7 August The Unity Synod held a meeting in England:
- The Synod made a significant change in the provinces' classification. Apart from existing unity provinces, the name of synodal and associate provinces was changed into mission provinces and mission areas respectively.
- Another unity province was granted the status: Costa Rica.

List of provinces in 2009

	Unity Provinces
1.	Alaska
2.	America, North
3.	America, South
4.	Great Britain
5.	Czech Province
6.	European Continental
7.	Honduras
8.	Jamaica
9.	South Africa
10.	Costa Rica
11.	Nicaragua
12.	Suriname
13.	Tanzania, Rukwa
14.	Tanzania, South
15.	Tanzania, South Western
16.	Tanzania, Western
17.	Eastern West Indies

Mission Provinces:

Guyana, Kigoma, D. R. Congo, Labrador, Malawi, Tanzania (North), Tanzania (East), Zambia, Zanzibar

Mission Areas:

Belize, Burundi, French Guiana, Kenya, Cuba, Peru, Rwanda, Uganda
The UF is active in four regions: European, American, Caribbean and African.

The membership is laid out as follows:
- European region 3 %
- American region 6 %
- Caribbean region 21 %
- African region 70 %

2010 1–8 October The Unity Board met in Calgary, Canada. (The Unity Board had already held regular meetings between synods.) Representatives from 14 provinces and 4 mission provinces were present.

The meeting showed increasing influence of the African region where the church was growing the fastest. African provinces became more and more economically self-sufficient and clearly expressed their views on practical theology. For example, the provinces are set against carrying out same-sex marriages or ordaining practicing homosexuals.

The Unity Board also approved D. R. Congo as a Unity Province increasing the number to eighteen Unity Provinces of the UF.

India was designated as a Mission Area of South Asia and Sierra Leone was designated as a Mission Area in Africa.

After 2012 more provinces were granted the status of a Unity Province:
Tanzania (Northern), Tanzania – Kigoma (Lake Tanganyika), Malawi, Zambia and Eastern Tanzania
Today the Unitas Fratrum comprises 23 provinces and the number of members exceeded one million in 2015.

PART IV

Part IV

Back in the Land of Fathers – from the promulgation of the Patent of Toleration to the Velvet Revolution

INTRODUCTION

1781 **13 October** The Patent of Toleration was promulgated and it granted limited freedom of worship to non-Roman Catholic Christians in the lands of the Austrian Empire. The Czech lands belonged to the empire. The Patent was a part of so-called enlightened reforms and was issued by the emperor Joseph II. The followers of Protestantism, amongst them the Czech Brethren, could, however, decide for only two branches of state recognized evangelical religions – Augsburg (Lutheran) or Helvetian (Calvinist). The Moravian Church was not recognized in the Austro-Hungarian Empire at that period of time. Its supporters who resisted 150-year-old re-Catholicization pressure especially in East Bohemia, in the Highlands of Bohemia and Northern Moravia, therefore became members of these emperor-approved Protestant churches.

1793 After the second division of Poland only eleven former Ancient Unity communities (settlements) remained out of sixty (three of them were German: Leszko, Skoky, Zichlin / Wola; and four were mixed: Poznan, Orzeszkowo, Heyersdorf, Waszko). The center of the surviving Polish Moravian Church was Leszno where a Brethren grammar school existed at that time.

1796 The Prussian government subordinated some matters of the Polish Moravian Church to the Council of Poznań and by means of that to a reformed church in Berlin.

1817 This work was canceled. But some Polish-Moravian communities (settlements)

Vilém Hartwig with his wife

lasted out following the traditions of the Ancient Unity (see p. 56).

1830 **12 December** Vilém Hartwig was born in Loužnice in Kladsko. He later became a collaborator of Friedrich Emanuel Kleinschmidt.

1844 **31 March** Eugen Schmidt was born and later became a pastor of the first Czech Moravian Church congregation in Potštejn.

1849 Some restrictions regarding the freedom of worship were canceled by an imperial order and later also by the new constitution of Austria-Hungary. Since then the Evangelicals kept calling louder and louder for rights that belonged to them according to the historical background.

- **1855 14 June** Theophilus Reichel was born in Silesian Gnadenberg. He was one of the crucial people of the Moravian Church in Czech lands.
- **1857 6 January** Václav Vančura was born in Čáslav. He later became a bishop of the Moravian Church.
- **1861 8 April** Another Edict of Toleration was issued, this time by the Emperor Franz Joseph I. The law enabled many Evangelicals to build legal and organizational foundations of their church and made the church equal with the still ruling Roman-Catholic Church. The law also enabled them to establish relationships with Evangelical churches abroad.

THE PIONEER FROM NOWA SÓL

- **1862 25 November** The Synod of the German province met in Herrnhut. The delegates discussed possibilities of the mission in Bohemia and Moravia, which is the Land of the Fathers. The Synod recommended to the Directory in Herrnhut to start work there officially. They established so-called Bohemian-Moravian Committee (BMC) and Brothers Heinrich L. Reichel, Gustav B. Müller, Theophilus Reichel and Theobald Wunderling were in charge of the Bohemian-Moravian Mission (BMM). Especially T. Wunderling, a pastor in Gnadenfrei and later a bishop, proved to have a true heart of a father in this mission.
  - ■ Moravian brothers devoted themselves to the scattered Evangelicals in diaspora (far from any evangelical congrega-

Theobald Wunderling and Heinrich Lewin Reichel – members of BMC

tions). They were making visits, house devotions, spread theological literature. Financial funds for this mission were collected in the way of collections and gifts in the Moravian Church in Europe which took care of organization, finance and administration of the whole Bohemian-Moravian Mission.

- Friedrich Emanuel Kleinschmidt became an important pioneer of the work in Nowa Sól as well as a great shepherd and a pastor. He encouraged clusters of scattered brothers and sisters in Bohemia and in Moravia to revive the work of Gospel. With time F. E. Kleinschmidt also recognized their spiritual and financial circumstances. During the years **1862–65** and **1866–69** he visited the majority of evangelical parishes. He had many talks with local Evangelicals, gave them clear testimony of the power of the resurrected Jesus Christ and prayed eagerly with them. But it was not easy to travel from one group to another. He encountered some obstacles which made him to stop the visits for some time. Kleinschmindt also helped the church a lot when he organized financial support from abroad for Czech priests, church teachers and congregations.

The manner of his preaching was described by G. Burghardt:

"Kleinschmidt was demanding conversion of individuals, he depicted different states of the hearers' hearts and he especially put the emphasis on that everyone must know if they gain forgiveness of their own sins. And though he spoke very quietly and simply and dealt with the matter always purely, the result of his words was mighty."[31]

Kleinschmidt, who remained a respectable and a highly-effective person

Friedrich Emanuel Kleinschmidt

and a friend of Bohemian and Moravian Evangelicals for a long time, was soon joined by other helpers, traveling preachers and those who spread Protestant literature. Those were Andreas Köther and Vilém Hartwig. Hartwig came from Silesia and was originally a Catholic. He later became a member of the Gnadenfrei congregation from where he was called to Bohemia by Wunderling's proposal. Hartwig was a common joiner's helper, but his power of faith and certainty of Christian conviction was striking. He was a faithful witness of the Gospel.

1866 The focus of the emerging Bohemian-Moravian Mission moved gradually to the region called Poorlicko. Vilém Hartwig, the most eager and the most distinctive Moravian Church worker of the first years, settled there. His main work was in the village of Horní Čermná.

- The Austro-Prussian War began and interrupted his missionary and diaspora work for some time. Local people showed aloofness and rejection towards him. Because he was a citizen of Prussia, many doors, which used to be open, hospitable and friendly, were then closed.
- **1 June** A missionary, František Chleboun, was born near Ústí nad Orlicí. He was a missionary in South Africa, first at a place where George Schmidt used to work*, and later he got independent work among the local Xhosa people. After the outbreak of so-called Boer wars, the Mission Board sent him to the Khoi congregation in Elim in the southernmost tip of Africa. After nine years he returned to his Xhosa people where he practically started from the beginning. He was on the missions until 1913 when he returned to Europe. The First World War then prevented him from returning to Africa. Later he mostly worked in the region of Turnov.

František Chleboun

1868 The Synod of the German Province** confirmed that the German Directory in Berthelsdorf would be in charge of the administration of the Bohemian-Moravian Mission through the Bohemian-Moravian Committee. The Committee would continue to manage the work, call new workers, but above all it would provide funds.

1869 **24 May – 8 July** The General Synod was happy to hear the news about the development of Bohemian-Moravian Mission and also discussed the proposal of American and British Provinces to make the mission independent. However, the proposal was not approved by German brothers. They wished the Bohemian-Moravian Mission continued only within existing Austrian Evangelical Churches. They feared the financial and administrative difficulties because the Moravian Church was not recognized in Austria yet.

The General Synod finally approved:
"1. Where in Bohemia and Moravia the Moravian Church is already helping within local Evangelical churches, it may keep helping unless proved otherwise.

---

*In the area of Cape Province serving the Khoikhoi people (also p. 93). / ** From 1869 European Continental Province (ECP)

2. The Mission of the Moravian Church in Bohemia and Moravia should be equal to the Moravian Church mission area work and should be held in that name and at cost of the whole Moravian Church.
3. If the Moravian Church receives a request of service of word and sacrament from any place in Bohemia or Moravia, especially if it is a place far from the existing Evangelical churches, it is supposed to be accepted after careful consideration.

The Synod decided so in the courage of faith that the Lord Himself would prepare the way for the return of the Moravian Church to the land of fathers, if it was His will.'[32]

So that is how the Bohemian-Moravian Mission became an undertaking of the whole Unitas Fratrum (UF) with the future possibility to set up their own congregations. 'It is interesting that it was not throughout the whole meeting that they named a particular Czech or Moravian site suitable for independent work and for starting a congregation. Even the Synod believed the Lord would show such a place of His will in the course of time."[32]

FIRST MORAVIAN CHURCH CONGREGATIONS

1870 The first group of people from Eastern Bohemia – Potštejn – asked for a spiritual service.
- **16 October** The first Moravian Church congregation was established. It became the cornerstone of the future growth of mission in Bohemia. Many blessings came from these subtle beginnings.

| *Eugen Schmidt with his family, the first pastor in Potštejn*

1872 **20 May** Another congregation was founded in Dubá near Česká Lípa.
- **13 October** Eugen Schmidt was called for service in Potštejn congregation; he was the first pastor in Bohemia.

1873 **1 January** The Moravian Church Daily Watchwords began to be published in the Czech language.

REGISTRATION

1874 **20 May** Act no. 68 of the Imperial Law Gazette was issued and enabled recognition of religious communities in the Austro-Hungarian Empire.
- **19 July** German Directory in Herrnhutt began to negotiate with Austrian authorities about the recognition of the Moravian Church in Bohemia. The request was surprising to some extent because the number of church members in Austria-Hungary was small (1875 – 200 members, 1876 – 212 members). That is why Austrian officials started to discuss the matter not until another application was submitted on February 5, 1876. The recognition, however, was not prolonged only by administrative procedure but also by political events.

1879 **26 May – 3 July** The General Synod decided that the Bohemian-Moravian Mission would continue to be under the Elders' Conference of Unitas Fratrum with the aid of Bohemian-Moravian Committee. The Committee would have nine members: five from the European Continental Province (ECP), two from the British Province and two from the American Province. Members would always be appointed by the General Synod.

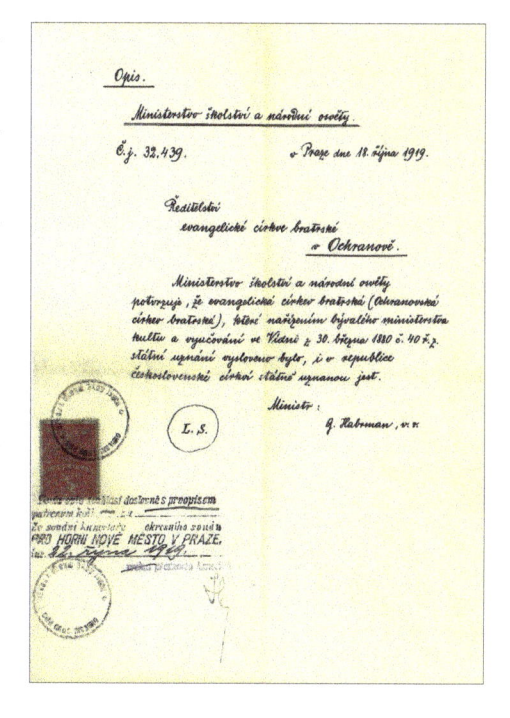

Decree of recognition of the Unitas Fratrum in the Austro-Hungarian Empire (a copy from 1919).

1880 **30 March** An official decree* was issued recognizing the Evangelical Brethren Church (Herrnhutt Brethren Church) as an independent church. The Directory wished explicitly not to use the name Jednota bratrská (Unitas Fratrum). The recognition meant new administrative changes for the Czech Unitas Fratrum.

1882 **16 March** Leontina Mašínová was born in Pilsen; she was a writer and a great devotee of the Moravian Church. She wrote a series of books about the church and Bishop Comenius. She died on February 10, 1975 in Lázně Bělohrad where she is also buried.

*The decree was archived in Reichenberg (present-day Liberec) according to the Imperial Law under the registration no. 40.

1883 Congregational statutes were prepared for the congregations in Potštejn and Dubá; the congregations were officially recognized after the statutes' approval.

- **Potštejn** – the congregation had 96 members at the time of its establishment. It was divided into the congregation in Potštejn and a 'subsidiary' congregation in Lanškroun. The pastor was Eugen Schmidt and his helper was Václav Medáček. Groups of believers in Čermná and Čenkovice with their own clergy belonged to Lanškroun congregation, as well as the new emerging group in Ústí nad Orlicí.
- **Dubá** – the congregation had 75 members. The pastor was Karl O. Bernhard.

The Moravian Church in the Czech Lands entered a new phase of its mission and development.

BRETHRENS' ORPHANAGES

Orphanages were one of the first independent works of the Unity in Bohemia. There was no existing plan for such an activity, it just started as a natural consequence due to Prussia-Austria war, after which there were many orphans left behind.

1867 4 June Vilém Hartwig from Čermná congregation received the first orphan. The Bohemian-Moravian Committee raised serious objections because they considered that the orphan boys would keep Hartwig from his work as a traveling preacher. Hartwig soon married Ludmila Samková who was a great help for the work with these children. She was strict, but a caring mother. Within one year, ten more orphans came to the

| Boys' orphanage in Čermná

family. There were no financial resources for the support of such a work; moreover, there was a need of a larger house owing to the growing number of these children.

1870 Thanks to generous donors from Germany and Switzerland and with the support of other friends, they could buy a homestead in Čermná. The boys and the Hartwigs were staying there and there was also some space for a new prayer room. Three years later the house burned down but thanks to the real unselfishness, the house was built again. Despite initial difficulties and the enmity of the neighborhood, the church gained trust and sympathy after some time. The number of boys gradually grew to forty.

1886 **26 May** Similar work as was in Čermná started in Potštejn but with girls. It was due to the fact that there was no space for girls in Čermná. In a very short time, the newly purchased house was filled with twenty girls. Such social service began thanks to Eugen Schmidt, the pastor of the Potštejn congregation. He loved this service and when he was called to move to Dubá in 1889, he helped the orphans even there. Later there was another orphanage opened in Dubá, especially for German boys.

1898 **2 December** A new orphanage was opened in Dubá for the first four girls. However, it was necessary to renovate the building. In 1904 the renovation was so good that the orphanage could accommodate fourteen girls.

The building of the girls' orphanage in Dubá

1899 The care for orphans was also approved by the Bohemian-Moravian Committee and by the General Synod (see p. 183) as a natural part of the mission of the emerging Moravian Church in Bohemia.

DIASPORA IN VOLHYNIA

1882 The head of the teaching institute in Stará Čava provided the Czech Unity with 500 marks so that it could support a diaspora worker (preacher) within Bohemian emigrants in Volhynia. When the Czechs lost their Czech preachers because of confession disputes, only Polish reformed preachers remained in service. After some time, the Czechs longed for Czech services again and for children being taught in Czech language.

- The inhabitants of Boratyn asked for help a pastor Eugen Schmidt who lived in Potštejn.
- **2 February** Eugen Schmidt summoned a conference of friends from different Evangelical churches for a common meeting in Prague. The conference established an administrative committee to find a suitable way of help and a person who could do the work in Volhynia. The committee decided to send a teacher who could not only teach children, but also do missionary-diaspora work in Boratyn. They found a candidate in Josef Motl who graduated from Moravian Pedagogium in Niesky. Josef Motl, son of Karel Motl, accepted it.
- **In September** Motl went to Boratyn. He did not come into easy circumstances. Squabbles between confessions were still alive. In addition, there were also efforts to join Czech emigrants to

The first letter written by Josef Motl from Volhynia

Orthodoxy. People from Boratyn received Josef Motl with joy and cared for him as much as they could. There was no school building and so he taught in a room of a tinsmith Josef Opočenský, a curator of the congregation. They also held worship meetings there. Motl arranged a Sunday school for older youth and taught them. Although he worked selflessly and devotedly, some of the Boratyns wanted to get rid of him. This is how far the confession hatred went. But the love of the vast majority of the people kept Josef Motl there and strengthened him in his hard work.

1884 A reformed teacher Václav Vančura from Čermná (later a Moravian pastor and a bishop), and Václav Medáček, an assistant of a Potštejn pastor Eugen Schmidt, visited Motl in Boratyn during the summer. Their visit was a great encouragement for Josef Motl in all the hard teaching and diaspora mission. He worked there for four years altogether. He fulfilled not only his teaching vocation faithfully, but also the mission of the spiritual worker in the diaspora.

1886 20 November Josef Motl returned from Volhynia to his homeland.

ÚSTÍ NAD ORLICÍ – THE RENEWAL OF THE CONGREGATION

The Ancient Unity was already active in Ústí nad Orlicí in the first half of the sixteenth century. The growing work in Ústí was, however, violently interrupted. Therefore brothers longed for the work to be renewed there again.

1882 The first members from Ústí were admitted to the Moravian Church. After a year, there were even more members and Pastor Schmidt recognized that a new work was being born there. In order to develop the work, he began to think about buying a house.

1884 6 March A house no. 293 was bought and with an apartment for Karel Motl who served there with evangelization and as a missionary. Not only an apartment was gained by buying a house, there was also a space for a prayer room.
- **11 May** A house of prayer was ceremonially opened and thus, solid foundations were given to the work of the Moravian Church in Ústí.

Ústí nad Orlicí – the still existing house of the congregation where even Jan Augusta preached

1886 Karel Motl left Ústí and went to Rychnov. The congregation in Ústí was taken over by his son Josef Motl, a teacher in Volhynia. But Josef moved to Prague after a year and from 1888 he worked as a news vendor in the English Bible Society.
- The congregation in Ústí got their first pastor, Josef Mikuláštík. He came from Jasenná in South Moravia. At first, he desired to go on a mission abroad, but the Lord prepared for him to go to the Eastern Bohemia. Josef Mikuláštík obeyed God's calling and remained faithful to this work all his life. It was not an easy work. Disfavor, hardness of hearts and indifference sometimes appeared in the congregation itself. The young pastor overcame these obstacles only because

he stayed deeply rooted in the faith of the Lord.

1895 Due to the poor technical state of the church house, Mikuláštík was looking for a more suitable place. It was difficult to get such a building, because the Catholic public in Ústí was not in favor of the Moravian Church. Still, they managed to buy a house no. 260.

1901 A house no. 53 which once belonged to the Ancient Unity was put on sale. Josef Mikuláštík did not hesitate a minute and bought the house. It was a significant step not only for the local congregation, but also for the whole church. They got the building of the Ancient Unity where even Jan Augusta had once preached. This building is still being used by the Moravian Church congregation to this day.

1902 **4 May** A house of prayer was opened with a wide participation of the public and a mayor himself Dr. František Vicena. The tolerant attitude of the mayor and the quiet and faithful work of the pastor Mikuláštík finally eased tensions and the town's bias towards the Moravian Church. It was a great success, needed for further gospel work and church growth. Josef Mikuláštík had served in the congregation for twenty-two years. He did a great deal of work and also got many friends, for example, a writer Alois Jirásek, at that time a professor in Litomyšl, or Ferdinand Schulz from Prague, the editor of *Zlatá Praha* (Golden Prague – Czech illustrated magazine).

1908 Mikuláštík left for the congregation in Potštejn where he replaced pastor The-

Josef Mikuláštík with his family, the oldest son Otto on the left

ophil Reichel who was called to Prague. Josef Mikuláštík was above all a shepherd and in such a way he worked in his new place of work too.

PROGRESS OF OTHER WORK

1889 27 May – 1 July The General Synod received a report on the recognition of the independence of the church within the Austro-Hungarian Empire with pleasure, based on which first congregations could be officially established in Bohemia. Synod also confirmed that Bohemian-Moravian Mission would continue to be under the Conference of Elders of the Moravian Church and in competency of the Bohemian-Moravian Committee. The Czech representative of the Synod was Eugen Schmidt, a pastor in Potštejn.

- **11 October** A house of prayer was opened in Mladá Boleslav.

1894 A magazine called *Bratrské Listy* (Brethren Papers) was published. Its editor was a pastor, Václav Betka.

1895 29 September Karel Reichel, later a bishop, was born in Potštejn.

1896 10 May Mission work began in Jablonec nad Nisou.

1898 15 August Another new congregation was established in Turnov.

1899 16 May – 30 June The General Synod met and discussed, beside other things, the work of Bohemian-Moravian Mission and issued a resolution on practical steps and further development of the mission.

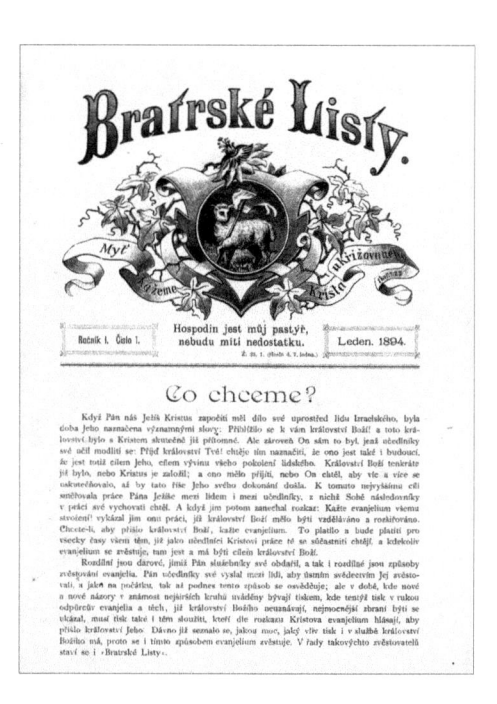

Front page of the first publication of a magazine Bratrské listy (Brethren Papers)

It concerned especially issues such as a practical procedure when establishing new congregations, obtaining financial resources, practical caring for orphans, publishing the magazine *Bratrské Listy* (Brethren Papers), supporting of the gospel work, accepting new members and education of new workers. A practical care for orphans was an important point approved by the Synod supporting the already working Moravian orphanages.
The Synod also called two Czech pastors to the Bohemian-Moravian Committee who continued to administer Czech mission work.

- Bohemian-Moravian Mission had a total of 985 members in four congregations (Potštejn, Dubá, Praha, Ústí nad Orlicí /

Lanškroun) at the time and other eight missionary areas.
- **10 September** A house of prayer was opened in Nová Paka.
- **15 October** A new house of prayer was opened ceremonially in Potštejn.

1900 A congregation in Herčivald* built its own church and four years later, a parsonage. The congregation had twenty-one members. At first it was just a preaching station belonging to Potštejn and Ústí nad Orlicí congregation. However, the long distance from the congregation and the fact that Herčivald was a German village required a change. František Spiegler was called there as a pastor and worked there until 1907.

1902 **21 September** A house of prayer was opened in Prague for the first time.

1904 **1 December** Vilém Hartwig, a traveling preacher and a father of orphans, died in Čermná.

1907 **9 May** After many years, an old brethren's congregation from the times of Ancient Unity was re-opened in Mladá Boleslav.
- Other congregations were growing in Železný Brod and Duchcov.
- **9 June** Adolf Ulrich, later a bishop, was born in Nová Paka.

1909 **18 May – 3 July** The General Synod decided that the newly established Provincial Board in Czech lands would continue to represent the interests of the Moravian Church within the Austro-Hungarian Empire and at the same time submit to a decision and approval of the Bohemian-Moravian Committee in Herrnhut. The Synod also addressed another important issue – finances – such as a fund for congregations gaining independence, insurance and pension fund. Czech representatives at the Synod were Theophil Reichel (pastor in Prague), Eugen Schmidt (pastor in Dubá) and Walther Eugen Schmidt (his son) as a reporter and a secretary of the Bohemian-Moravian Committee.
- **8 September** The first members of the Provincial Board were elected: Theophil Reichel, Josef Mikuláštík, Václav Vančura and one of the oldest pastors Eugen Schmidt was delegated by the Bohemian-Moravian Committee.
- General Bohemian-Moravian Convention, which consisted of Czech pastors and congregation representatives, began

Church house in Potštejn

Herzogwald – no longer existing village in the area of Kružberk dam.

to meet regularly. In addition to educational programs, Brethren also dealt with administrative issues. However, the convention had no decision-making power.

1913 **12 May** A house of prayer was opened in Turnov.

1914 **14 May 14 – 13 June** The General Synod adopted, among others, a resolution from which it was obvious that Bohemian-Moravian Mission was in a very difficult financial situation. The Synod invited all the provinces to *"support the mission and its new board with all seriousness and dedication."*[33] The Synod also elected new members of the Bohemain-Moravian Committee. Eugen Schmidt, a pastor in Dubá, represented the Czech branch of the Moravian Church at the Synod again.

- **20 December** Eugen Schmidt, a Provincial board chairman and a pastor, died.

Theophil Reichel became a chairman. He died two years later. Then the following brothers took the lead: Josef Mikuláštík, Jindřich Schiller, Václav Vančura, Gottfried Schmidt (son of Eugen Schmidt) and Bohumil Vančura (son of Václav Vančura).

UNEASINESS BETWEEN TWO WORLD WARS

After the dissolution of the Austro-Hungarian Empire, the Bohemian-Moravian Mission found itself under pressure because of the following social changes:
- the establishment of Czechoslovakia,
- discrimination of national minorities,
- efforts to unite some evangelical churches within a newly established, republic,
- a significant increase in the membership of the Moravian Church thanks to so-called "transfer movement"*,

Opening of a church house in Turnov (1913)

---

* *Departure from the Catholic Church which was associated with Austro-Hungarian Empire; highlighting patriotic ideals and establishing new non-Catholic churches.*

- a crisis of identity of the German Moravian Church,
- increasing pressure between the Czech and German congregations because of the onset of Nazism.

All these facts led to the realization that such a growing church cannot be managed from abroad. The General Bohemian-Moravian Convention also needed more rights and a greater degree of responsibility. It was necessary to negotiate a new, more independent establishment and to carry out administrative and financial reorganization of the mission.

1918 **19 November** A new Provincial Board (PEC) consisting of Josef Mikuláštík, Václav Vančura and Jindřich Schiller was elected at a meeting of all pastors in Potštejn. They decided that the church would use the original name Jednota bratrská (Czech version of Unitas Fratrum).

1919 – 1920 The Moravian Church took part in negotiations about possible unification with other evangelical churches within the newly emerging republic. However, it wanted to remain in the UF world union. In the end, only cooperation with the Evangelical Church of Czech Brethren, formed by the merger of the two Evangelical Churches of Augsburg and Helvetian Confession, remained. The Moravian Church, however, kept its distance from the then patriotic-religious and liberal endeavors of the Evangelical Church.

■ German congregations within the Bohemian-Moravian Mission sought closer connection with Herrnhut. They were dependent on Herrnhut financially and

| *Provincial Board of the Bohemian-Moravian Mission – from the left Josef Mikuláštík, Václav Vančura, Jindřich Schiller*

they also expected national support. They remained a minority in Czechoslovakia and expressed certain jealousy of the rapid growth of Czech congregations. Yet neither the Czech nor the German congregations wished to break the mutual unity or ties with the UF.

- The Bohemian-Moravian Mission strived for its own more flexible leadership, less dependent on foreign countries, and brothers also wanted to resolve relations with the German congregations in their own way.

1921 31 July Czechoslovak government acknowledged the church a historical name Jednota bratrská (Unitas Fratrum).

1922 11 August – 21 August The conference of the German Province took place and there was a change in the Church Order regarding the work in the countries formed after the collapse of Austria-Hungary. The work of the Bohemian-Moravian Mission was redefined in the following proposal:

"The congregations in Bohemia and Moravia will continue to be represented by: a Czech Unity convention and a German Unity convention (congregations formed mostly in the area of Sudetenland) in Czechoslovakia. Each convention will elect its own board and both elected boards will vote together and elect the Provincial Board from among their number in a ratio of two from the Czech board and one from the German board. The Directory will continue to appoint the Chairman of the Moravian church. The PEC will then have the highest representation of the Moravian church in Czechoslovakia."[34] This proposal was, however, discussed in the following years with no final resolution.

Church house in Nová Paka

1923 23 January A Czech theologian and historian, Amedeo Molnár, was born in Prague Amedeo Molnár served in the Moravian Church in the years 1944 and 1945. Since 1950 he was an associate professor of Evangelical Comenius Faculty of Theology in Prague. He died on January 31, 1990 in Prague. As a historian he focused on topics such as: Luke of Prague, the second generation of Ancient Unity, brethren from Boleslav.

1924 8 August Czech pastors' conference met in Prague and unanimously approved its own proposal for a new solution of church establishment – to give greater authority to the Provincial Board and to the General Bohemian-Moravian Convention. This proposal was written by Bohumil Vančura and Jindřich Schiller.
- The Bohemian-Moravian Committee refused this proposal. It came up with a proposal to divide the Czech mission into two areas again (Czech and German), with two separate boards and two separate regional conferences and one common Provincial Board. The Czechs, however, refused it because the decision making would be too much complicated.

1925 7 July A resolution was passed with the agreement of Bohemian-Moravian Committee after long-term inconsistencies at the General Bohemian-Moravian Convention: *"Czech mission will continue to be administered by the Directory of the Moravian Church in Czechoslovakia based in Herrnhut. The Directory appoints its representative for Czechoslovakia. The Directory will continue to:*
- *keep track of church finances, approve budgets of congregations and changes in financial funds,*

From the left: Bohumil Vančura and Gottfried Schmidt Sitting: Jindřich Schiller and Walther Eugen Schmidt

- *call or remove pastors on the proposal of the Provincial Board,*
- *establish or disband congregations in Czechoslovakia.*

Other internal administration will remain within the competence of the Provincial Board (for Czech and German congregations) that will answer to General Bohemian-Moravian Convention."[35]

The Directory was appointed from the members of German and British provinces. Walther Eugen Schmidt was appointed a secretary, a treasurer and a representative for Czechoslovakia. He was also appointed a chairman of the Provincial Board. Members of the PEC were elected: Václav Vančura and Jindřich Schiller for Czech congregations and Gottfried Schmidt for German congregations.

- Thus, the leading of the mission was primarily in the hands of W. E. Schmidt. Negotiations, however, remained very long and complicated and no congregation was happy with it, not even the German ones. So the negotiations continued; for Czech congregations there were J. Schiller and B. Vančura, for the German congregations there was W. E. Schmidt.
- **28 October** A house of prayer was opened ceremonially in Dobřív

1931 **28 May – 22 June** The General Synod took decisions regarding the Bohemian-Moravian Mission: *"This Czech mission received calling from the whole church and took the challenge to spread the gospel in the Catholic-oriented Czechoslovakia, involve all the members in this mission and prepare conditions for the future establishment of Czechoslovakian province."*[36]

The General Synod also declared Bohemian-Moravian Mission a growing branch of the Moravian Church and defined responsibilities given to the Directory of the Moravian Church in Czechoslovakia more precisely:
- to call and remove pastors in the Bohemian-Moravian Mission after an agreement with the Provincial Board,
- to administer gifts and donations given to the Bohemian-Moravian Mission from other provinces,
- to oversee the administration of congregational and church property,
- to administer orphanages and diakonia.

Everything else, including the election of the chairman, was administered by the Provincial Board.

Jindřich Schiller and Walther Eugen Schmidt represented the Czech Moravian Church at the Synod.

- **29–30 November** The General Bohemian-Moravian Convention took place in Prague. The Convention elected Jindřich Schiller (as a chairman), Otto B. Mikuláštík and Bohumil Vančura to the Provincial Board. Gottfried Schmidt was elected to the Provincial Board to represent German congregations.

The meeting of the General Bohemian-Moravian Convention (1931)

1933 Adolf Hitler seized power and was appointed a chancellor of Germany and a rapid rise of fascism occurred. Even in Czechoslovakia, especially in the borderlands, German nationalism grew.
- It was a difficult test for the Bohemian-Moravian Mission again. Moreover, the situation in the church worsened due to overall economic crisis. The Provincial Board and Walther Eugen Schmidt were lost and helpless. It was obvious that Czech and German congregations would have to separate. Brothers were looking for a way and a new form of working in two separate groups.
- **20 August** A new congregation was opened in Ujkovice.

1934 The function of the representative of the Directory for Czechoslovakia was canceled and Walther Eugen Schmidt left for Switzerland. The Czech congregations found themselves in a deep crisis because of Schmidt's absence, new constitutional negotiations and difficult financial circumstances. There were serious concerns about whether it would be possible to keep the mission financially going. Two pastors left the church due to disagreement on the upcoming administrative changes and also because of the dismal financial situation. The situation was serious. Families of the pastors literally scratched out a living. They often lived from just one Sunday collection, from week to week. In the end, Czech congregations pulled themselves together and overcame the crisis.

1935 1 January The new establishment of the Moravian Church in Czechoslovakia began to exist. The church was divided into two districts: Czech and German – due to the growing German nationalism and hostility of both nationalities. It was the only possible solution in a given situation. Division of the groups had, yet, a deeper spiritual context.

General Convention of the Moravian Church (Ústí nad Orlicí, 1936)

The Czech district

Czech congregations grew faster than the German ones since the beginning of the twentieth century. They spread the gospel in Czech language and claimed allegiance to the legacy of the Ancient Unity (as it was known before the battle of White Mountain). However, some congregations did not resist the so-called transfer movement after the establishment of the Czechoslovak Republic.

People who en masse left the Catholic Church and joined the Moravian Church, however, lived without inner relationship with God. So Czech congregations became bigger and bigger in this way, but at the same time it largely became so-called folk church.

1935 A new congregation was established in the Czech district and it was in town of Holešov. A part of an evangelical congregation in Prusinovice, including the priest Karel V. Pavlinec, joined the Moravian Church after long-standing disagreements with their own church. So the group then searched an opportunity to join another church. Town council in Holešov recommended them to join the Moravian Church. After the talks with the Provincial Board (J. Schiller and B. Vančura), they were accepted into the Moravian Church.

The German district

The transfer movement originally began among the Czech Germans at the turn of the century. People converted from Catholic Church in masses and new German Lutheran Evangelical congregations grew rapidly. German congregations of the Bohemian-Moravian Mission were not affected by the movement as much due to pietistic emphasis and personal piety of Herrnhut people. Nevertheless, they failed to resist the growth of German nationalism after the emergence of Czechoslovakia with growing tensions between the Czechs and the German national minority and also with the world economic crisis. Nationalism was promoted mainly by Alfred Präger

Moravian Church in Herčivald (Herzogwald)

in the German district. His nationalist thinking grew into Nazism. Only two German congregations resisted this – Herčivald and Dubá. The congregation in Herčivald finally protested and left the German district and at the synod of the German Province in 1939 in Herrnhut, they were allowed to join them.

1936 A congregation was established in Rossbach (present-day Hranice u Aše). It was established due to a quarrel inside a local German Lutheran congregation. Its pastor Othmar Müllner did not hesitate to oppose public opinion when it came to clear distinguishing between religion and politics. Many members left the church together with the pastor; they sought help in the German district of the Moravian Church. First, they became a mission area of the church in Podmokle, later they became independent. Othmar Müllner served there until 1937 when he left for church in Herčivald. The congregation came to an end by expulsion of the Germans in 1945.

1937 26 October All Czech congregations claimed allegiance to and approved the Constitution of the Moravian Church in Czechoslovakia. It helped to resolve the crisis and the autonomy of the administration of the Czech district was completed.

GERMAN OCCUPATION AND THE WAR YEARS

During the World War II, the Moravian Church did not hesitate to support emerging resistance against the occupier, for example resistance center in the area of Český Ráj (Pavel Glos from Turnov). Pastors Otto B. Mikuláštík from Ústí, Miroslav Plecháč from Nová Paka and Karel V. Pavlinec from Holešov participated in the resistance, each in their own region. These three were even interned in concentration camps. Other

Moravian Church congregations in 1937

	Congregation	Pastor	Year of establishment
1., 2.	Dobřív, Duchcov	Without pastor	1927, 1912
3.	Holešov	Karel V. Pavlinec (*17 October 1902)	1937
4.	Mladá Boleslav	Jindřich Schiller (*19 November 1883)	1907
5.	Nová Paka	Stanislav Čech (*12 November 1893)	1899
6.	Potštejn	Karel Reichel (*29 September 1895)	1879
7.	Prague	Bohumil Vančura (*2 May 1894)	1902
8.	Turnov	Pavel Glos (*4 December 1903)	1898
9.	Ujkovice	Josef Korbel (*16 April 1883)	1933
10.	Ústí nad Orlicí	Otto B. Mikuláštík (*1 October 1891)	1884
11.	Železný Brod	František T. Petr (*6 December 1900)	1907
	Czech congregations: 5,358 members		
1.	Dubá	Johann Bayer	1872
2.	Herčivald (Herzogwald)	Othmar Müllner	1891
3.	Jablonec nad Nisou	Joachim Voelkel	1910
4.	Podmokly	Alfred Präger	1936
5.	Rossbach (Hranice)	Heinz Schmidt	1932
	German congregations: 1,960 members		

pastors were arrested for anti-Reich attitude: Karel Reichel and Gustav Zvěřina from Potštejn. In these conditions, the administration of the church was very difficult.

At this time, the Moravian Church became financially self-sufficient for the first time since returning to the land of forefathers. The finance commission, led by Jaroslav John from Nová Paka, deserves credit for solving the finances. The Commission drew up a plan requiring great dedication from the side of all congregations. Church management had a balanced budget for the first time, and even managed to repay old debts.

Occupation and collective repressions helped to break down boundaries between individual evangelical churches. Difficult conditions of church life during the war reopened discussions about uniting churches. First ideas revolved around union of the Moravian Church and the Evangelical Church of Czech Brethren. The questions of bishopric, name of the united church and connections with the Unitas Fratrum remained sticking points in the discussion. The Methodist Church also joined this platform for unification as a third partner.

These ideas were not implemented in the end but the negotiations helped to bring the churches together and to deepen their cooperation which continued developing even in the Ecumenical Council of Churches and the Konstanz Union (Kostnická Jednota).

1938 With the border territories annexed by Nazi Germany, the Czech part of the

Miroslav Plecháč and Pavel Glos

Czechoslovak Moravian Church lost its work in Liberec* and the charity work in Čermná. The congregation in Dobřív was left unoccupied. The church administration remained in the hands of the Provincial Board which was often personally changed by outside interventions.

1943 The church prepared an outlook of three ministries: **mission ministry** was to continue with support from František Chleboun; **spiritual ministry** was to care for continuous studies of the grounds of brethren reformation; **charity ministry** was determined for orphanages and care for the poor and sick.

- The congregation in Železný Brod was divided into several mission stations:

*Mission station of the Turnov congregation.

Loučky (Koberovy) with 408 members, Huntířov with 454 members and Bratříkov. František Polma became a pastor in Loučky and Vladimír Habr in Huntířov. The services were held at schools in both places.

1944 Until 1944, Czech pastors were ordained by foreign bishops. Ordinations thus took place in Germany or in Great Britain. During the war, there was an urgent need to ordain new workers. The circumstances did not allow Bishop Samuel Baudert from Herrnhut to ordain brothers personally. Therefore, he authorized the oldest Czech pastor Václav Vančura in writing to carry out the ordination on his behalf.

- **9 August** Three brothers were ordained in Mladá Boleslav: Miroslav Plecháč, Radim Kalfus and Jan Dušek.
- **In September**, the Board of Elders in Rovensko decided to establish a congregation and the PEC confirmed their decision.

1945 After the war, the Moravian Church in Czechoslovakia was faced with new tasks concerning broader ministry and considerable growth of membership. People who were resettling abandoned borderlands were joining local evangelical parishes but many of them were not participating on the church life actively.

- **17 June** The first constitutive committee met in Liberec to start a new congregation. The mission in Liberec, violently interrupted in 1938, was renewed. The congregation was given a former Lutheran church at its disposal.

Church house in Mladá Boleslav

However, that church was not suitable for the work at the beginning. The first pastor was Radim Kalfus and after him Boris Uher. In 1950, Josef Votrubec became a pastor and had been serving in Liberec for 36 years.

- **6 July** The Moravian Church met in a memorable rock maze called Kalich near Koberovy for a celebration of the end of the war. This celebration expressed the sense of belonging of the Moravian Church to a nation from which it once originated and where it wants to live in good times and bad.
- **28 October** Moravian missionary František Chleboun died in Přerov. He is buried in Turnov.

POST-WAR PERIOD

The war helped the church to develop deeper relationships with God and with each other. The years after and the renewal of civil liberties were bringing lukewarmness and stagnation to the Moravian Church. Many members needed to be searched for and invited to participate in church life. Official statistics did not correspond with the real number of active church members.

Furthermore, some church houses in the border regions were left empty after expulsion of Germans (Dubá, Jablonec, Herčivald). The Moravian Church attempted to restore its work there but not always with success.

1946 **1 March** Václav Vančura, aged 89, was elected the first Czech bishop at the synod in Železný Brod.

- **3–7 July** In Montmirail in Switzerland, the UF General Conference took place and replaced the long-awaited General Synod. The Conference mapped the situation after the war in the UF.

Bohumil Vančura was a Czech delegate and he informed about the situation of the Czech part of the Moravian Church. He also requested consecration of Václav Vančura to become the first Czech bishop because the church was taking on new workers and they needed to be ordained. The General Conference granted the request and sent greetings to the Czech and Moravian brothers and sisters.

Church house in Dubá

PART IV

Václav Vančura

- **20 July** In Mladá Boleslav, a celebration was held in an old Moravian church building. Bishops Clarence H. Shawe and George W. Mc Leavy from London, and Dr. Samuel H. Capp from the USA came to ordain the new Bishop Vančura.

After 1945, the Moravian Church in Czechoslovakia worked in seven congregations and seven mission stations. The number of members was growing fast.

Year	Members
1945	4,524
1946	6,457
1947	6,657

ARRIVAL OF TOTALITARIAN REGIME

1948 25 February With the beginning of socialism in Czechoslovakia, the church and the state were dictated by the new ideology of Marxism-Leninism. New acts determining the relationship of the church and the state were passed. The state confiscated church property and took over its financing. Salaries for the clergy were deeply below average. The state also took over all social care and defined limited possibilities for the church to engage in the society (for example in the so-called peace movement).

- **1 March** A second bishop, Karel Reichel, was elected at the synod in Ústí nad Orlicí. The consecration was performed by Bishop Václav Vančura with the assistance of two presbyters* Pavel Glos and Josef Korbel who were authorized by UF bishops. The Moravian Church took another step to full independence of the Czech mission.

Consecration of Vančura in an old church house in Mladá Boleslav

- **1 July** A new pastor Gustav Zvěřina took on the abandoned parsonage in Dubá. At the beginning, his ministry was purely missionary and he started with empty hands. Gradually a few mission works were formed in Střezivojice, Tuhaň and in Česká Lípa. Mission in Česká Lípa was growing in particular and local church members even bought a house to have a prayer room and later also a flat for the pastor.

1950 The congregation in Česká Lípa became independent with a pastor Petr Baumgartner. Nevertheless, from 1957 the congregation had not had a pastor for many years.

*Second degree of spiritual ordination

- The church main office moved to Nová Paka for a long time. It was an important decision because until then the Provincial Board and archive had been moving from one place to another. The church office resided in Nová Paka until 2008.

1951 9 December A new church house was ceremonially opened in Koberovy. Rudolf Borski became the pastor.

1952 26 May The first Czech bishop Václav Vančura died in Poděbrady aged 95.

1953 4 March Jan Klas was born in Jilemnice. He later became a Moravian bishop.

1955 20 March The Synod approved a new constitution of the Moravian Church in the Czechoslovak Socialist Republic.

1956 A new congregation was established in Tanvald. Rostislav Chlubna became its administrator. He bought an older house for the church and gradually adjusted it for church house.

1957 24–26 May A ceremonial synod of the Czechoslovak Moravian Church was held in Železný Brod. It was later designated as the first synod. Bishop Karel Reichel was elected to the church leadership. The Synod was also attended by 34 foreign delegates.

INDEPENDENCE OF CZECHOSLOVAK PROVINCE

1957 13 August – 10 September The General Synod met again after twen-

Ceremonial synod in Železný Brod (May 1957)

ty-six years. It took place overseas in Bethlehem (Pennsylvania, USA) for the first time. This Synod was fundamental for the modern history of the Moravian Church in the land of fathers. On September 5, 1957, the Czechoslovak Moravian Church was pronounced the fifth independent UF Province. One of the reasons was also the fact that the Czechoslovak government would recognize and respect the Moravian Church as an independent church that celebrated 500th anniversary at that time.

1958 The Czechoslovak Province held a second synod which elected a new Provincial Board: Bishop Karel Reichel as the chairman, Radim Kalfus as the secretary, Jindřich Halama as the head of educational department.

1959 **9 January** Evald Rucký, later a bishop, was born in Frýdek-Místek.
The Moravian Church in Czechoslovakia was also a member of the Ecumenical Council of Churches, Christian Peace Conference and Konstanz Union.

At that time, all Czechoslovakian churches were in a tight grip of the communist dictatorship and they had to submit to the Ministry of Culture and its church secretaries. The churches were also helpless against the system of the so-called state security (StB), the powerful instrument of the regime. They could not develop naturally and their strength, energy and time were often devoted to official requirements of the regime.
This involuntary state affected the Moravian Church as well. Candidates for the Pro-

Karel Reichel with his wife

vincial Board were screened by the state to receive official consent before the actual election in the church. The Moravian Church itself did not hold fruitful discussions about where the church is heading. Little by little, tensions had been growing among the pastors. Some were influenced by pre-war transfer movement; some grew up with evangelical and pietistic influences with emphasis on rebirth, personal relationship with Christ and consecrated active life within the church.

SPIRITUAL AND SOCIAL CROSSROAD

1961 5 March The third Provincial Synod took place in Nová Paka. The Provincial Board gave a report on its activities for the past period. The members of the Provincial Board were newly elected after three years in office: Vladimír Habr as the chairman, Karel Reichel and Radim Kalfus as other members. The Synod focused on upcoming meeting of the Unity Synod that was planned for 1967

List of congregations in 1961

	Congregation	Mission station	Pastor
1.	Česká Lípa	Teplice	served from Dubá
2.	Dobřív		Emanuel Pokorný (*21. 7. 1916)
3.	Dubá	Tuhanec, Nedvězí	Gustav Zvěřina (*17. 01.1906)
4.	Holešov	Hulín, Brno	Adolf Ulrich (*4. 6. 1909)
5.	Huntířov		Rudolf J. Trousil (*14. 9. 1905)
6.	Jablonec n. N.	Smržovka	Vladimír Habr (*14. 10. 1913)
7.	Liberec	Nové Měto p. S., Mníšek u Liberce	Josef Votrubec (*14. 8. 1919)
8.	Loučky	Koberovy	Rudolf Borski (*2. 7. 1927)
9.	Mladá Boleslav	Dolní Bousov	Jindřich Halama (*14. 3. 1925)
10.	Nová Paka	Lázně Bělohrad	Miroslav Plecháč (*7. 11. 1900)
11.	Potštejn	Kunvald v Čechách, Rychnov nad Kněžnou, Vamberk	Jan Niebauer (*3. 5. 1918)
12.	Prague	Karlovy Vary	Karel Reichel (*29. 9. 1895)
13.	Rovensko pod Troskami		Miroslav Hloušek (*9. 2. 1927)
14.	Tanvald		served from Nová Paka
15.	Turnov	Sedmihorky-Nová Ves	Pavel Glos (*4. 12. 1903)
16.	Ujkovice		František J. Polma (*24. 4. 1914)
17.	Ústí nad Orlicí	Havlíčkův Brod, Choceň, Pardubice	Adolf Vacovský (*10. 5. 1926)
18.	Železný Brod	Bozkov, Bratříkov, Semily	František Tim. Petr (*6. 12. 1900)

in Czechoslovakia in honor of the vote of the first Brethren priests in 1467.
- **25 December** Petr Krásný, later a bishop, was born in Třebíč.

1964 **22–23 May** The Province held a fourth Provincial Synod in Nová Paka. Members of the Provincial Board were re-elected as follows: Bishop Karel Reichel became a chairman, Vladimír Habr took up the Christian Education ministry and Radim Kalfus became a secretary and foreign affairs officer. He was charged with setting up a preparatory committee for the upcoming 1967 Unity Synod. Bishop Karel Reichel also put emphasis on the synod and proposed election of another bishop. Some pastors were part of working committees and presented their reports to the synod. Pastor Josef Votrubec was engaged in the Prayer and also in the Evangelization Committee. Jindřich Halama was the head of Committee on Theology and he proposed to the Synod a renewal of the Cup of Covenant*. The final resolution of the synod was rather in line with the times: emphasizing the peace efforts of the so-called Christian Peace Conference. These activities were supported by the communist regime. The churches were thus diverted from their initial calling of Christ to bear witness to His mighty actions through Resurrection. Instead, they were called to participate actively on the world peace. However, this was only a state propaganda.
- **In July**, a regional European committee of the UF held its session in Czechoslovakia. These regional working sessions took place in the inter-synodal period

Emblem with a lamb – symbol of the Moravian Church

- successively in the four regions: Africa, Caribbean, America and Europe. This particular European committee declared March 28 (day of birth of John Amos Comenius) to be a memorial day of the whole Unity. The committee also recommended pursuing the question of the office of a Moravian bishop and reminded to be forthcoming to former mission areas (such as Jamaica) so that they could become independent unity provinces.

1967 **In spring**, Bishop Karel Reichel defined the mission of the church of the time:
1. to honor the authority of God's Word
2. faithful obedience
3. congregationalism
4. order and discipline

---
*A tradition from the times of Herrnhut awakening that is becoming a tradition in the UF at the end of provincial synods or congregational conferences.

5. freedom of the church
6. relationship to the world

In the author's opinion, it all remained a theory. The church was in deep stagnation despite the communist regime's internal changes that resulted in Prague Spring in 1968. That year, the First Secretary of the Communist Party of Czechoslovakia, Alexander Dubček, together with other reformers of the party took steps towards liberalization of socialism. Freedom of the press was proclaimed and even the church had more freedom at that time. The Moravian Church, however, did not use the opportunity and did not come to an inner reform.

- **26 May** A special pastors' conference elected new bishop, Adolf Ulrich, who was a student of the first Bishop Václav Vančura. Ulrich served in a congregation in Holešov.
- **25 June** Adolf Ulrich was consecrated by Bishop Karel Reichel and two presbyters, Jan Niebauer and Josef Korbel.
- **6 July – 13 August** The General Synod* met in Potštejn, Czechoslovakia. The Czechoslovak Province was represented by Rudolf Borski, Jindřich Halama, Radim Kalfus and Bishops Karel Reichel with wife Bedřiška and Adolf Ulrich. Every province gave report about its activities (see also p. 165).

The author appreciates the effort of representatives of the Czech Moravian Church that they took on themselves organizational and financial responsibility for the Synod. It was a special gift for all participants. Many of them would not have other opportunity to visit the land where the Moravian Church emerged.

Adolf Ulrich

1968 26–28 April The fifth Provincial Synod of the Czechoslovak Province took place in Nová Paka. The synod elected a new provincial board: Bishop Adolf Ulrich became a chairman, František J. Polma took charge of economic affairs of the church, and Jindřich Halama took on the responsibility for theological and educational matters.

1970 29 October Bishop Karel Reichel died in Mladá Boleslav.

1971 18–19 September The sixth Provincial Synod was held in Železný Brod. The Provincial Board was re-elected with Bishop Adolf Ulrich, František J. Polma and Jindřich Halama.

---

* *The term* General Synod *was gradually replaced by* Unity Synod.

1974 **23 June – 10 July** The Unity Synod took place in Kingston, Jamaica. The Czechoslovak Province was represented by Bishop Adolf Ulrich and Jindřich Halama.
- **18–20 October** The seventh Czechoslovak Synod met in Holešov on the occasion of anniversary of brethren's synod held in the same town in 1574. The Provincial Board was re-elected again in the same composition: Bishop Adolf Ulrich, František J. Polma and Jindřich Halama.

1977 **In September**, František J. Polma, member of the Provincial Board, died, aged 63 years.
- **14–16 October** The eighth synod was held in Prague and elected new Provincial Board: Jindřich Halama as a chairman, Rudolf Borski who was responsible for church management until 1989 and Adolf Vacovský was responsible for publishing and education. Members of the church got older and congregations lacked a young generation. There was also a shortage of young spiritual workers. That is why the synod appealed to congregations to part with lukewarmness and indifference, to be in prayers for inner change inside congregations and to seek selfless young servants.

1980 **17–19 October** Prague hosted the ninth Provincial Synod. The Provincial Board was re-elected in the same composition.

Pastors and representatives of congregations at the Synod in Holešov (1974)

1981 29 August – 13 September The Unity Synod met in Herrnhut. The delegates for the Czechoslovak Province were: Jindřich Halama, the chairman of the Board, Bishop Adolf Ulrich, and Irena Kuželová, pastor of Prague congregation.

1983 7–9 October The tenth Provincial Synod was held in Prague. The situation in the leadership did not change and the Provincial Board remained in the same composition. Unfortunately, Adolf Vacovský died a year later aged only 57 years. In him, the church lost an expert and lecturer in the Moravian Church history.

1984 6 October A special Provincial Synod was summoned to Rovensko and elected Miroslav Hloušek, pastor in Železný Brod, for the vacant seat in the Provincial Board. Hloušek took over education and publishing after Vacovský. There was, however, a tension among the Board members.
- The chairman of the Board, Jindřich Halama, sought new candidates for spiritual service in other Christian denominations.

1986 3–4 October The eleventh Provincial Synod in Prague elected a new Provincial Board: Jindřich Halama, Rudolf Borski and Bohumil Kejř, pastor in Mladá Boleslav.

1987 1 July Evald Rucký, who originally served in Evangelical Brethren Church*, took over the congregation in Liberec. He received permission from the state and assumed the office in the congregation after deceased Josef Votrubec.

The Provincial Board – from the left: Rudolf Borski, Jindřich Halama, Adolf Vacovský (1983)

- Several young pastors started work; some of them came from different denominations. Relations at joint sessions of pastors (pastoral or annual conferences and synods), which took place several times a year, were not very heartening. Especially the older generation was accusing the younger one of disrespecting church history and traditions. This generational crisis culminated in 1998.

1988 3–16 July The Unity Synod was held in Antigua in the Caribbean. The Czechoslovak Province was represented by pastor in Jablonec congregation, Jindřich Halama, Jr., and members of the Board, Rudolf Borski and Bohumil Kejř.

---

* Protestant, reformed, evangelical church established at the end of nineteenth century.

1989 17–18 November The twelfth Provincial Synod took place in Prague right at the time of great political changes later called *The Velvet Revolution*. Jindřich Halama, Sr., left the position of the chairman and the Provincial Board was elected as follows: Rudolf Borski – chairman, Ondřej Halama – financial department, Bohumil Kejř – educational department. List of congregations in 1989.

List of congregations in 1989

	Congregation	Mission station	Pastor
1.	Česká Lípa		Served from Dubá
2.	Dobřív		Petr Horáček (*1. 2. 1960)
3.	Dubá	Tuhanec	Josef Marek (*1. 11. 1942)
4.	Holešov	Hulín, Brno	Jaroslav Pleva (*20. 7. 1955)
5.	Jablonec n. N.		Jindřich Halama ml. (*23. 11. 1952)
6.	Koberovy		Václav Kačer (*17. 7. 1931)
7.	Liberec	Nové Město p. S., Český Dub	Evald Rucký (*9. 1. 1959)
8.	Mladá Boleslav	Dolní Bousov	Bohumil Kejř (*14. 1. 1952)
9.	Nová Paka	Lázně Bělohrad	without pastor
10.	Potštejn	Vamberk, Kunvald Rychnov n. K.	Ondřej Halama (*8. 4. 1956)
11.	Prague	Vysočany	Irena Kuželová (*10. 5. 1931)
12.	Rovensko pod Troskami		Hana Jalušková (*30. 11. 1947)
13.	Tanvald	Kořenov, Velké Hamry II	Rudolf Borski (*2. 7. 1927)
14.	Turnov	Olešnice, Nová Ves	Jiří Polma (*25. 2. 1950)
15.	Ujkovice	Libáň	Eliška Šolcová (*25. 10. 1938)
16.	Ústí nad Orlicí	Choceň, Pardubice, Havlíčkův Brod	Svetozár Slavka (*19. 8. 1952)
17.	Železný Brod	Semily, Střevelná, Bratříkov – Pěnčín	Miroslav Hloušek (*9. 2. 1927)

PART V

PART V

Current mission of the Moravian Church
in its homeland

EVENTS OF THE PAST YEARS IN THE MORAVIAN CHURCH

The last chapter of the Moravian Church life is written by the present young generation which is very different from that which reached the end of the totalitarian regime. But there are also several spiritual fathers, bonded in peace and love with the younger generation, who remember communism and the painful crisis of the 1990s.

However, this period of the Moravian Church's current ministry will still be tested by the time and only the future will show what it really was.

After the fall of the totalitarian regime in 1989, new possibilities opened up for all churches, including the Moravian Church. We select only a few events from this period that are important or fundamental to us.

Class of the Church Primary and nursery school of John Amos Comenius (1995)

1992 After several centuries, the Moravian Church established its first primary and nursery school. It was founded in Liberec on the occasion of the 400th anniversary of the birth of Bishop Comenius after whom it was named.
- A post-secondary extension study called the Mission School of N. L. Zinzendorf was established. The school was later transformed into the Jan Blahoslav Academy. Today, it is the internal educational institute of the Moravian Church where new church workers are trained for ministry.
- Several new churches were formed by missionary work.
- Social care for the elderly also began to develop and subsequently other activities and organizations focused on services for people were established in individual congregations.

However, there were also unresolved disputes in the church from the communist era when the church did not address various theological and ecclesiological issues. Disputes also grew due to various spiritual trends that passed not only through the Moravian Church but also through other churches. There was an influence of liberal attitudes from some pastors and subsequently the charismatic movement which addressed mainly the younger generation.

1998 Disputes over further direction of the
– Czech Province escalated. There was a
1999 conflict that resulted in a minority group

joining the Evangelical Church of Czech Brethren and a creation of the Herrnhut Seniorate within the church. The Herrnhut Seniorate gradually transformed into the mission province of the Moravian Church.
However, this chapter of the church's life will be objectively evaluated only by the historical view of future generations.

2000 At the time when the Moravian Church celebrated 300 years since the birth of Count Nicholas Ludwig Zinzendorf, the college of pastors went through a certain self-reflection and also sought a vision for the province. The vision was developed in the following years: *Following the example of our fathers, to build a church on an apostolic and prophetic foundation.*

2001 – 2002 The synods also formulated the mission of the church and set values that became binding for the whole province.

2003 17 November On the fourteenth anniversary of the fall of the communist dictatorship, the Czech Province concluded a Covenant of Loyalty with the Lord. It was inspired by the so-called *Agreement on the mountains of Rychnov* in 1464 and also by the Memorial Day of Repentance and Restoration on August 13, 1727. This Covenant of Loyalty eventually gave impetus to a gradual shift from the charismatic movement to preaching Christ crucified and risen. This emphasis began to be applied at various meetings of the church from the following year.

Educating new generation

Preaching Christ crucified is an integral part of what shaped the history of the Moravian Church. Without this inner understanding, the Moravian Church would never be able to make the personal commitment and sacrifices it has made. As a result, life of the church has always been renewing. Many generations found a new identity in Him, a new source of life.

"I am crucified with Christ: nevertheless I live; yet not I, but Christ lives in me: and the life which I now live in the flesh I live by the faith of the Son of God." Galatians 2:19-21
We were crucified with Him at the same time that He Himself was crucified for us because God put us in Him. The rule of our own ego, which was born independent of God, was ended through His cross.

For the Moravian Church, Christ crucified means that with His crucifixion, our crucifixion also took place. We have died with Christ and at the same time we are actively numbing our SELF. *"For you died... Therefore put to death your members which are on the earth..."* Colossians 3:3-5

Death is the end of existence. We die to ourselves, to our self-centeredness – to our ego. The passive form in Greek shows that it is something that happened to me undeservedly. Not what I did on my own, with my skills or abilities. It is a grace to die to oneself and to live a new life in Christ that is fruitful, joyful and bears the fruit of the Spirit (Galatians 5:22-23). The present generation rediscovers the power of this sermon on Christ crucified and risen. Thanks to this

| *Touring exhibition prepared for the 550th anniversary of the founding of the Moravian Church (2007)*

message, it began to discover its history and identity and also received an answer to a question, just like the generation that found itself in crisis after the Napoleonic Wars in the nineteenth century: *"Why does God still have us here?"*

2007 The Moravian Church celebrated the 550th anniversary in the presence of a number of statesmen, politicians and people from the state administration. The church prepared a touring exhibition under the auspices of the Senate President, Přemysl Sobotka, and the Minister of Culture, Martin Štěpánek. The exhibition traveled through 34 cities in the Czech Republic during the year. It met with a positive response everywhere and was inspiring for many. Thanks to this, the Moravian Church was able to establish relations with the state and the local administration, and it started a dialogue which led to further steps in cooperation in many places, whether in the field of education, prevention or social work. The Moravian Church thus proved that it is not a closed church, which only remembers its glorious history, but it lives today and is here for others.

On the occasion of the anniversary, the Czech Province published a brochure dealing with its current events and activities. The brochure was also available to all interested parties during the exhibition.

2008 In November, the Moravian Church began to think of Poland as its future mission field. Poland was a second

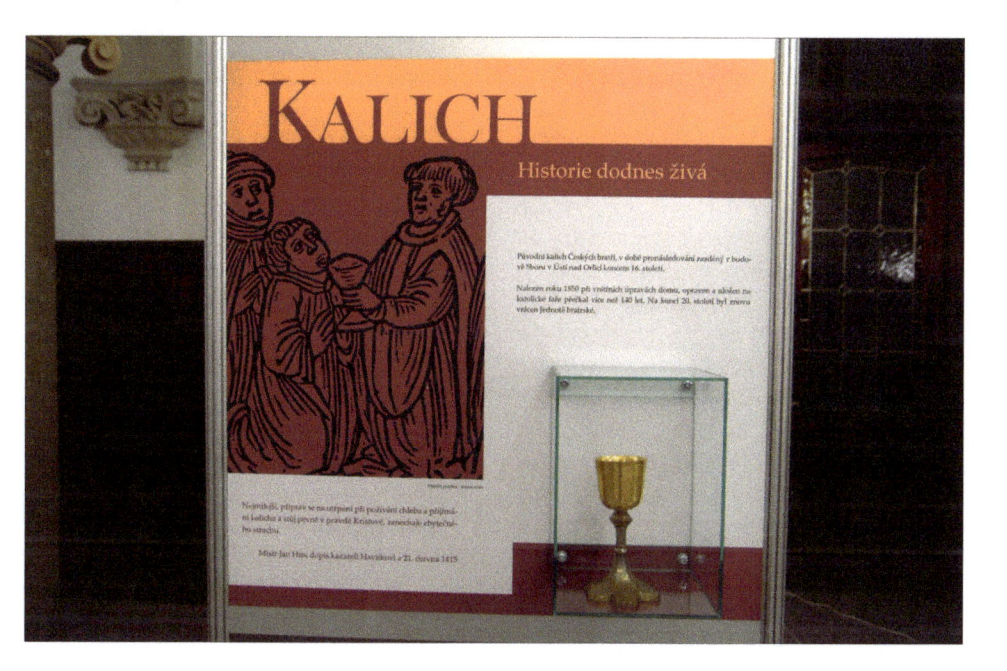

The original chalice from the sixteenth century from the church in Ústí nad Orlicí which was part of the exhibition

home not only for the Ancient Unity. In the 1840s, new Brethren villages were established on the territory of modern-day Upper and Lower Silesia (see Chapter II). One of them was founded in Nowa Sól (Neusalz). Brothers from the Provincial Board were visiting the town from 2009 negotiating with the local city and district administration (powiat). The town also saw the travelling exhibition on the history of the Moravian Church translated into Polish. Later, a young family moved to Nowa Sól to start a new ministry.

2009 Following the example of fathers, the Moravian Church in Czech Republic also adopted a threefold form of membership which expresses the depth of involvement of individual members in congregations and the understanding of life in church.

2011 28 March After more than forty years, two new bishops, Evald Rucký and Petr Krásný, were consecrated. Bishops Samuel Gray from the USA and Kingsley Lewis from Antigua came to carry out the consecration with participation of Paul Gardner from Jamaica, Chairman of the UF Unity Board. The consecration was also attended by representatives of the state administration – the first vice-president of the Senate, Přemysl Sobotka, Minister of Culture, Jiří Besser, and other important guests and representatives of the local administration. A year later, a third bishop, Jan Klas, was consecrated. The consecration was carried out by Bishops Samuel Gray, Evald Rucký and Petr Krásný. The third bishop was once again greeted by the Chair-

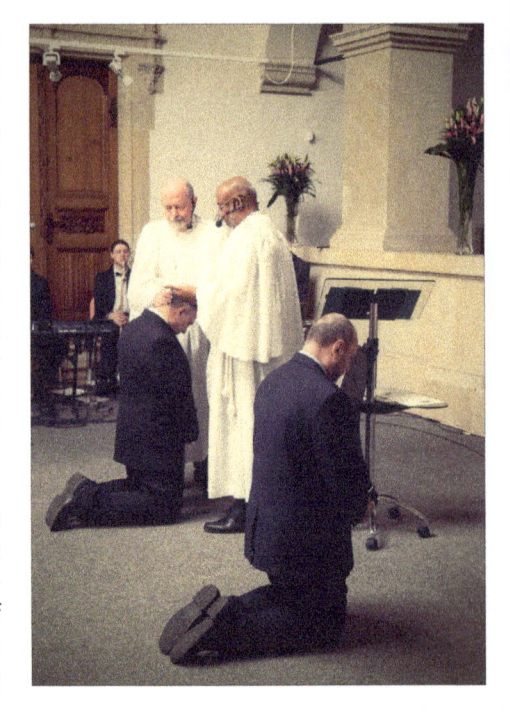

Bishops S. Gray and K. Lewis consecrate new bishops

man of the UF Unity Board, Paul Gardner from Jamaica.

2012 15 January A congregation called Nevo Dživipen (New Life) was established in Nové Město pod Smrkem. It is mainly a Roma church working on a mission in this ethnic group in the region. It is intended for those who are close to the Romani lifestyle or Romani culture; the church is the fruit of many years of work among the Roma people.

- **6 March** At the occasion of the 555th anniversary of the Moravian Church, the so-called *Study Day* dedicated to the legacy of the Moravian Church took place on the grounds of the Senate of the Czech Republic under the auspices of its

PART V

A solemn assembly in Liberec, during which E. Rucký and P. Krásný were consecrated as Bishops of the Unitas Fratrum (2011)

vice-president Přemysl Sobotka. Speakers presented historical personalities of the Moravian Church, its contribution to education, medicine and Czech language, as well as the previous and current mission work. Bishop Samuel Gray and Chairman of the Unity Board Paul Gardner took part in the event.

- **11 June** A jubilee synod was held in Rokytnice. The synod was to evaluate fulfilled goals and values of the vision of the church so far. This solemn synod highlighted the two highest virtues of the Moravian Church: meekness and obedience to God, with which all delegates of the synod unanimously agreed. This synod also approved the new Orders of the Czech Province, which among other things prepared conditions for the gradual economic self-sufficiency of the church independent of the state. The delegates of the synod hoped that the long-term injustice to the churches would be resolved in the near future with a restitution act.

- **8 November** The Parliament of the Czech Republic approved Act No. 428/2012 on property settlement with churches and religious societies. This law came into force on January 1, 2013. The so-called *original property* began to be returned to the churches. That property once belonged to churches, religious societies and ecclesiastical legal entities and they lost it as a result of property wrongs done by the regime in the period from February 25, 1948 to January 1, 1990. In addition to the return of specific items, on the basis of so-called *settlement agreements* between the state and individual

| *Bishop Petr Krásný and Prime Minister of the Czech Republic Petr Nečas signing the settlement agreement (2013)*

churches or religious societies, regular financial compensation is paid for thirty years, the total amount of which is determined by law. At the same time, the state contribution to the operation of churches and religious societies is gradually reduced. After seventeen years, the state will completely stop financing the operation of churches and this will lead to the definitive separation of church and state.

2013 The Moravian Church thus opens its new chapter. The current generation of ministers, unburdened by the past of communism or the post-revolutionary internal crisis of the church, is facing a new challenge. It must become economically self-sufficient. And not only for the sake of their congregations, but above all for the sake of many works that arose from these congregations thanks to twenty-five years of civil liberty.

So a generation otherwise unburdened by the past will eventually have to humble itself again and learn to rely entirely on the Chief Elder of the Moravian Church, Jesus Christ. He has been leading this church for more than 555 years. As its Shepherd, he took good care of it not only in ancient times of oppression and persecution, but also in the period of mission development in the eighteen century, when the church was without the support of other churches and relied only on Christ through its own church business with profits supporting the mission and social service. Why would he not take care of His church today if we are humble and obedient to His voice!

APPENDIX

APPENDIX

LIST OF UNITAS FRATRUM BISHOPS UNTIL 2014

Number	Name	Place of Consecration	Date	Consecrated by	He died
1	Matěj z Kunvaldu	Lhotka u Rychnova	1467		1500
2	Tůma Přeloučský	Prostějov	1499		1517
3	Eliáš z Chřenovic	Prostějov	1499		1503
4	Lukáš Pražský (Luke of Prague)	Rychnov nad Kněžnou	19. 4. 1500	Tůma z Přelouče, Eliáš z Chřenovic	1528
5	Ambrož ze Skutče	Rychnov nad Kněžnou	19. 4. 1500	Tůma z Přelouče, Eliáš z Chřenovic	1520
6	Martin Škoda		15. 8. 1517		1532
7	Václav Bílý	Brandýs nad Orlicí	21. 9. 1529		1533
8	Ondřej Ciklovský	Brandýs nad Orlicí	21. 9. 1529		1529
9	Jan Roh z Domažlic	Brandýs nad Orlicí	21. 9. 1529		1547
10	Jan Augusta		14. 4. 1532		1572
11	Beneš Bavoryňský		14. 4. 1532		1535
12	Vít Michalec		14. 4. 1532		1536
13	Martin Michalec		1537		1547
14	Mach Sionský		1537		1551
15	Jan Černý	Prostějov	8. 6. 1553	Matouš Strejc, Pavel Paulinus	1565
16	Matěj Červenka	Prostějov	8. 6. 1553	Matouš Strejc, Pavel Paulinus	1569
17	Jiří Izrael	Sležany	24. 8. 1557		1588
18	Jan Blahoslav	Sležany	24. 8. 1557		1571
19	Ondřej Štefan	Ivančice	11. 10. 1571		1577
20	Jan Kálef	Ivančice	11. 10. 1571		1588
21	Jan Lorenc	Ivančice	11. 10. 1571		1587
22	Zachariáš Litomyšlský	Holešov	30. 8. 1577		1590
23	Jan Eneáš Boleslavský	Holešov	30. 8. 1577		1594
24	Jan Abdiáš	Lipník na Moravě	1587		1588
25	Šimon Teofil Turnovský	Lipník na Moravě	1587		1608
26	Jan Efraim		5. 6. 1589		1600
27	Pavel Jessen (Jessenius)		5. 6. 1589		1594
28	Jakub Narcissus	Přerov	14. 7. 1594		1611
29	Jan Němčanský	Přerov	14. 7. 1594		1598
30	Samuel Sušický		6. 7. 1599		1599
31	Zachariáš Ariston		6. 7. 1599		1606
32	Jan Lanecius	Mladá Boleslav	? 11. 5. 1601		1626
33	Bartoloměj Němčanský	Mladá Boleslav	? 11. 5. 1601		1609

BISHOPS

#	Name	Date	Place	Consecrator(s)	Year
34	Jan Cruciger	1609			1612
35	Matěj Rybinski	1608	Lipník na Moravě		1612
36	Martin Gratianus	1608	Lipník na Moravě		1629
37	Matouš Konečný	1609			1622
38	Matěj Cyrus	1611			1618
39	Jan Turnovský	1612			1629
40	Jiří Erastus	1612			1643
41	Jan Cyrill Třebíčský	1618	Brandýs nad Labem		1632
42	Daniel Mikolajewski	6. 7. 1629	Leszno		1633
43	Pavel Paliurus	6. 7. 1629	Leszno		1632
44	Vavřinec Justýn	6. 10. 1632	Leszno	Jiří Erastus	1648
45	Matěj Prokop	6. 10. 1632	Leszno	Jiří Erastus	1636
46	John Amos Comenius	6. 10. 1632	Leszno	Jiří Erastus	1670
47	Pavel Fabricius	6. 10. 1632	Leszno	Jiří Erastus	1649
48	Martin Orminus	17. 4. 1633			1643 / 1644
49	Jan Rybinski	17. 4. 1633			1638
50	Martin Gertich	15. 4. 1644			1657
51	Jan Bythner	15. 4. 1644			1675
52	Mikuláš Gertich	5. 11. 1662	Milenczyn		1671
53	Petr Figulus Jablonský	5. 11. 1662	Milenczyn	Jan Bythner	1670
54	Adam Samuel Hartman	28. 10. 1673			1691
55	Jan Zugehör	13. 8. 1676			1698
56	Joachim Gulich	26. 6. 1692			1703
57	Daniel Ernest Jablonský	10. 3. 1699			1741
58	Jan Jakobides	10. 3. 1699			1709
59	Salomon Opitz	11. 7. 1712		Daniel Ernest Jablonský	1716
60	David Cassius	4. 11. 1712		Daniel Ernest Jablonský	1716
61	Paul Cassius	26. 2. 1725		Daniel Ernest Jablonský	?
62	Kristian Sitkovius	1734		Daniel Ernest Jablonský	1762

Numbering from 1735

#	Name	Date	Place	Consecrator(s)	Year
63 / 1	David Nitschmann	13. 3. 1735	Berlin	D. E. Jablonský, (K. Sitkovius)	1772
64 / 2	Mikuláš L. Zinzendorf	20. 5. 1738	Berlin	D. E. Jablonský, D. Nitschmann, (K. Sitkovius)	1760
65 / 3	Polycarp Müller	9. 7. 1740	Marienborn	D. Nitschmann, M. L. Zinzendorf	1747
66 / 4	Johann Nitschmann	22. 7. 1741	Herrnhaag	M. L. Zinzendorf, P. Müller	1772
67 / 5	Friedrich von Watteville	25. 8. 1743	Gnadeneck/Silesia	D. Nitzendorf, P. Müller	1777
68 / 6	Martin Dober	15. 6. 1744	Herrnhaag	M. L. Zinzendorf, P. Müller	1748
69 / 7	August G. Spangenberg	15. 6. 1744	Herrnhaag	M. L. Zinzendorf, P. Müller, D. Nitschmann, J. Nitschmann	1792

219

BISHOPS

70/8	David Nitschmann – syndikus	14. 6. 1746	Zeist / Netherlands	M. L. Zinzendorf, F. von Watteville	1779
71/9	Friedrich Wenzel Neisser	14. 6. 1746	Zeist	M. L. Zinzendorf, F. von Watteville	1761
72/10	Christian Frederick Steinhofer	14. 6. 1746	Zeist	M. L. Zinzendorf, F. von Watteville	1777
73/11	Joh. Frederick Cammerhof	25. 9. 1746	London	M. L. Zinzendorf, M. Dober, C. F. Steinhofer	1751
74/12	Johannes von Watteville	4. 6. 1747	Herrnhaag	M. L. Zinzendorf, D. Nitschmann, J. Nitschmann	1788
75/13	Johann Leonhard Dober	4. 6. 1747	Herrnhaag	M. L. Zinzendorf, D. Nitschmann, J. von Watteville, A. Spangenberg, P. Böhler	1766
76/14	Albert Anton Vierort	4. 6. 1747	Herrnhaag	M. L. Zinzendorf, M. Dober, C. F. Steinhofer	1761
77/15	Frederick Martin	10. 1. 1748	Herrnhaag	M. L. Zinzendorf, J. von Watteville, J. Nitschmann	1750
78/16	Peter Böhler	10. 1. 1748	Herrnhaag	M. L. Zinzendorf, J. von Watteville, J. Nitschmann	1775
79/17	Georg Waiblinger	6. 12. 1750	Herrnhut	J. von Watteville, L. Dober	1774 / 1775 ?
80/18	Matthew Hehl	24. 9. 1751	London	J. von Watteville, A. Spangenberg, P. Böhler	1787
81/19	John Gambold	14. 11. 1754	London	J. von Watteville, L. Dober, J. Nitschmann	1771
82/20	Andreas Grassmann	5. 7. 1756	Herrnhut	J. von Watteville, L. Dober, J. Nitschmann	1783
83/21	Johann Nitschmann ml.	12. 5. 1758	Herrnhut	M. L. Zinzendorf, J. von Watteville, L. Dober	1783
84/22	Nathanael Seidel	12. 5. 1758	Herrnhut	M. L. Zinzendorf, J. von Watteville, L. Dober	1782 / 1784 ?
85/23	Martin Mack	18. 10. 1770	Bethlehem / USA	D. Nitschmann, M. Hehl, N. Seidel	1784
86/24	Michael Graff	6. 6. 1773	Bethlehem	M. Hehl, N. Seidel	1782
87/25	Johann Friedrich Reichel	8. 10. 1775	Barby	J. von Watteville, A. Spangenberg, A. Grassmann	1809
88/26	Paul Eugene Layritz	8. 10. 1775	Barby	J. von Watteville, A. Spangenberg, A. Grassmann	1788
89/27	Philipp Heinrich Molther	8. 10. 1775	Barby	J. von Watteville, A. Spangenberg, A. Grassmann	1780
90/28	Heinrich von Bruiningk	2. 10. 1782	Herrnhut	J. von Watteville, A. Spangenberg, J. F. Reichel, P. Layritz	1785
91/29	Gottfried Clemens	2. 10. 1782	Herrnhut	J. von Watteville, A. Spangenberg, J. F. Reichel, P. Layritz	1788
92/30	Johann Jeremias Risler	2. 10. 1782	Herrnhut	J. von Watteville, A. Spangenberg, J. F. Reichel, P. Layritz	1811
93/31	George Traneker	14. 8. 1783	Zeist	J. von Watteville	1802
94/32	John Ettwein	25. 6. 1784	Bethlehem	J. von Watteville, M. Hehl	1802
95/33	Gustavus Ewald Schaukirch	25. 6. 1784	Bethlehem	J. von Watteville, J. Ettwein	1805
96/34	Burghard George Müller	11. 1. 1786	Herrnhut	A. Spangenberg, P. Layritz	1799
97/35	Christian Gregor	25. 8. 1789	Herrnhut	A. Spangenberg , J. F. Reichel, J. Risler	1801
98/36	Samuel Liebisch	25. 8. 1789	Herrnhut	A. Spangenberg , J. F. Reichel, J. Risler	1809
99/37	Jacob Christoph Duvernoy	25. 8. 1789	Herrnhut	A. Spangenberg , J. F. Reichel, J. Risler	1808
100/38	Christian David Rothe	25. 8. 1789	Herrnhut	A. Spangenberg , J. F. Reichel, J. Risler	1802
101/39	Johannes Andreas Hübner	11. 4. 1790	Bethlehem	J. Ettwein, (A. Spangenberg)	1809
102/40	John Daniel Koehler	9. 5. 1790	Lititz / USA	J. Ettwein, J. Hübner	1805
103/41	Thomas Moore	26. 8. 1801	Herrnhut	J. F. Reichel, S. Liebisch, J. Duvernoy	1823
104/42	Christian Salomon Dober	26. 8. 1801	Herrnhut	J. F. Reichel, S. Liebisch, J. Duvernoy	1827
105/43	Samuel Traugott Benade	13. 11. 1801	Fulneck / UK	G. Traneker, T. Moore	1830
106/44	Charles Gotthold Reichel	6. 12. 1801	Bethlehem	J. Ettwein, (J. Risler)	1825

BISHOPS

107 / 45	Georg Heinrich Loskiel	14. 3. 1802	Herrnhut	J. F. Reichel, S. Liebisch, J. Hübner	1814
108 / 46	Johann Gottfried Cunow	26. 12. 1808	Herrnhut	J. F. Reichel, S. Liebisch, J. Hübner	1824
109 / 47	Hermann Richter	26. 12. 1808	Herrnhut	J. F. Reichel, S. Liebisch, J. Hübner	1821
110 / 48	John Herbst	12. 5. 1811	Lititz	G. Loskiel, Ch. G. Reichel	1812
111 / 49	Lorenz Wilhadus Fabricius	24. 8. 1814	Herrnhut	C. S. Dober, J. Cunow, H. Richter	1825
112 / 50	Christian Gottlieb Hüffel	24. 8. 1814	Herrnhut	C. S. Dober, J. Cunow, H. Richter	1842
113 / 51	Carl August Baumeister	24. 8. 1814	Herrnhut	C. S. Dober, J. Cunow, H. Richter	1818
114 / 52	Johann Baptist von Albertini	24. 8. 1814	Herrnhut	C. S. Dober, J. Cunow, H. Richter	1831
115 / 53	Jacob van Vleck	7. 5. 1815	Bethlehem	Ch. G. Reichel, (J. Cunow)	1831
116 / 54	Gottlob Martin Schneider	2. 9. 1818	Herrnhut	J. Cunow, T. Moore, H. Richter	1849
117 / 55	Frederick William Foster	2. 9. 1818	Herrnhut	J. Cunow, T. Moore, H. Richter	1832 / 1835 ?
118 / 56	Benjamin Reichel	27. 9. 1818	Herrnhut	L. Fabricius, T. Moore, Ch. G. Reichel	1835
119 / 57	Andreas Benade	15. 9. 1822	Lititz	Ch. Hüffel, J. van Vleck	1859
120 / 58	Hans Wied	18. 8. 1825	Herrnhut	C. Baumeister, G. Schneider, F. Foster	1837
121 / 59	Johann Ludolf Fabricius	18. 8. 1825	Herrnhut	C. Baumeister, G. Schneider, F. Foster	1838
122 / 60	Peter Friedrich Curie	18. 8. 1825	Herrnhut	C. Baumeister, G. Schneider, F. Foster	1855
123 / 61	John Holmes	18. 8. 1825	Herrnhut	C. Baumeister, G. Schneider, F. Foster	1843
124 / 62	John Daniel Anders	26. 9. 1827	Herrnhut	J. von Albertini, H. Wied, P. Curie	1847
125 / 63	Frederick Louis Kölbing	13. 3. 1835	Herrnhut	Ch. Hüffel, H. Wied, P. Curie	1840
126 / 64	Johann Christian Bechler	17. 5. 1835	Lititz	J. Anders, A. Benade	1857
127 / 65	Charles August Pohlmann	5. 9. 1836	Herrnhut	P. Curie, H. Wied, J. Anders	1842
128 / 66	Hans Peter Hallbeck	5. 9. 1836	Herrnhut	P. Curie, H. Wied, J. Anders	1840
129 / 67	Jacob Levin Reichel	5. 9. 1836	Herrnhut	P. Curie, H. Wied, J. Anders	1853
130 / 68	Daniel Friedrich Gambs	5. 9. 1836	Herrnhut	P. Curie, H. Wied, J. Anders	1854
131 / 69	William Henry van Vleck	20. 11. 1836	Bethlehem	A. Benade, (J. Anders)	1853
132 / 70	John King Martyn	23. 12. 1836	Ockbrook / UK	Ch. Pohlmann, H. Hallbeck	1849
133 / 71	John Ellis	29. 12. 1836	Fulneck	J. Holmes, H. Hallbeck	1855
134 / 72	Johann Martin Nitschmann	17. 9. 1843	Herrnhut	P. Curie, H. Wied, J. Anders	1862
135 / 73	Christian Conrad Ultsch	17. 9. 1843	Herrnhut	P. Curie, H. Wied, J. Anders	1862
136 / 74	John Stengörd	17. 9. 1843	Herrnhut	P. Curie, H. Wied, J. Anders	1848
137 / 75	William Wisdom Essex	30. 3. 1844	Ockbrook	J. Martyn, (P. Curie)	1852
138 / 76	Peter Wolle	28. 9. 1845	Lititz	A. Benade, W. van Vleck	1871
139 / 77	John Gottlieb Hermann	27. 9. 1846	Herrnhut	P. Curie, L. J. Reichel, J. M. Nitschmann	1854
140 / 78	Benjamin Seifferth	26. 10. 1846	Ockbrook	J. Martyn, J. Hermann	1876
141 / 79	Christian Wilhelm Matthiesen	5. 9. 1848	Herrnhut	P. Curie, L. J. Reichel, W. van Vleck	1869
142 / 80	Franz Joachim Nielsen	5. 9. 1852	Herrnhut	J. M. Nitschmann, L. J. Reichel, Ch. Matthiesen	1867
143 / 81	John Rogers	19. 9. 1852	Ockbrook	B. Seifferth, J. Ellis	1862
144 / 82	Johann Christian Breutel	26. 6. 1853	Herrnhut	Ch. Matthiesen, P. Curie, J. Bechler	1875

BISHOPS

145 / 83	Heinrich Theodor Dober	26. 6. 1853	Herrnhut	Ch. Matthiesen, P. Curie, J. Bechler	1867
146 / 84	George Wall Westerby	5. 7. 1853	Fulneck	B. Seifferth, J. Rogers	1886
147 / 85	John Christian Jacobson	20. 9. 1854	Lititz	P. Wolle, (A. Benade)	1870
148 / 86	Gottfried Andreas Cunow	30. 8. 1857	Herrnhut	J. M. Nitschmann, Ch. Matthiesen, F. Nielsen	1866
149 / 87	William Edwards	30. 8. 1857	Herrnhut	J. M. Nitschmann, Ch. Matthiesen, F. Nielsen	1879
150 / 88	Carl Wilhelm Jahn	30. 8. 1857	Herrnhut	J. M. Nitschmann, Ch. Matthiesen, F. Nielsen	1858
151 / 89	Heinrich Rudolf Wullschlägel	30. 8. 1857	Herrnhut	J. M. Nitschmann, Ch. Matthiesen, F. Nielsen	1864
152 / 90	Samuel Reinke	3. 10. 1858	Lititz	P. Wolle, J. Jacobson	1875
153 / 91	George Frederick Bahnson	13. 5. 1860	Bethlehem	P. Wolle, J. Jacobson	1869
154 / 92	Ernst Friedrich Reichel	13. 7. 1862	Herrnhut	Ch. Matthiesen, G. Cunow, H. T. Dober	1878
155 / 93	Ernst Wilhelm Cröger	31. 8. 1862	Niesky	J. M. Nitschmann, Ch. Matthiesen, G. Cunow	1878
156 / 94	James La Trobe	18. 7. 1863	Ockbrook	W. Edwards, B. Seifferth	1897
157 / 95	David Bigler	31. 7. 1864	Bethlehem	S. Reinke, P. Wolle, J. Jacobson	1875
158 / 96	Henry August Schultz	31. 7. 1864	Bethlehem	S. Reinke, P. Wolle, J. Jacobson	1885
159 / 97	Gustav Theodor Tietzen	22. 4. 1866	Herrnhut	Ch. Matthiesen, E. F. Reichel, E. Cröger	1882
160 / 98	Levin Theodore Reichel	7. 7. 1869	Herrnhut	E. F. Reichel, J. La Trobe, G. Bahnson	1878
161 / 99	Augustus Clemens	7. 7. 1869	Herrnhut	E. F. Reichel, J. La Trobe, G. Bahnson	1874
162 / 100	Gustav Bernhard Müller	7. 7. 1869	Herrnhut	E. F. Reichel, J. La Trobe, G. Bahnson	1898 / 1899 ?
163 / 101	John England	7. 7. 1869	Herrnhut	E. F. Reichel, J. La Trobe, G. Bahnson	1895
164 / 102	Edmund A. de Schweinitz	28. 8. 1870	Bethlehem	D. Bigler, H. Schultz, A. Reinke, P. Wolle, J. Jacobson	1887
165 / 103	Amadeus Abraham Reinke	28. 8. 1870	Bethlehem	D. Bigler, H. Schultz, A. Reinke, P. Wolle, J. Jacobson	1889
166 / 104	Emil Adolphus de Schweinitz	11. 10. 1874	Salem / USA	H. Schultz, D. Bigler, E. de Schweinitz	1879
167 / 105	Johann Friedrich Wilhelm Kühn	7. 7. 1878	Herrnhut	G. Müller, G. Tietzen	1890
168 / 106	William Taylor	10. 7. 1878	Fairfield / UK	J. La Trobe, J. England, W. Edwards	1900
169 / 107	Heinrich Levin Reichel	29. 6. 1879	Herrnhut	G. Tietzen, J. England, E. de Schweinitz	1905
170 / 108	Heinrich Müller	29. 6. 1879	Herrnhut	G. Tietzen, J. England, E. de Schweinitz	1912
171 / 109	Theobald Wunderling	29. 6. 1879	Herrnhut	G. Tietzen, J. England, E. de Schweinitz	1893
172 / 110	Henry J. van Vleck	18. 9. 1881	Bethlehem	H. Schultz, A. Reinke, E. de Schweinitz	1906
173 / 111	Alexander Cossart Hassé	5. 7. 1883	Fulneck	J. La Trobe, W. Taylor	1894 / 1895 ?
174 / 112	Marc Théophile Richard	25. 6. 1888	Herrnhut	H. Müller, H. L. Reichel, T. Wunderling	1893 / 1894 ?
175 / 113	Konrad August Beck	25. 6. 1888	Herrnhut	H. Müller, H. L. Reichel, T. Wunderling	1908
176 / 114	Louis Theodor Erxleben	25. 6. 1888	Herrnhut	H. Müller, H. L. Reichel, T. Wunderling	1894
177 / 115	Hermann Friedrich Jahn	25. 6. 1888	Herrnhut	H. Müller, H. L. Reichel, T. Wunderling	1899
178 / 116	Clement Leander Reinke	30. 9. 1888	Bethlehem	A. Reinke, H. J. van Vleck	1922
179 / 117	Henry Theophilus Bachmann	30. 9. 1888	Bethlehem	A. Reinke, H. J. van Vleck	1896
180 / 118	Joseph Mortimer Levering	30. 9. 1888	Bethlehem	A. Reinke, H. J. van Vleck	1908
181 / 119	George Henry Hanna	31. 8. 1889	Bristol / UK	J. La Trobe, W. Taylor	1901
182 / 120	Benjamin Romig	3. 8. 1890	Herrnhut	H. Müller, M. Richard, K. Beck	1903

BISHOPS

183 / 121	Charles Edward Sutcliffe	7. 8. 1890	Ockbrook	J. La Trobe, W. Taylor, A. Hassé	1913
184 / 122	Edward Rondthaler	12. 4. 1891	Salem	H. J. van Vleck, H. Bachmann, J. Levering	1331
185 / 123	Henry Matthew Weiss	? 28. 5. 1891	Gracehill / Antigua	B. Romig	1895
186 / 124	Charles Buchner	21. 8. 1892	Herrnhut	H. Müller, B. Romig, K. Beck	1907
187 / 125	Henry Edwards Blandford	8. 8. 1894	Baildon / UK	W. Taylor, Ch. Sutcliffe	1899
188 / 126	Frederick Ellis	8. 8. 1894	Baildon	Ch. Sutcliffe, W. Taylor	1920
189 / 127	Hermann Otto Padel	28. 9. 1896	Herrnhut	H. Müller, B. Romig, Ch. Buchner	1906
190 / 128	Edmund Adolphus Oerter	18. 9. 1898	Lititz	C. L. Reinke, E. Rondthaler, J. Levering	1920
191 / 129	Charles L. Moench	18. 9. 1898	Lititz	C. L. Reinke, E. Rondthaler, J. Levering	1927
192 / 130	Reinhold Becker	30. 6. 1899	Herrnhut	K. Beck, H. Müller, E. Rondthaler	1929
193 / 131	Paul Leonhard Dober	30. 6. 1899	Herrnhut	K. Beck, H. Müller, E. Rondthaler	1917
194 / 132	Ernst Arved Senft	30. 6. 1899	Herrnhut	K. Beck, H. Müller, E. Rondthaler	1903
195 / 133	Friedrich Stähelin	22. 10. 1899	Herrnhut	Ch. Buchner, B. Romig, H. Padel	1922
196 / 134	Paul Otto Hennig	22. 10. 1899	Herrnhut	Ch. Buchner, B. Romig, H. Padel	1928
197 / 135	Ernest van Calker	22. 10. 1899	Herrnhut	Ch. Buchner, B. Romig, H. Padel	1929
198 / 136	Albert Martin	22. 10. 1899	Herrnhut	Ch. Buchner, B. Romig, H. Padel	1934
199 / 137	Edwin Carpenter Greider	27. 6. 1900	Nazareth / USA	E. Oerter, J. Levering, Ch. Moench	1933
200 / 138	John Herbert Edwards	16. 10. 1900	London	F. Ellis, Ch. Sutcliffe	1906
201 / 139	Benjamin La Trobe	25. 2. 1901	Herrnhut	Ch. Buchner, B. Romig, H. Padel	1917
202 / 140	Peter Larsen	18. 4. 1901	Springfield / Jamaica	E. Greider	1904
203 / 141	August H. Berkenhagen	19. 11. 1902	Salem	E. Rondthaler, J. Levering, E. Oerter	1931
204 / 142	August Westphal	27. 9. 1903	Bethlehem	J. Levering, Ch. Moench, E. Oerter	1939
205 / 143	Evelyn Renatus Hassé	4. 8. 1904	Horton / UK	F. Ellis, Ch. Sutcliffe, J. Edwards	1918
206 / 144	John Taylor Hamilton	19. 2. 1905	Herrnhut	Ch. Buchner, B. La Trobe, H. Müller	1951
207 / 145	Hermann Theodor Bauer	4. 6. 1905	Herrnhut	R. Becker, P. L. Dober, B. La Trobe	1919
208 / 146	Hermann Walter Reichel	4. 6. 1905	Herrnhut	R. Becker, P. L. Dober, B. La Trobe	1924
209 / 147	Paul Adolf Asmussen	13. 6. 1907	Dublin / Ireland	E. Hassé, F. Ellis	1939
210 / 148	Morris William Leibert	13. 9. 1908	Lititz	E. Oerter, C. L. Reinke, E. Rondthaler, Ch. Moench	1919
211 / 149	Karl Anton Mueller	13. 9. 1908	Lititz	E. Oerter, C. L. Reinke, E. Rondthaler, Ch. Moench	1962
212 / 150	Clement Hoyler	13. 9. 1908	Lititz	E. Oerter, C. L. Reinke, E. Rondthaler, Ch. Moench	1957
213 / 151	Paul Marx	14. 8. 1911	Herrnhut	P. L. Dober, H. Bauer, P. Hennig	1945
214 / 152	Richard Voullaire	14. 8. 1911	Herrnhut	P. L. Dober, H. Bauer, P. Hennig	1944
215 / 153	Herbert Russell Mumford	28. 10. 1914	London	E. Hassé, M. Asmussen	1937
216 / 154	John Edwin Zippel	8. 8. 1919	Fulneck	H. Mumford, M. Asmussen, J. Hamilton	1936
217 / 155	Arthur Ward	8. 8. 1919	Fulneck	J. Hamilton, M. Asmussen, H. Mumford	1935
218 / 156	Paul Theodor Jensen	22. 5. 1922	Herrnhut	H. W. Reichel, P. Marx, P. Hennig	1938
219 / 157	Leonhard A. Bourquin	22. 5. 1922	Herrnhut	H. W. Reichel, P. Marx, P. Hennig	1931
220 / 158	Theodor Marx	22. 5. 1922	Herrnhut	H. W. Reichel, P. Marx, P. Hennig	1963

BISHOPS

221 / 159	John Emanuel Weiss	16. 5. 1924	St. John´s / Antigua	E. Greider, A. Ward	1936
222 / 160	Guido Grossmann	21. 6. 1925	Bethlehem	E. Rondthaler, Ch. Moench, E. Greider, K. Mueller, C. Hoyler, P. Jensen	1945
223 / 161	Hermann Georg Steinberg	11. 5. 1926	Herrnhut	P. Hennig, Th. Marx, P. Jensen	1945
224 / 162	Friedrich Eugen Peter	20. 2. 1927	Kleinwelka	P. Hennig, A. Berkenhagen, A. Martin	1958
225 / 163	Richard Johannes Marx	17. 5. 1928	Herrnhut	Th. Marx, P. Marx, E. van Calker	1947
226 / 164	Samuel Libbey Connor	5. 7. 1928	London	H. Mumford, J. Zippel, A. Ward	1956
227 / 165	Samuel Baudert	7. 4. 1929	Herrnhut	Th. Marx, E. van Calker, R. Voullaire	1940
228 / 166	Edward Shober Crosland	19. 6. 1930	Bethlehem	J. Hamilton, K. Mueller, C. Hoyler	1967
229 / 167	John Kenneth Pfohl	26. 4. 1931	Winston-Salem / USA	J. Hamilton, E. Greider, E. Crosland	1959
230 / 168	Felix Oskar Gemuseus	21. 8. 1932	Herrnhut	S. Baudert, Th. Marx, G. Grossmann	1957
231 / 169	Clarence Harvey Shawe	16. 10. 1934	London	H. Mumford, J. Zippel, S. Connor	1938
232 / 170	Nils Hansen Gaarde	23. 2. 1936	Horton	S. Connor, H. Mumford, A. Shawe	1940
233 / 171	Paul de Schweinitz	14. 3. 1937	Bethlehem	J. Hamilton, K. Mueller, J. Pfohl	1959
234 / 172	John Henry Blandford	20. 10. 1937	Bristol	S. Connor, P. Asmussen, A. Shawe	
235 / 173	Walter Vivian Moses	10. 5. 1942	Bethlehem	J. Hamilton, C. Hoyler, J. Pfohl	1962
236 / 174	Samuel Henry Gapp	10. 5. 1942	Bethlehem	J. Hamilton, C. Hoyler, J. Pfohl	1967
237 / 175	John Kneale	4. 10. 1942	Bethlehem	J. Hamilton, J. Pfohl, S. Gapp, W. Moses	1961
238 / 176	Herbert Pearce Connor	19. 5. 1943	Kingston / Jamaica	J. Kneale	1963
239 / 177	George William M. MacLeavy	4. 7. 1944	Bristol	J. Blandford, S. Connor, A. Shawe	1978
240 / 178	Soeren Haahr Ibsen	26. 6. 1946	London	S. Connor, S. Gapp, J. Blandford, A. Shawe	1952
241 / 179	Václav Vančura	20. 7. 1946	Mladá Boleslav	A. Shawe, S. MacLeavy, S. Gapp	1957 / 1975 ?
242 / 180	Kenneth Gardiner Hamilton	16. 2. 1947	Bethlehem	S. Gapp, J. Pfohl, K. Mueller	1981
243 / 181	Immanuel Richard Mewaldt	6. 4. 1947	Watertown / USA	K. Mueller, S. Gapp, C. Hoyler	1976
244 / 182	Willy Senft	21. 8. 1947	Herrnhut	S. Baudert, G. MacLeavy, F. Gemuseus	
245 / 183	Johannes Christian Vogt	21. 9. 1947	Winston-Salem	Th. Marx, F. Gemuseus, (Hahn – Bishop of Saxon Church)	1956
246 / 184	Howard Edward Rondthaler	11. 1. 1948	Winston-Salem	J. Pfohl, W. Moses, K. G. Hamilton	1970
247 / 185	Karel Reichel	1. 3. 1948	Ústí nad Orlicí	V. Vančura, (presbyteři J. Korbel a P. Glos)	1999
248 / 186	Paul Willibald Schaberg	19. 9. 1948	Königsfeld	S. Baudert, H. Steinberg, (presbyter K. Krüger)	1953 / 1954 ?
249 / 187	Johannes Raillard	22. 5. 1949	Basel / Switzerland	W. Senft	1981
250 / 188	Peter Madson Gubi	10. 4. 1951	St. John´s	K. G. Hamilton, (S. Gapp, J. Kneale)	1952
251 / 189	Walther Baudert	21. 10. 1951	Niesky	J. Vogt, Th. Marx, F. Gemuseus	1953
252 / 190	Paul Gerhard Reichel	18. 11. 1951	Neuwied	A. Shawe, W. Senft, H. Steinberg	1972
253 / 191	Carl John Helmich	27. 4. 1952	Lititz	S. Gapp, J. Pfohl, I. Mewaldt	1982
254 / 192	Ernest Walter Porter	4. 10. 1955	Bristol	H. P. Connor, J. Blandford, G. MacLeavy, (presbyter F. E. Birtill)	1959 ?
255 / 193	Edmund Paul Schwarze	30. 12. 1956	Winston-Salem	J. Pfohl, K. G. Hamilton, C. Helmich	1980
256 / 194	Elmo Knudsen	18. 8. 1957	Bethlehem	E. Porter, H. Steinberg, E. Schwarze	1992
257 / 195	Theodor Siebörger	27. 4. 1959	Bad Boll	J. Vogt, E. Knudsen, (presbyter E. Marx)	

224

BISHOPS

258 / 196	Walther Herbert Spaugh	27.12.1959	Charlotte / USA	J. Pfohl, K. G. Hamilton, C. Helmich, (W. Moses)		1964
259 / 197	Adolf Hartmann	19. 6. 1960	Mvenyane / S. Africa	S. Ibsen, P. Schaberg, (presbyter W. Bourquin)		1971
260 / 198	Frederick Wolff	8. 10. 1961	Lake Mills / USA	I. Mewaldt, K. G. Hamilton, C. Helmich		1991
261 / 199	Selwin U. Hastings	11. 10. 1961	Kingston	E. Porter, C. Helmich, W. Spaugh		1997
262 / 200	Allen W. Schattschneider	5. 11. 1961	New Dorp / USA	C. Helmich, K. G. Hamilton, I. Mewaldt		1980
263 / 201	Rudolf E. C. Doth	11. 2. 1962	Paramaribo / Nicar.	H. Steinberg, S. Hastings, (presbyter V. Müller)		1987
264 / 202	Hedley Ewart Wilson	25. 3. 1962	Bilwaskarma / Nicar.	K. G. Hamilton, W. Spaugh, S. Hastings		1999
265 / 203	John Humphrey Foy	30. 9. 1964	London	E. Porter, J. Kneale, E. Knudsen		1994
266 / 204	George G. Higgins	?1. 1. 1966	Winston-Salem	W. Spaugh, K. G. Hamilton, C. Helmich		
267 / 205	Sigurd Nielsen	7. 7. 1966	Mvenyane	P. Schaberg, (presbyteři W. Dube a H. Motel)		2002
268 / 206	Edwin Wunderly Kortz	23. 10. 1966	Bethlehem	K. G. Hamilton, C. Helmich, A. Schattschneider		1977
269 / 207	Edward Wilde	13. 11. 1966	Wisconsin / USA	I. Mewaldt, F. Wolff, E. Kortz		2007
270 / 208	Percival R. Henkelmann	20. 11. 1966	Edmonton / Canada	F. Wolff, (I. Mewaldt, K. G. Hamilton)		1982
271 / 209	Teofilo Hiyobo Kisanji	27. 11. 1966	Tabora / Tanzania	S. Ibsen, J. Foy		2002
272 / 210	Adolf Ulrich	25. 6. 1967	Holešov	K. Reichel, (presbyters J. Korbel, J. Niebauer)		1983
273 / 211	Samuel Jones Tesch	12. 12. 1968	Winston-Salem	K. G. Hamilton, W. Spaugh, G. Higgins		1997
274 / 212	Bernhard Krüger	13. 7. 1969	Genadendaal / S. Africa	P. Schaberg, S. Nielsen, (P. Pakendorf a R. Rapoo – Lutheran)		2005
275 / 213	G. Oliver Maynard	17. 7. 1969	St. John's / Antigua	E. Kortz, P. Gubi, S. Hastings		
276 / 214	Milo Alvin Loppnow	4. 10. 1970	Lake Mills / USA	I. Mewaldt, F. Wolff, (K. G. Hamilton)		1989
277 / 215	James Gordon Weingarth	25. 10. 1970	Bethlehem	K. G. Hamilton, F. Wolff, E. Wilde, M. Loppnow		1978
278 / 216	Günther Hasting	6. 12. 1970	Herrnhut	J. Vogt, A. Ulrich, (presbyter E. Förster)		2003
279 / 217	Wilbur William Behrend	10. 11. 1974	Wisconsin	E. Kortz, J. Weingarth, M. Loppnow, E. Wilde		
280 / 218	James C. Hughes	17. 11. 1974	Lititz	E. Kortz, K. G. Hamilton, J. Weingarth, A. Schattschneider		1990
281 / 219	John Knight	12. 10. 1975	Antigua	S. Hastings, E. Kortz, H. Wilson		1980
282 / 220	August Wilhelm Habelgaam	17. 10. 1976	Landsdowne / S. Africa	B. Krüger, S. Nielsen, P. Schaberg, (A. Bruhnke, P. B. Mhlungu)		2005
283 / 221	Joseph Henry Cooper	10. 11. 1976	Belfast / UK	J. Foy, P. Gubi, E. Porter		1986
284 / 222	Edward T. Mickey	5. 6. 1977	Winston-Salem	W. Spaugh, G. Higgins, S. Tesch		
285 / 223	Hellmut Reichel	26. 6. 1977	Königsfeld	T. Siebörger, B. Krüger, A. Ulrich, G. Hastings, E. Knudsen, S. Ibsen, P. Schaberg		
286 / 224	John Franklin Wilson	14. 8. 1977	Bluefields / Nicaragua	H. Wilson, J. Knight		
287 / 225	Anosisye Jongo	29. 7. 1979	Rungwe / Tanzania	T. Kisanji, H. Reichel, (presbyter Msinjili)		1981
288 / 226	Theodor Gill	2. 3. 1980	Herrnhut	H. Reichel, T. Siebörger, A. Ulrich		
289 / 227	Joseph R. Kalindimya	27. 4. 1980	Tabora / Tanzania	T. Kisanji, A. Jongo, (E. Eweka – luter., A. Mohamed – Anglican)		2000
290 / 228	Clayton H. Persons	15. 6. 1980	Winston-Salem	S. Tesch, G. Higgins, E. Kortz, E. Mickey		1988
291 / 229	Albert Andreas Cloete	16. 11. 1980	Bridgetown / S. Africa	S. Nielsen, P. Schaberg, (P. Rapoo a Hart – Lutheran)		2005
292 / 230	Guillaume Emile E. Polanen	30. 11. 1980	Paramaribo	S. Hastings, J. Knight		1982
293 / 231	Emile Cornelis Ritfeld	30. 11. 1980	Paramaribo	J. Knight, S. Hastings		
294 / 232	Geoffrey Edward Birtill	27. 10. 1982	Fulneck	J. Foy, J. Cooper, T. Gill, (K. Woollcombe – Anglican		2004

225

BISHOPS

#	Name	Date	Place	Consecrators	Year
295 / 233	Stanley Fitz-Roy Thomas	14. 11. 1982	New Dorp / USA	M. Loppnow	2008
296 / 234	Stephen Mwakasyuka	9. 1. 1983	Rungwe	J. Kalindimya, H. Reichel, (Mwakagali – Lutheran)	2009
297 / 235	Neville S. Neil	16. 1. 1983	St. Elizabeth / Jamaica	G. Hastings, J. Knight, A. Schattschneider, S. Thomas	2014
298 / 236	Jacob Nelson	13. 3. 1983	Bethel / Alaska	W. Behrend, M. Loppnow, (C. Harris)	1999
299 / 237	Yohana Wavenza	24. 7. 1983	Mbeya / Tanzania	T. Gill, (Ch. Mwaigoga – angl.)	1991
300 / 238	A. A. Breeveld	20. 11. 1983	Paramaribo	J. Knight, N. Neil, E. Ritfeld	
301 / 239	Johannes Jacobus Ulster	18. 11. 1984	Mamre / S. Africa	S. Nielsen, P. Schaberg	
302 / 240	Victor N. Mazwi	17. 2. 1985	Mvenyane	J. Ulster, S. Nielsen	2005
303 / 241	Edwin A. Sawyer	14. 9. 1986	Bethlehem	W. Behrend, E. Kortz, A. Schattschneider, J. Weingarth	
304 / 242	Warren A. Sautebin	5. 10. 1986	Wisconsin	W. Behrend, M. Loppnow, J. Weingarth	2014
305 / 243	Henning Schlimm	31. 1. 1988	Bern / Switzerland	H. Reichel, B. Krüger, T. Gill, (T. Siebörger, P. Schaberg)	
306 / 244	Walter Navarro Allen	28. 10. 1988	Cocobila / Honduras	J. Wilson, S. Thomas	1989
307 / 245	Emmanuel Martin Temmers	30. 10. 1988	Capetown / S. Africa	J. Ulster, A. Cloete, V. Mazwi, (N. Rohwer – Lutheran)	
308 / 246	Robert A. Iobst	14. 5. 1989	New Philadelphia / USA	G. Higgins, J. Hughes, J. Wilson	2012
309 / 247	Arthur James Freeman	11. 11. 1990	Bethlehem	E. Kortz, E. Sawyer, A. Schattschneider, G. Higgins, S. Thomas	2013
310 / 248	Paul A. Graf	5. 5. 1991		W. Sautebin, M. Loppnow, E. Sawyer	
311 / 249	Burton Jones Rights	7. 6. 1992	Clemmons / USA	G. Higgins, J. Hughes, R. Iobst	2000
312 / 250	Neville Brown	11. 11. 1993	Antigua	S. Thomas, N. Neil, J. Wilson	
313 / 251	Robert Godfrey Foster	11. 9. 1994	Mandeville / Jamaica	N. Neil, N. Brown, G. Birtill, J. Wilson	2015
314 / 252	Isaac Robert Nicodemo	18. 9. 1994	Tabora	E. Temmers, J. Kalindimya, S. Mwakasyuka, Y. Wavenza	
315 / 253	Alexander Theodor Darnoud	4. 12. 1994	Paramaribo	E. Ritfeld, H. Schlimm	
316 / 254	Graham H. Rights	16. 7. 1996		B. Rights, J. Hughes, R. Iobst, J. Wilson	
317 / 255	Theodor Clemens	17. 11. 1996	Berlin	T. Gill, E. Ritfeld	
318 / 256	Lusekelo B. Mwakafwila	28. 9. 1997	Rungwe	G. Birtill, S. Mwakasyuka, I. Nicodemo, Y. Wavenza	
319 / 257	Stanley Goff	26. 10. 1997	Brus Laguna / Honduras	R. Iobst, J. Wilson	
320 / 258	C. Hopeton Clennon	25. 10. 1998	Schoeneck / USA	S. Thomas, E. Sawyer, N. Neil, W. Sautebin	2002
321 / 259	Kay Ward	1. 11. 1998	Lititz	M. Loppnow, P. Graf, E. Kortz	
322 / 260	Kingsley Lewis	13. 11. 1999	Antigua	N. Brown, R. Foster, S. Thomas	
323 / 261	William Webster	6. 5. 2001	Puerto Cabezas / Nicar.	J. Wilson, G. Rights	
324 / 262	Walter Oliver Hodgson	13. 5. 2001	Bluefields	J. Wilson, G. Rights, W. Webster	
325 / 263	Alinikisa Cheyo	12. 8. 2001	Mbeya	L. Mwakafwila, T. Clemens, I. Nicodemo, S. Mwakasyuka	
326 / 264	Bernhard Ch. Petersen Lottring	21. 10. 2002	Eluyengweni / S. Africa	E. Temmers, A. Cloete, J. Ulster	
327 / 265	Eagle Mzuvelile Ndabambi	7. 7. 2002	Winston-Salem	E. Temmers, A. Cloete, B. Lottring, V. Mazwi, S. Nielsen, J. Ulster	
328 / 266	Lane Sapp	16. 9. 2001	Mamre	G. Rights, R. Iobst, J. Hughes	
329 / 267	Jonas David Kasitu	14. 7. 2002	Sumbawanga / Tanz.	I. Nicodemo, T. Clemens, L. Mwakafwila, S. Mwakasyuka, A. Cheyo	
330 / 268	D. Wayne Burkette	21. 7. 2002	Winston-Salem	G. Rights, K. Ward, J. Hughes	
331 / 269	John McOwat	21. 9. 2002	Fulneck	J. Cooper, G. Birtill, T. Gill	
332 / 270	Douglas H. Kleintop	13. 10. 2002	Palmer Township / USA	W. Behrend, W. Sautebin, E. Sawyer, S. Thomas	

BISHOPS

333 / 271	M. Blair Couch	Bethlehem	3. 11. 2002	E. Sawyer, K. Ward
334 / 272	John Kent	Paramaribo	2. 2. 2003	T. Darnoud, E. Ritfeld, R. Foster
335 / 273	Humbert Hessen	Zeist	21. 11. 2004	H. Schlimm, J. Kent, J. McOwat
336 / 274	Errol Sydney Moos	Port Elizabeth / S. Africa	5. 12. 2004	B. Lottring, E. Temmers, E. Ndabambi, J. Ulster, A. Cloete
337 / 275	Samuel Gray	Winston-Salem	25. 6. 2006	G. Rights, M. Couch, C. Clennon
338 / 276	Elizabeth Torkington	Oxford / UK	2. 12. 2006	J. McOwat, T. Clemens
339 / 277	Wincap Cassy	Honduras	14. 1. 2007	S. Gray, C. Clennon
340 / 278	Stanley G Clarke	Kingstown / Jamaica	16. 9. 2007	
341 / 279	William Nicholson	Anchorage / Alaska	4. 5. 2008	A. Freeman, J. Nelson
342 / 280	Volker Schulz	Basel	17. 10. 2010	H. Schlimm, T. Clemens, E. Torkington , J. McOwat
343 / 281	Chris Giesler	Bethlehem	13. 11. 2010	
344 / 282	Frieder Waas	Herrnhut	14. 11. 2010	T. Clemens, T. Gill, H. Hessen
345 / 283	Evald Rucký	Liberec	28. 3. 2011	S. Gray, K. Lewis
346 / 284	Petr Krásný	Liberec	28. 3. 2011	S. Gray, K. Lewis
347 / 285	Jan Klas	Praha	4. 3. 2012	S. Gray, E. Rucký, P. Krásný
348 / 286	C. M. Tschimanga	Dar Es Salaam / Tanz.		L. Mwakafila, J. Kasitu
349 / 287	Peter Green	Bethel	26. 5. 2013	S. Gray, J. Nelson
350 / 288	Augustine Joemath	Landsdowne / S Africa	16. 6. 2013	E. Temmers
351 / 289	Lennox Mcubusi	S. Africa	7. 7. 2013	E. Ndabambi
352 / 290	Sithembiso Ngqakayi	Johannesburg / S. Africa	4. 8. 2013	E. Moos
353 / 291	Evelio Romero	Brus Laguna / Honduras	18. 8. 2013	O. Hodgson, K. Lewis
354 / 292	Sandoval Maetinez	Honduras	13. 10. 2013	K. Lewis, W. Webster
355 / 293	Conrad Nguvumali	Sumbawanga/Tanz.	25. 5. 2014	A. Cheyo, I. Nicodemo
356 / 294	Joachim Kreussel	London	29. 11. 2014	J. McOvat, V. Schulz, F. Wass

The accuracy of some of the data shown is not guaranteed due to different sources.

BIBLIOGRAPHY

Publications and Brochures

Bartoš, František M.: *Biskupství v Jednotě bratrské*, Praha 1944.

Bidlo, Jaroslav: *Akty Jednoty bratrské*, Brno 1915.

Bílek, Jakub: *Jan Augusta v letech samoty 1548–1564*, Praha 1942.

Bray, John: *A History of the Moravian Church in India*, The Himalayan Mission, Leh 1985.

Brown, M. T.: *Jan Blahoslav – humanista, filolog, muzikolog, Boží muž*, Praha 2010.

Dworzaczkowa, Jolanta: *Bracia czescy w Wielkopolsce w XVI i XVII wieku*, Wydawnictwo Naukowe Semper 2001.

Glos, Pavel: *Misie Františka Chlebouna*, KEBF 1995.

Hamilton J. Taylor und Kenneth G.: *Die Erneuerte Unitas fratrum 1722–1957*, Band I, Herrnhuter Verlag 2001.

Hamilton J. Taylor und Kenneth G.: *Die Erneuerte Unitas fratrum 1722–1957*, Band II, Herrnhuter Verlag 2003.

Hrejsa, Ferdinad: *Sborové Jednoty bratrské*, Praha 1939.

Hrejsa, Ferdinad; Bednář, František a Hromádka J. L.: *Zásady Jednoty českých bratří*, Praha 1939.

Hýbl, František a Szymańska, Kamila: *Jan Amos Komenský a Polsko*, Leszno 2009.

Jednota bratrská, knížka o vzniku, učení, řádech a zřízení, Úzká rada 1947.

Kalfus, Radim: *Jednota bratrská v obrazech 1457–1957*, Praha 1957.

Kaňák, Miloslav: *Význačné postavy Jednoty bratrské a jejich dílo*, Praha 1957.

Karczyńska, Helena: *Odnowiona Jednota Braterska w XVIII-XX wieku*, Wydawnictwo Naukowe Semper 2012.

Knihovna Bratrských listův IX.: *Obrazy z dějin Jednoty bratrské*, díl druhý, Praha 1911.

Knižnice Biblické Jednoty, číslo 2.: *Česká emigrace v Polsku a na Volyni*, Brno 1924.

BIBLIOGRAPHY

Komenský, Jan Amos: *Smutný hlas zaplašeného hněvem Božím pastýře k rozplašenému, hynoucímu stádu, ostatní již rady dáním se všemi se žehnající*, Vyškov 1946.

Kumpera, Jan: *Jednota bratrská – Odkaz evropské duchovní kultuře*, 555. výročí vzniku (1457–2011), Plzeň 2012.

Kybal, Vlastimil: *M. Matěj z Janova. Jeho život, spisy a učení*, Brno 2000.

Loula, David: *Studna lásky k pravdě*, Praha 2012.

Loula, David: *České studny aneb hloubání o české identitě*, Praha 2007.

Malínský, František: *Život Jana Blahoslava – jubilejní vzpomínka*, Praha 1923.

Mannsbart, Claus: *David Nitschmann. První biskup obnovené Jednoty bratrské*, Suchdol nad Odrou 1995.

Molnár, Amedeo: *Boleslavští bratří*, Praha 1952.

Molnár, Amedeo: *Bratr Lukáš bohoslovec Jednoty*, Praha 1948.

Molnár, Amedeo: *Českobratrská výchova před Komenským*, Praha 1956.

Molnár, Amedeo: *Čeští bratří a Martin Bucer, Listy kritického přátelství*, Praha 1972.

Müller, J. Th.: *O souvislosti obnovené církve bratrské se starou Jednotou bratří českých*, Český Hus 1885.

Müller, J. Th. a Bartoš, F. M.: *Dějiny Jednoty bratrské I*, Praha 1923.

Müller, Karl: *200 Jahre Brüdermission, I. Band*, Herrnhut 1931.

Niebauer, Jan: *August Gottlieb Spangenberg biskup obnovené Jednoty*, 1980.

Padesát zastavení. Jednota bratrská 1457–1957, určeno pro vnitřní potřebu Kostnické jednoty, 1957.

Pěnčík, Josef: *Prsten věrnosti*, Třebíč 2008.

Přeloučský, Tůma: *O původu Jednoty bratrské a o chudých lidech*, Praha 1947.

Reichel, Hellmut: *David Nitschmann Syndikus a první archivář Jednoty bratrské*, Suchdol nad Odrou 2003.

Rokyta, Jan: *Doba a dílo Petra Chelčického*, Brno 2013.

Říčan, Daniel: *David Zeisberger – Apoštol indiánů*, Suchdol nad Odrou 2008.

Říčan, Gustav Adolf: *Moravští bratři ze Suchdolu*, Suchdol 2012.

Říčan, Rudolf: *Dějiny Jednoty bratrské*, Praha 1957.

Říčan, Rudolf; Molnár, Amedeo a Flegl, Michal: *Bratrský sborník. Soupis prací přednesených při symposiu konaném 26. a 27. září 1967 k pětistému výročí ustavení Jednoty bratrské*, Praha 1967.

Říčan, R.; Bartoš, F. M.; Molnár, A.; Smolík, J.; Čapek, J. B.; Ďurďovič J. P. a Hromádka, J. L.: *Jednota bratrská 1457–1957. Sborník k pětistému výroční založení*, Praha 1956.

Schiller, Jindřich: *Vypravujme si o obnovené Jednotě*, Železný Brod 1945.

Schulze, Adolf: *200 Jahre Brüdermission, II. Band*, Herrnhut 1931.

Smolík, Josef: *Bratr Jan Augusta*, Praha 1984.

Srba, Ondřej: *David Schneider 1693–1755*, Suchdol nad Odrou 2006.

Szymańska, Kamila: *Bracia Czescy w Lesznie Przewodnik po zbiorach Muzeum Okręgovego w Lesznie*, Leszno 2007.

Štěříková, Edita: *Jak potůček v jezeře. Moravané v obnovené Jednotě bratrské v 18. století*, Praha 2009.

Štěříková, Edita: *Christian David zakladatel obnovené Jednoty bratrské*, Suchdol nad Odrou 2008.

Štěříková, Edita: *Matouš Stach moravský misionář v Grónsku*, Suchdol nad Odrou 2012.

Vacovský, Adolf: *Obnovení Jednoty bratrské v zemi otců*, (v rámci časopisu JB), ÚR Jednoty bratrské 1997.

Weinlick, John R.: *Hrabě Zinzendorf*, Jindřichův Hradec 2000.

Moravian Church materials
The Moravian Church: *Handbook for Bishops*, Unity Board 1996.

The Moravian Church: *Church Order of The Unitas Fratrum*, Unity Synod, Hoddesdon 2009.

Magazines
Bratrské listy. Ročníky 16 a 17, Praha 1910 a 1911.
Jednota bratrská (roky 1921–1986)

Synod materials
Verhandlungen des Synodus der evangelischen Brüder-Unität 1836, Gnadau, 1838.

Verlass des Synodus der evangelischen Brüder-Unität 1848, Gnadau 1848.

Verlass der Allgemeinden Synode der Brüder-Unität 1857, Gnadau 1857.

Verlass des Allgemeinden Synode der Brüder-Unität 1879, Gnadau 1880.

Verlass der General Synode der Evangelischen Brüder-Unittät, Gnadau 1914.

Synodal materials and minutes from General and Unity Synods 1914–2009.

Synodal materials and minutes from general conferences and synods of the Moravian Church Czech Province 1922–2012.

Atlases
Reichel, L. Th.: *Missions-Atlas der Brüder-Unität*, Herrnhut 1860.

Missions-Atlas der Brüdergemeinde, Herrnhut 1907.

BIBLIOGRAPHY REFERENCE LIST

PART I

1. Bartoš, F. M.: *Poslání papeži Urbanu V.*, Praha 1948.
2. Komenský, Jan Amos: *Stručná historie církve slovanské*, Melantrich 1942.
3. *Br. Jana Blahoslava spis O původu Jednoty bratrské a řádu v ní*, Český časopis historický, 1902.
4. *Br. Jana Blahoslava spis O původu Jednoty bratrské a řádu v ní*, Český časopis historický, 1902.
5. Kumpera, Jan: *Jednota bratrská – Odkaz evropské duchovní kultuře (1457–2011)*, Plzeň 2012.
6. Kumpera, Jan: *Jednota bratrská – Odkaz evropské duchovní kultuře (1457–2011)*, Plzeň 2012.
7. Kumpera, Jan: *Jednota bratrská – Odkaz evropské duchovní kultuře (1457–2011)*, Plzeň 2012.
8. Kumpera, Jan: *Jednota bratrská – Odkaz evropské duchovní kultuře (1457–2011)*, Plzeň 2012.
9. Gindely, J.: *Dekrety Jednoty bratrské*, vydavatelství Kober 1865.
10. Kaňák, Miloslav: *Význačné postavy Jednoty bratrské a jejich dílo*, Praha 1957.
11. Kumpera, Jan: *Jednota bratrská – Odkaz evropské duchovní kultuře (1457–2011)*, Plzeň 2012.
12. Kumpera, Jan: *Jednota bratrská – Odkaz evropské duchovní kultuře (1457–2011)*, Plzeň 2012.
13. Kumpera, Jan: *Jednota bratrská – Odkaz evropské duchovní kultuře (1457–2011)*, Plzeň 2012.
14. Kaňák, Miloslav: *Význačné postavy Jednoty bratrské a jejich dílo*, Praha 1957.
15. Kaňák, Miloslav: *Význačné postavy Jednoty bratrské a jejich dílo*, Praha 1957.
16. Kumpera, Jan: *Jednota bratrská – Odkaz evropské duchovní kultuře (1457–2011)*, Plzeň 2012.
17. Kumpera, Jan: *Jednota bratrská – Odkaz evropské duchovní kultuře (1457–2011)*, Plzeň 2012.
18. Fiedler, J.: *Todtenbuch der Geistlichkeit der Böhmischen Brüder*, Wien 1863.
19. Kumpera, Jan: *Jednota bratrská – Odkaz evropské duchovní kultuře (1457–2011)*, Plzeň 2012.

20. Kumpera, Jan: *Jednota bratrská – Odkaz evropské duchovní kultuře (1457–2011)*, Plzeň 2012.
21. Kaňák, Miloslav: *Význačné postavy Jednoty bratrské a jejich dílo*, Praha 1957.
22. Fiedler, J.: *Todtenbuch der Geistlichkeit der Böhmischen Brüder*, Wien 1863.
23. Fiedler, J.: *Todtenbuch der Geistlichkeit der Böhmischen Brüder*, Wien 1863.
24. Komenský, J. A.: *Smutný hlas zaplašeného hněvem pastýře*, Vyškov 1946.
25. Br. Jana Blahoslava spis *O původu Jednoty bratrské a řádu v ní*, Český časopis historický, 1902.

PART II

26. Weinlick, John R.: *Hrabě Zinzendorf*, Stefanos 2000.
27. Štěříková, Edita: *Jak potůček v jezeře*, Kalich 2009.

PART III

28. Knihovna Bratrských listův IX.: *Obrazy z dějin Jednoty bratrské, díl druhý*, Praha 1911.
29. *Verlass der Allgemeinen Synode der Brüder-Unität 1869*, § 115, Gnadau 1869, překlad.
30. Vacovský, Adolf: *Obnovení Jednoty bratrské v zemi otců*, Úzká rada Jednoty bratrské 1997.

PART IV

31. Bratrské Listy, ročník I., č. 5, 1894
32. Vacovský, Adolf: *Obnovení Jednoty bratrské v zemi otců*, (v rámci časopisu JB), ÚR Jednoty bratrské 1997.
33. *Verlass der General Synode der Evangelischen Brüder-Unität*, Gnadau 1914, překlad.
34. *Prohlášení české konference Jednoty bratrské 8. srpna 1924.*
35. *Zápis ze zasedání Všeobecné českomoravské konference 7. července 1925.*
36. *Allgemeine Kirchenordnung der EBU und Beschlüsse und Erklärungen Ihrer Generalsynode 1931*, překlad.

LIST OF IMAGES

PAGE	
16	Chelčický, Petr: *Siet viery pravé* 1521 (faksimile).
17, 19, 22, 24, 29, 30, 33, 34, 39, 45–48, 51, 54, 55	Kalfus, R.: *Jednota bratrská v obrazech*, Praha 1957.
18	Míka, Alois: *Petr Chelčický*, Svobodné slovo 1963.
20, 28	*Slovem obnovená, čtení o reformaci*, Kalich 1977.
21	Kadlčík, Fr. B.: *Děje i paměti Brandejsa nad Orlicí*, Praha 1885.
23, 36, 37, 41, 60–64, 66, 69, 75, 76, 81, 83, 88, 94, 99–101,103, 104, 106, 107, 112, 114–116, 120, 121, 124, 145, 146, 153–157, 160, 175, 176	Unitätsarchiv, Herrnhut
25	*Tůmy Přeloučského spis o Původu Jednoty bratrské a o chudých lidech*, Melantich 1947.
27, 31, 38, 43	Denis, Arnošt: *Konec samostatnosti české*, Praha 1932.
40	Photo Martin Klaus
42	Fialová, Vlasta: *Historie Kralic nad Oslavou*, Krajské nakladatelstství Brno 1959.
44	Zoubek, Fr. J.: *Život J. A. Komenského*, Praha 1892.
49	Photo Zdeněk Chotaš
50	Pavel Skála ze Zhoře: *Král Fridrich Falcký a bitva na Bílé hoře*.
52	Bahlcke J.; Dybaš B. a Rudolph H.: *Daniel Arnošt Jablonský život a dílo dílo vnuka JAK*, NPMK, 2011.

LIST OF IMAGES

57	Hrejsa, Ferdinad: *Sborové Jednoty bratrské*, Praha 1939.
65, 77, 78, 82, 89–93, 95–98, 102, 105, 111, 118, 119, 125–128, 130–133, 135–144, 147, 148, 158, 159, 161–164, 166, 168, 174, 177–193, 195–206, 210, 213–217	Archiv Jednoty bratrské, Liberec
67	Reichel, L. Th.: *Missions-Atlas der Brüder-Unität*, Herrnhut 1860.
68, 71, 134	*The Moravian Atlas*, Fulneck Academy 1853.
70, 72–74	*Misions-Blatt aus der Brüdergemeinde*, měsíčník (1850–1870).
79, 80, 86	Photo Hlavsa
84, 110	Štěříková, Edita: *Jak potůček v jezeře*, Praha 2009.
85, 87	Müller, Karl: *200 Jahre Brüdermission*, I. Band, Herrnhut 1931.
108, 109	Jacques-Nicolas Bellin (1703–1772).
113, 134	*Die Brüder – aus der Vergangenheit und Gegenwart der Brüdergemeinde*, Herrnhut 1914.
117	Moravian Church Archive and Library, London
122, 152	Photo L. Halamová
123	Joanne Portantio (1573–1578).
129	*Missions-Atlas der Brüdergemeinde*, Herrnhut 1907.
149	Photo archive Sam Gray
211, 212	Photo Tomáš Růžička a Daniel Krejčík